Discovery Guide to

# THE UNITED ARAB EMIRATES

by Diana Darke

IMMEL
Publishing

*To Jamie, Chloë and Max*

*Grateful acknowledgments* are due to the following:
Engineer Mohamed Rashad Bukhash of Historic Buildings Department,
Dubai Municipality; Dr Sabah and Mr Issa of Sharjah Archaeology
Museum; Walid Yasin of Al-Ain Department of Antiquities; Nabil,
guardian at the Kalba Fort; Taalib of the Hatta Municipality; the Majlis
Gallery; Dubai Natural History Group and  Gary Fuelner, Martin Parker,
Valerie Chalmers, Sandy Fowler, Carolyn Lehmann in particular;
Dr Marycke Jongbloed; Colin Richardson; Alison Simms; David Wiggins;
Shaun Crawley; Simon Crisford; Evan Arkwright and Alma Taylor

*Transliteration Note*
There are no set rules for the method of writing Arabic names in English
script, so the author has simply opted for the most commonly used
spellings. The purist may be offended by the lack of consistency this
entails, but the general reader will find it easier.

*Editorial Note*
No hospitality or favours have been accepted in the preparation of this
book, which therefore has complete editorial integrity. This is a relatively
rare phenomenon in the region, where many publications have local
sponsors.

**Discovery Guide to The United Arab Emirates**, first edition

Published by Immel Publishing Limited,
20 Berkeley Street, London W1X 5AE
*Telephone:* 0171 491 1799
*Facsimile:* 0171 493 5524

Design by Anthony Nelthorpe
Printed at the Bath Press

A CIP catalogue record for this book
is available from the British Library

ISBN 1 898162 41 7

# CONTENTS

# MAPS

## UNITED ARAB EMIRATES

❖ Site of historical importance
✳ Place of interest
✈ International airport
🏔 Mountainous region

0 km       50

THE ARABIAN GULF

MUSANDAM

Rams
RAS AL KHAIMAH    Shimmel, Julfar & Kush
Ras Al Khaimah Airport   Khatt   Dibba
UMM AL QUWAIN
Ad Dour
AJMAN   Tell
SHARJAH   Abraq   Falaj Al Mu'alla   Badiyah
Sharjah Airport   Masafi   Khor Fakkan
Dubai Airport   DUBAI   Dhaid   Bithnah
Jumeirah   Maleihah   Fujairah Airport   FUJAIRAH
Qarn Nazwa   Faya   Kalba
Jebel Ali Port   Buheis   Khor Kalba
Madam   GULF OF OMAN

SCRUB DESERT   Hatta

ABU DHABI ISLAND   Umm Al Nar
Abu Dhabi Airport   SULTANATE OF OMAN   Sohar

Al Ain   Buraimi

To Muscat

Ain Al Faydah   Mazyad

To Liwa & Qatar    Jebel Hafeet

UNITED ARAB EMIRATES

# INTRODUCTION

This book affords the most comprehensive coverage yet published in one book of what to see in the United Arab Emirates. The author describes at first hand, in detail, the archaeological sites and places to visit, bringing them to life through the eyes of earlier travellers, local people and a wealth of cultural and social insights. She includes twenty off-road drives, chosen because there is something worth driving to see: a fort, a ruin or natural feature like a waterfall set among barren mountains. No special driving experience is required, and a carefully handled saloon car will cope on most occasions. Where 4WD is essential, this is made clear. Timings of drives and itineraries are given throughout to help you plan, as well as eight town maps to pinpoint places of interest. The guide also covers places of leisure and entertainment, along with practical information for each Emirate.

The UAE is a fast-changing society, so events may in some instances overtake what is described. Your help in enabling future editions to be as accurate and exhaustive as possible will be all the more appreciated, as will any suggestions you have for additional content. Please write to the publisher at:

Immel Publishing Limited
20 Berkeley Street, Berkeley Square
London W1X 5AE

# OVERVIEW OF THE EMIRATES

The UAE has become, within the space of 25 years, a prosperous, tolerant country with a multi-cultural and multi-ethnic society, thanks first to its oil wealth and second to the enlightened leadership of Shaikh Zayed bin Sultan Al-Nahyan, who has used the oil revenues for the benefit of the country.

**From survival ...** For centuries here life continued for the local people largely unchanged. It was a life of great hardship and dire poverty. Apart from occasional feuding with rival tribes, each family's preoccupation was simply how to survive the next season. In the 1960s, and while the USA was preparing for a walk on the Moon, Abu Dhabi had no general hospital and no tarmac roads. Had oil never been discovered, that lifestyle would probably have remained unchanged.

**... to oil wealth** Although oil was discovered in commercial quantities in Abu Dhabi as early as 1959 the then ruler Shaikh Shakhbut (elder brother of the current ruler Shaikh Zayed) horded the revenues in his Palace, distrustful of innovation and change. Only when Shaikh Zayed took over from Shakhbut on 6 August 1969, did their lives change dramatically. "Money is of no value", he said, "unless it is used to benefit the people." By 1972 they had mobile phones, much the same time as they were introduced in the West.

**Resolving borders** With the arrival of the prospecting oil companies it became necessary for the first time to establish which ruler owned which desert hinterland and which shallow seas. This was an elaborate process, in which two Arabic-speaking British diplomats travelled by camel from one settlement to another questioning the village headman in order to establish to which Shaikh the village owed its allegiance. It took many years to arrive at the first ever formal boundaries, and border disputes continued to erupt periodically till as late as 1979.

The true character of the Emirates as a country is elusive. Each of the seven Emirates is changing so quickly and each of its relationships with the other six developing so constantly that it is hard to keep track. The character of each Emirati ruler has an enormous bearing on the character of the emirate, no more so than in the case of Shaikh Zayed himself. Perhaps even more elusive are the nationals themselves, the Emiratis as they are known. The average expatriate living in the Emirates comes into contact with remarkably few Emiratis, especially Emirati women, in a normal social context, making it difficult to establish conventional social links. Those who work in Arabic schools or in government departments have an all too rare exposure to nationals which most expatriates are denied.

Conscious that they have been propelled headlong, and by their own admission, ill-prepared into the future, many, especially the higher echelons, have accepted the opportunities and technologies of the twentieth century with remarkably little sentimentality. For others, the pace of change **Pace of change** has been too much, and they long for the simpler less materialistic days when everyone knew his neighbour and when each day was the same as the one before.

Of all the Emirates it is Dubai that has carved out its role as top destination for the businessman and tourist, investing millions in leisure and sporting infrastructures. To western visitors the key attractions of the UAE, especially Dubai, are **Dubai's** the weather, the stability of the political climate and the **commercial** absence of crime and burglary. Eighty-two companies offer a **role** range of packages from golfing holidays to business conferences.

With all vistas dominated by construction work, Dubai is a civil engineer's dream come true. More than 40 British tour operators now feature Dubai in their winter sun brochures. In 1996 110,000 British visitors came, most of them middle-aged. Eighty international airlines now operate the Dubai route, due to its Open Skies policy. Dubai has 223 hotels, 76 percent of the total in the UAE, Abu Dhabi has 39, Sharjah 19, Fujairah and Ras Al-Khaimah have about 10 together, while Ajman and Umm Al-Quwain have about 6 together.

Abu Dhabi was the first to export oil in 1962, yet Abu Dhabi had been till that time the most desert oriented of all the Emirates, with the people living mainly in the desert and the oases. Next was Dubai's turn in 1969, with oil in much smaller quantities, though enough to boost the active merchant community. Though originally from the same Bani Yas tribe as the Abu Dhabians, the people of Dubai were never desert dwellers, but traders settled round the Creek. When in the early twentieth century many Persian families from Lingah and other coastal districts of Iran emigrated to Dubai, a new element was introduced into the population, making it more cosmopolitan. They strengthened the trading network not just with Asia but also with India, East Africa and the Gulf.

From the 1960s onwards there were also other Arab immigrants, Palestinians, Lebanese and Syrians who moved here to escape the political turmoil of their own countries. Some of the earliest of these were granted UAE nationality, but those who came after 1971 and the federation were never granted nationality, nor the right to stay forever. As a result the population of nationals, estimated at 100,000 in 1960, has still stayed relatively small at 560,000 and the rest are essentially transient, here to do a job after which they leave. This has had **Outnumbered** a marked effect on the character of the UAE, and increasingly, **by foreigners** the nationals, grossly outnumbered by immigrant workers in all fields from top to bottom are retreating into their own circles, mixing less and less with the foreigners who live and work here. For the foreigners this also has a distancing effect, and many feel they work in isolation from local nationals, surrounded by and mixing with other foreigners throughout their time here, having little or no exposure to the local culture. The administration of so much wealth necessitated the import of foreign labour, a situation which had its parallel earlier this century, when the pearling industry was booming and slaves **Imported** were brought in to fill the labour shortage. The oil boom has **labour** resulted in a similar set-up with foreigners imported to do the work. Whilst they do of course receive salaries for their work, there is an extent to which nationals regard foreign workers as slaves, with white western workers simply representing the top rung, moving down to Asians on the bottom rung.

## UAE's 25th ANNIVERSARY

Extraordinary celebrations marked the anniversary in December 1996 of 25 years since the Emirates Federation in 1971, especially in Abu Dhabi where it coincided with the 30 year anniversary of Shaikh Zayed's accession as ruler. Streets in towns everywhere were decked with photos of Shaikh Zayed and the other rulers. Newspapers, TV and radio were full of eulogies. Fireworks, laser shows, giant cakes and parades abounded. The anniversary cake was 2.5 kilometres long, made of date and banana, topped with white icing, and took 25 days to make. Rumours that the key of a prize Mercedes was hidden inside led to extraordinary scenes of devastation. The key turned out to be a hoax. Shaikh Zayed issued a decree raising by 15–30 percent the salaries and bonuses of all UAE nationals working in federal government, armed forces, police and security. Pages were bought in major newspapers throughout the world and filled with editorial cataloguing the achievements of the UAE. The figures are indeed phenomenal. In the 25 year period the GDP has risen 22 times over, a rate which most countries would have to wait over a century to achieve. Not all of this is due to the oil and gas sector, for while the crude oil sector's contribution to the GDP has grown 12 times, the non-oil sector has grown over 40 times, accounting for over two thirds of the total, and Dubai has announced its intention to have a 100 percent non-oil economy by the year 2010.

**Phenomenal figures**

Before the federation in 1971  99% of national income was from pearl sales to Indian merchants. There was some trading and subsistence farming but no roads, no hospitals and no schools. Now it is counted among the 10 richest nations in the world with one of the highest per capita incomes. At the time of federation, the world was sceptical, fearing it would not last because the warring rivalries of the tribes and their rulers would prove too great. The fact that rivalries were overcome speaks volumes of Shaikh Zayed's generosity in sharing out Abu Dhabi's phenomenal oil revenues for the benefit of the other Emirates. All of them recognise that they are best off inside the federation.

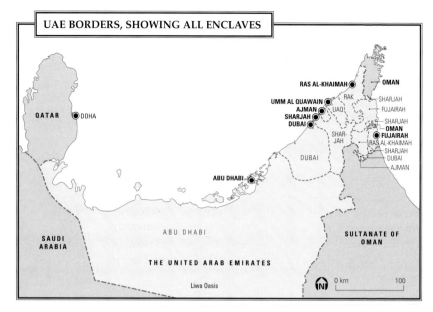

UAE BORDERS, SHOWING ALL ENCLAVES

# FACTS AND FIGURES

| Total Area | 75,150 sq km |
|---|---|
| Abu Dhabi | 64,750 |
| Dubai | 3,900 |
| Sharjah | 2,600 |
| Ras Al-Khaimah | 1,690 |
| Fujairah | 1,170 |
| Umm Al-Quwain | 780 |
| Ajman | 260 |
| | |
| Total Population (approximate) | 2,500,000 |
| of whom UAE nationals | 560,000 |
| Expatriates of which: | 1,940,000 |
| Indians | 835,000 |
| Pakistanis | 400,000 |
| Other Asians | 345,000 |
| Other Arabs | 300,000 |
| Europeans | 35,000 |
| British | 25,000 |

70% of the population is expatriate, 30% is national.

Islam is the official religion, with UAE nationals belonging to the Sunni (orthodox) sect. Religions of expatriates are tolerated, though no religious teaching other than of Islam is permitted in schools.

Friday is the weekly holiday and many organisations take a two-day Friday/Saturday weekend.

Time is GMT +4 hours.

**Office hours**
Public sector 0730–1330 Sat–Wed, 0730–1100 Thurs
Private sector variable, average timings 0800–1300, 1600–1930, though some shops open at 1000 and stay open till 2200, especially shopping malls. Many shops stay open on Friday, as do all markets, since Friday is the main shopping day for working residents.

**Ramadan**
Working hours are generally shorter. Hotels continue to sell alcohol, but activity only really begins after dark. Most nationals make an effort to be in the country for Ramadan and it is therefore a good time to see people and make business contacts among nationals, provided you can accept the slower pace of work.

Ramadan dates

| | |
|---|---|
| 1998 | 29 Dec 1997–27 January 1998 |
| 1999 | 18 Dec 1998–16 January 1999 |

**Religious Holidays** *(variable dates because of the lunar calendar)*
Eid al-Fitr (after Ramadan):

| | |
|---|---|
| 1998 | 28,29,30 January |
| 1999 | 17,19,19 January |

Eid al-Adha (after Pilgrimage)

| | |
|---|---|
| 1998 | 6,7,8,9 April |
| 1999 | 26,27,28,29 March |

*New Diving
Village on
Dubai's
creekside*

**National Holidays**
New Year: 1 January
Accession of Shaikh Zayed: 6 August
National Day: 2–3 December

**Currency**
UAE dirham pegged to $US. At time of going to press,
exchange rates were 1$US = Dh3.67 and £1 = Dh6.01.
Each dirham is divided into 100 fils.

**Visas**
None required for stays of up to 30 days for nationals of the
UK, Saudi Arabia, Oman, Bahrain, Kuwait and Qatar. All
others need visas, obtainable at the relevant embassies.

*Section 1*
# Practicalities

## Climate

Day trips and camping expeditions tend to be pleasant from mid-October, when the summer heat has begun to recede and the humidity drops, till April. Then from late April when the heat begins to intensify again and the humidity shoots up, all but the hardiest stay indoors between 11.00am and 4.00pm throughout the summer till September. In the winter months heavy rains can occur anytime unexpectedly but most commonly in December, January, February and March. With this in mind, never camp in a wadi bed however fine the weather appears. In winter an extra layer is often needed in the evenings when the temperature drops sharply.

*Aboul Fort near Al-Ain*

## Health

There are no compulsory vaccinations for visitors to the UAE, but everyone should check with their doctor what the recommendations are. Certainly all visitors would be wise to be up to date with tetanus and polio. Long-term visitors or expatriate residents are usually advised to have Hepatitis A and B injections. There is a very low incidence of malaria and so anti-malarial precautions are not generally taken. A control programme is in force and carefully monitored.

The standard of medical care and hospitals is extremely high, if expensive. Doctors and specialists from all over the world come to practice at clinics here to earn more money than they could make in their home countries.

## Pets

Pets can be brought into the UAE as long as they have a Rabies vaccination certificate less than 6 months old, together with a health certificate from a vet in your home country that is no more than 7 days old. There are no quarantine rules. Standards of veterinary clinics are extremely high. Dogs are banned in parks and in theory on the beach.

## Taxis

Taxis are cheap and metered and the Dubai taxi fleet has increasingly been taken over by government controlled taxis. You can ring 313131 in Dubai to call for a taxi or 447787 in Abu Dhabi. The only other form of public transport is bus, which tends to be crowded and infrequent and used almost exclusively by Asian labourers.

## Car Hire and Driving

Car hire in the UAE is straightforward and requires only a minimum age of 21 and production of your National driving licence from your home country. Rates range from about £25–£45 pounds a day depending on the size of car. Europcar, based in Dubai, is one of the most reliable firms (tel. +971 4-520033  fax +971 4-527692). Car hire firms have offices at the airports and in many of the large four and five star hotels.

*Off-road in Wadi Bih – with convoy travel three is the ideal number, more than ten becomes very cumbersome*

For resident expatriates, driving your own car is generally considered essential, as there is no public transport system except taxis, which are difficult to get to come to your home, as so many new villas have no address. Describing your exact location over the phone to a driver who speaks no English is a recipe for frayed tempers and the taxi, if it ever finds you, has been known to be three hours late! There is a thriving second-hand car market and most Japanese, European and American models are available new at prices much cheaper than elsewhere. Many expatriates choose 4 wheeldrive vehicles, not simply because of the off-road capability, but also because of the solidity, so that injury is less likely in an accident. Traffic accidents are very common in the UAE, due to a combination of an inexperienced driving population of nationals and Asians, and the speed at which the excellent road network encourages people to drive. Traffic accidents account for 20% of all deaths in the UAE, and most of the victims are young. No law yet exists stipulating the use of seat-belts for adults or children. Women drive and there are women driving instructors.

Speed limits are 120 kph on dual carriageways outside town and 60 kph in towns. Speed cameras trap you once you have exceeded the speed limit by 20 kph and all fines have to be settled before your annual vehicle registration licence is renewed. Drunken driving penalties are severe.

### Petrol
Petrol is very cheap. Petrol stations serve you and the choice is between diesel (generally just for trucks and therefore tucked round the back in a separate, usually rather tacky, area with no shade), red leaded PREMIUM petrol (97 octane) for most normal saloon cars, black lead NORMAL petrol (95 octane) for trucks and pickups, and green UNLEADED petrol (99 octane) for newer expensive saloon cars.

### Expatriates
The expatriate population of the UAE accounts for 70% of the whole. By sustaining the  huge growth in the economy and services of the country, this large expatriate community has been crucial to the development of the UAE since 1971. In Dubai alone the expatriate population is predicted to reach 1.8 million by 2012. The Municipality has calculated that to meet the needs of this increase, it must build an extra 401 mosques, 9 more fire stations, 3 new police stations and 4 more hospitals.

Of the western expatriates, the British are dominant with around 25,000 UK nationals based here, more than twice that of all other western expatriate communities combined. Over

500 British companies including a number of law firms, have permanent representation in Abu Dhabi and Dubai, testimony to the strong commercial links that Britain has historically had with the UAE. It is Britain's second largest trading partner in the Arab world after Saudi Arabia.

## Administration
Be prepared in the early weeks after your arrival for much tedious and time-consuming administration spent queueing in government offices to get driving licences and identity cards sorted out. "Patience is beautiful" runs the Arab proverb.

## Food
Virtually every ingredient you could wish for is available in the supermarkets and there are no shortages or restrictions. Many luxury items are imported and expensive, but local produce is becoming better now and is considerably cheaper. Chicken is the only local meat. Beef is imported from Australia, Ireland and Holland, as is lamb and pork. There is a good range of local fish, available at supermarkets or at the fish market (souq) if you have a strong stomach for the smell.

## Alcohol
Hotel restaurants and bars serve alcohol with the exception of Sharjah, which has been dry since 1985. Restaurants which are not attached to hotels are not usually licensed, but nightclubs are. Resident expatriates can buy alcohol once they have obtained a licence from their sponsor, issued by the police department on payment of an annual fee. This is subject to a monthly quota, based on salary. There is a wide range of wines, beers and spirits available from the shippers and prices are similar to the UK and US.

## Electricity and gas
There is no mains gas, so cooking is by bottled gas or electricity. The supply is 20/40V, 50 cycles and Standard British 13 amp square pin plugs are the norm with bayonet or screw light fittings.

## Housemaids

Most families find a live-in full-time housemaid indispensable. Philippinos tend to be the most expensive, followed by Sri Lankans, then Indians. The salary range is Dh600–1500 a month depending on experience, standard of English and length of service. They generally expect a small room with WC and shower facilities separate to the family, and cook separately on two-ring gas cookers in this little room, into which the longer-established ones also squeeze a TV, radio cassette and sometimes even a husband. The larger villas have separate servants' quarters in the garden. All domestic servants get a return air ticket and two months leave every two years.

## Dress

The surroundings may appear so Western and familiar to many expatriates that they dress as they would in any hot climate, without considering that they are in an Islamic country. In truth the local people are often so little in evidence that it is only the many mosques and the call to prayer that serve as reminders that the UAE is a Muslim country. Wearing of shorts and skimpy T-shirts is fine on the beach, at the Sports Club or at home, but is not appropriate for public places like the supermarket or shopping mall. Women should avoid sleeveless dresses and low necklines, and should be especially aware of this if travelling in rural areas of the interior, where local people are less used to Western dress habits.

## Entertainment

There is a handful of Western theatre-dinners and concerts which come through the UAE on their tours, but most expatriates rely on satellite and cable TV, which is cheaply available.

## Clubs

Most Western expatriates join at least one club. Sports and the pursuit of fitness often becomes the major pastime. Sports facilities are excellent and there are many social events organised around sport, which becomes a good way of meeting friends. Golf, tennis and water sports are the most popular.

## Ramadan

Although the fasting restrictions do not apply to non-Muslims, foreigners are expected not to eat, drink or smoke in public in daylight hours. This can especially affect lunchtime picnics in the desert or trips into the wadis, when extreme care should be taken to choose a spot well away from any villages or settlements.

## Pork

Most supermarkets sell pork products, but in a separate area, away from the other meats, so that Muslims do not have to come into close contact with it. Some supermarkets like the French Continent in Dubai's City Centre, simply do not sell it at all.

## Tipping

15% service charge is usually included on hotel and restaurant bill. Dh5 is appropriate for a small service.

## Visas

UK nationals can enter the UAE for stays of up to 30 days with no visa. The passport is simply stamped at the airport on arrival, and then checked on departure to make sure you have not overstayed the 30 day limit. The same applies to nationals of Saudi Arabia, Oman, Bahrain, Kuwait and Qatar. All other nationalities need to obtain visas from the UAE embassy in their home country.

## Maps

Geoprojects do the best maps of the UAE and also do ones of Al-Ain, Abu Dhabi and Sharjah. Dubai Municipality produces the best one of Dubai. All are available at local bookshops in the UAE. For field trips and off-roading you can buy Tactical Pilotage Charts as used by aircraft. These are only available from Stanfords Bookshop, London, not in the UAE.

## Travel to the UAE

Air is the way 99% of visitors come (the other 1% comes by bicycle!). The national carrier Emirates Airlines has the most comprehensive network of direct flights, with three a day from London alone. For the best deals from the UK call your local travel agent. Royal Brunei and Malaysian Airlines often have good rates. In London two of the best are Trailfinders tel: 0171-938 3366 and STA Travel tel: 0171-937 9962. For packages, there are now over 40 tour operators featuring Dubai in their winter sun brochures. On arrival at the airport you can bring in a limited amount of alcohol (1 litre of spirits per person) and lots of cigarettes (200 per person). Do not bring videos in your luggage as they may be confiscated and checked for pornographic material no matter what the label says. There is no departure tax on leaving.

### Travel within the UAE
Taxis are plentiful and relatively inexpensive. They are metered in Abu Dhabi and Dubai, but not in Sharjah and the other emirates. There are no railways and buses are not worth considering as they run so infrequently. Service (shared) taxis taking up to 6 passengers are the cheapest way of covering the longer distances between the emirates.

### Accommodation
Dubai has 76% of the UAE's hotels with 223; Abu Dhabi has 39; Sharjah has 19; Fujairah and Ras Al-Khaimah have about 10 together; and Ajman and Umm Al-Quwain have about 6 between them. Most are at the expensive end, and all the big international chains are here like Meridien, Marriott and Forte Grand, with prices to match. There are no youth hostels or organised camp sites. Room prices are cheapest in the less affluent emirates, so if you want to economise you might consider basing yourself in Ajman or Umm Al-Quwain.

### Budgetting and Currency
This is not the place for a cheap holiday. Petrol is about the only thing cheaper than in the UK. If you are staying in a 3 star hotel in Dubai, you must budget at least £100 per day to include the room, food and taxis. You can reduce costs by staying in one of the Umm Al-Quwain or Ajman hotels, but even then it would be difficult to get your daily budget below £70. The UAE dirham is pegged to the US dollar. Exchange rates at the time of going to press were £1 = Dh 6.01 and $US1 = Dh 3.67. Credit cards like American Express and Diners Club are accepted, but Visa and Access are not unless you have a

local bank account to which they are attached. Travellers' cheques are the safest way to bring money.

## Security and Safety
The UAE prides itself on its crime-free reputation and certainly it is one of the safest and most politically stable places in the Middle East. Women travelling alone are no problem and Dubai especially is a very tolerant and liberal place in which women do everything men do.

## Opening Hours
*See Facts and Figures.*

## Public Holidays
*See Facts and Figures.*

## Useful items to take
Suncream and hat. Supermarkets sell factors up to 25 but prices are higher than in the UK.

Comfortable shoes that you can walk in sand with. Walking anywhere even within the cities is often a sandy experience.

On day trips and outings, get into the habit of taking plenty of water bottles, your mobile phone and a medicine kit which includes painkiller, anti-histamine and Waspeze (for scorpion, snake and insect bites), plasters and antiseptic cream. If you are going near a beach also put in some white vinegar in case of jellyfish stings.

## Where to go for information
There is no Tourist Office in the UK, only the embassy in London   tel: 0171-581 1281. In the USA the embassy is tel: Washington DC 338 6500.

Within the emirates, Dubai is planning 3 Tourist Offices. In practice your hotel gives you any information you need.

## Itineraries
Dubai is the best emirate to be based in for centrality and ease of road communication to the other emirates.   Detailed itineraries are given with timings at the front of the chapters on each emirate.

*Al-Hayl*
*watchtower*

### Walking

There is a lot of excellent hill, mountain and wadi walking to be enjoyed in the UAE. Details of the best areas are given at the end of the Practical Information section for each emirate. Terrain can be loose and care should be taken to wear good comfortable shoes or trainers at the very least.

*Section 2*
# Social Issues, Past & Present

**Coping with change**

The UAE's quick transition from a traditional society to sudden affluence and urbanisation has created a demographic imbalance which is the unavoidable consequence of the sheer pace of development. The federal Planning Department has conducted its own research to establish ways of dealing with this and is actively seeking ways of rectifying it. Those elements of the national population which benefited from the oil wealth have inevitably become a highly consuming society, dependent on a large expatriate workforce, thereby creating this demographic and gender imbalance. Credit is due to the local press which regularly airs such issues, and press articles published in 1996 and 1997 have been the source material for all the subjects treated in this section.

Arab traditions and culture are increasingly exposed to external sources such as satellite TV, video, electronic games, music and fashions. The more these come to dominate, the more the local identity is watered down and weakened. Nationals also employ large numbers of domestic helpers from Sri Lanka and the Indian Sub-Continent who have come to the UAE with their own customs and values, having detrimental social and linguistic effects on national children. Mixed marriages occur between national men and foreign women, and large numbers of them have ended in divorce.

**Government solutions**

The solution, and this is what the government is working towards, is to reduce the demographic imbalance by adopting gradual nationalisation through the employment of qualified nationals, and producing a national population that consumes less and contributes more to the country's development. A major problem in achieving this is the absence of any work ethic among many young nationals. When wealth has come so easily there is little will to strive for anything, indeed, no perceived need. The real problem, as the government readily acknowledges, is how to implement a policy in favour of employing nationals, without adversely effecting economic performance. Many nationals still have unrealistic expectations from entering the labour market, but attitudes will gradually change.

**Lifestyles before and after oil**

Shaikh Zayed himself said "A nation without a past has neither a present nor a future". The pre-oil era lifestyles were similar for all the Emirates, but since oil wealth probably the most severe contrast has been for Abu Dhabi, originally the least blessed but now the most wealthy by far, with proven oil reserves of at least 100 years, more than any other country in the world. In order to appreciate fully the colossal progress made by the UAE states since 1971, an effort should be made to understand how Emiratis lived before and the factors that used to dominate their lives.

**Massive reserves**

Remarkably little has been documented of the early stories of everyday life in the Emirates, and it is important to remember that the culture of the Arabian peninsula had a strong oral tradition, with such stories passing by word of mouth from one generation to the next. The coming of oil has of course put paid to this tradition. Modern technology with its faceless means of communication have taken over, and so it is only from rare eye witness accounts of Emiratis such as Mohammed al-Fahim in his book *From Rags to Riches*, that we are able to glean a picture of the hardships that were experienced by the tiny indigenous population as it eked out its subsistence living.

**From rags to riches**

In the eighteenth and nineteenth centuries the population is thought never to have exceeded 100,000 scattered about in small villages mainly on the coast at Ras al-Khaimah, Dubai, Sharjah and Abu Dhabi. These coastal settlements depended almost entirely on the sea for their living, working as fishermen, pearl divers or boat builders.

Inland life could only be supported in the scattered desert oases such as Liwa and Al-Ain, while limited agriculture was possible in parts of Ras al-Khaimah, Fujairah, Khor Fakkan and Kalba where increased levels of rainfall or springs existed. The main staple was dates of the palm trees, camels' milk and fish. Other basic necessities such as rice and cloth were bought with pearls traded through the Iranian ports like Bandar Abbas and Lingah just on the other side of the Persian Gulf.

**Subsistence living**

**Oh to be a national**

### ADVANTAGES OF BEING A NATIONAL

The nationals of the UAE are among the best looked-after and most privileged of any in the world. In addition to free health care of the highest quality, heavily subsidised water and electricity, marriage grants, and extra benefits for large numbers of children and generous pensions for the older nationals, there are a number of privileges which enable them to earn money from trade agencies, or from renting property built with government-provided loans on freely distributed land. Some nationals who have taken advantage of these privileges wisely, find themselves owning considerable property yet choose to live in their traditional ways. Nationals are given priority in job allocations, and it is a great source of concern to the authorities that national manpower should be given the opportunity to prepare itself for the future, when the number of foreign workers in the country will eventually decline. Only nationals can own land, and many of the less well-off families were given People's Houses. Low interest building loans are available to nationals for property of their own or property they will rent out.

## Women's activities

The women's duties concentrated on the home where they had total control. Shopping at the markets was done by the men, it being considered quite unseemly for the women to be seen in public out at the souq. The men therefore bulk-bought most items and brought them to the house. In most families the women were expected to make all clothing for the family, while the wealthy households might have servants to do this for them. No cotton grew locally, so all the material was imported from India and bought by the men.

**No shopping**

Cooking, apart from coffee-making, was entirely the business of the women, and fuel collecting was a major time-consuming chore, which fell to them before cooking could begin. Brushwood had to be collected from the wadis near their houses and brought back. Wealthier families were able to buy charcoal or fuel wood in the souq to avoid this task. During the pearling season when most able-bodied men were away at sea for four to five months, the women were in charge of the date harvest, the younger ones sometimes even climbing the trees to do the picking.

The exception to women at the markets were fishermens'

wives – it was their job to take their husbands' early morning catch to the market to sell or exchange for other commodities.

Now that there are women working beyond the home, there are far more women out shopping for themselves, in the malls, buying clothes, perfumes, make-up, jewellery and other luxuries. They even sit now without their husbands in the mall cafes, with other female members of the family or friends, behaviour which would have been considered shameful till very recently. One grandmother related "At that time, no woman went out shopping alone. A man had to be with her. Now she's out earning her own money, she is out in the streets, buying for herself without a man's protection". In rare cases in pre-oil days, a woman who inherited money might buy a business, even a pearling boat, but would use a male employee as agent in all her business dealings whilst she took the decisions behind the scenes.

**New woman**

The segregation of men and women was not a specifically Islamic question. The Koran does not in fact stipulate it, but it is intertwined with tribal customs. Houses were designed so that male guests could be received in the *majlis,* (sitting area) but only the close male relations were allowed beyond the *majlis* to the courtyard, kitchen, sleeping and living areas. The women could thus go about their daily routine even while strangers were visiting. Far from restricting women, such measures are seen as protecting women. Within the home the women frequently dominate, especially the senior woman of the household, who can lay down rules for the entire household on praying, fasting, marriage and social contacts. The customs of marriage and divorce, whilst conforming to Islam are also the backbone of the tribal society. Marriage of first cousins was the ideal, and girls were married off as soon as possible after puberty at 13, with the husbands themselves frequently being no more than 16. In practice the young brides would often stay living within the same extended family, because of the closeness of the relations of her husband. Today most women prefer to finish their education and work a few years before marrying, usually at the age of 22–25. Their husbands are commonly aged 25–30 at the time of marriage.

**Domestic privacy and protection**

---

### WOMEN'S MAGAZINES

UAE National women now have a series of specialised publications which give them an opportunity to express their views through letters and contributions, as well as raising cultural awareness and interest in women's and family issues. Many women are themselves employed in the media, and the magazines are not just vehicles for advertising entertainment and leisure, but also cover serious issues affecting women's lives in the UAE. The first magazine was *Zahrat al-Khaleej* (Flower of the Gulf), and another is *Durret al-Emarat* (Pearl of the Emirates).

---

A substantial proportion of enlightened women can cope with the pace of change of the last 25 years, but recognise that they may have to be less picky in future about what jobs they chose. One young Emirati woman confirms "It's true, everybody wants to be a manager, but gradually that too will change. In fact it's already happening, as the buffer created by the state which offers secure jobs to nationals slowly disappears and there are more nationals and fewer secure jobs."

In the home among Arab families, Sri Lankan or Indian maids are the norm, while Pakistanis and Beluch do the outdoor work of tending gardens and seeing to livestock. Supervising the servants falls to the women.

### Children's activities

There were no schools for the children till the 1970s and the Koranic schools were attended by boys only. Boys and girls were expected to help their parents as soon as they were able. Up to the age of five the mother and other females of the household were very tolerant of their children and the men did not interfere. After this they were encouraged to behave like adults as soon as possible, and motivated to live up to this expectation from an early age so that by their early teens they could accept the responsibilities of adult life including marriage. Today there are equal educational opportunities for boys and girls, often in segregated schools.

**Equal opportunities**

### Ageing population

The number of UAE nationals who retain first hand memories and experiences of their lives pre-oil are dwindling. Though life was full of physical hardships, it was a great deal simpler. "Life was very different then", recalls one elderly national. "Everyone knew who his neighbour was and your home was always open. It was a very social and enjoyable time".

Another said "We weren't wealthy, but I think we were healthier then".

There is a shift away from the extended family which used to provide basic care for the elderly, and families are becoming increasingly nuclear, creating the need for the first time for old age homes and community centres as society changes. Many of the older men in such homes talk with longing of their past simpler lives.

The incidence of serious illness such as cancer or heart disease has increased dramatically in recent years and has been linked to newly emerging lifestyle and eating habits. Obesity-related diseases now account for over 50% of total deaths in the country. Nationals living in the rural areas are now healthier than those in cities because they do more exercise and eat less fatty foods. Thanks to medical advancement, life expectancy has increased in spite of the less healthy lifestyle, from 45 in the 1960s to a remarkable 72 today.

**Medical advances**

### Safety

The Emirates and especially Dubai are understandably anxious to preserve their crime-free reputation, where tourists can walk in safety day or night. At present violent crime is minimal, with vehicle theft, credit card and cheque fraud accounting for the bulk of recorded crime, and even this is very slight compared to most developed countries. Such crime as exists is aired regularly in the press, debated and condemned, as the view is very sensibly taken that if people know the punishment, they will be deterred. Shame is another tactic used, where the press publishes photos of men caught harrassing women on the streets, for all their friends and relations to see.

**Minimal crime**

The practice of prostitution, largely by women from Russia and the CIS countries, has been on the increase in recent years, and the authorities are trying to control it. In Sharjah a moral squad was recently created and now patrols beaches and markets to ensure that foreign women – largely from CIS countries – do not violate local culture and values through

**Keen to curb**

their behaviour and dress. Some Sharjah beach corniche hotels are well known, and some Umm al-Quwain beach hotels are also active. In Dubai the so-called Russian beach in Jumeirah has acquired a long-standing reputation, as have some of the Deira hotels and squares. The remaining Emirates are relatively free of it. The matter is aired quite openly from time to time in the local press and there is little attempt to deny it exists. The problem in controlling it is how to tell the difference between prostitutes and foreign women who dress scantily. Many an expatriate mother dressed in a sleeveless top and tight trousers or shorts has a story to tell about being mistaken for a Russian, and one group of elderly German lady tourists were very put out when they were refused entry at the airport. The government realises the issue is damaging to its image and is keen to curb it. Several successful prosecutions and deportations were recently made in Dubai and Sharjah.

**Telling the difference**

Crimes such as drug-smuggling carry severe prison sentences, but the death penalty – execution by firing squad – is rare, in contrast to neighbouring Saudi Arabia, and is generally reserved for acts of murder.

### Marriage

A Marriage Fund, set up in 1994 by Shaikh Zayed to help young national couples with the cost of a traditional wedding, has allocated over $100 million so far to eligible couples, and raised the rate of marriages between UAE nationals by 100% since its inception five years ago. A full grant is Dh70,000, thereby relieving the groom of the huge expenses associated with getting married to a national woman, such as the high dowry. A new draft law has now set dowries at Dh20,000 and divorce compensation at Dh30,000. Another law is currently being drafted specifically to curtail the number of UAE nationals marrying expatriate women (at present 30% of all nationals), mainly Asian women. Marriages to European women are the most likely to end in divorce, statistics show, so that the large number of UAE spinsters of marriagable age (currently 22%), will fall. Many nationals still prefer arranged marriages and feel that their parents' advice is valuable in guiding them to find the kind of partner whose characteristics are in line with the religious and social traditions of the family. Among the ill effects cited of marrying an expatriate woman,

**Nationals are best**

are that the children will speak the mother's language and their Arabic will become broken. The children will also be brought up closer to the mother's beliefs and customs and will therefore not feel strong patriotism to their father's homeland. Non- Muslim mothers will also have children who will not grow up true Muslims and will not conform to Islamic rules and practices. If their mother is from the West, the children find themselves torn between the values of two different cultures. The marriage fund regularly sends letters to UAE nationals who are studying abroad warning them of these dangers, and urging them to marry national women in order to preserve the UAE's cultural identity. What this of course fails to address, is that the same problem can be found where nationals marry each other, as so many national women give their housemaids, 53% of whom are non-Muslims and come from Sri Lanka, India, the Philippines or Bangladesh, the job of bringing up the children. The maids feed them, play with them and even help them in so far as they are able, with their homework, even though 23% are illiterate and 42% semi-illiterate. All this of course impedes the children's assimilation of Arabic and Islamic culture.

**Cultural values**

Dubai Police have taken a lead in many such social issues, including anti-divorce campaigns. They have published statistics showing that 36 out of every hundred marriages of UAE nationals ends in divorce, a surprising statistic in a Muslim society. 31% are due to personality differences, 26% due to interference of the family, 19% due to infertility, 10% due to financial problems, 7% due to wife's disobedience, and 5% due to age differences. The increased divorce rate is seen as a threat to social stability and security, since studies have shown that the children of divorced parents are more likely to become anti-social and aggressive. Of those with personality differences, 26% of the total 30% were divorces between national men and foreign wives. A staggering 90% of divorces were requested by women.

**Statistics**

If a woman comes to the marriage with her own inheritance, she is always careful to keep it separate, so that in the event of divorce, she takes it back. No stigma attaches to divorce in the way that it can in western societies, and a woman will take back to her father's house any boy children under the age of seven and girl children under puberty. Boys

**No stigma**

over seven stay with the father. The marriage contract is arrived at with the agreement of both sides and thus the rights of the woman are strictly safeguarded in accordance with Islamic tradition.

**Future solutions**

In the 1980s only 10% of marriages ended in divorce. The Dubai Police have said they would support an institution being established where national men and women could get to know one another through social gatherings attended by mothers. "What we are doing now", said the Chief of Police, "is keeping men and women "jailed" away from each other for 25 years. After that we expect them to suddenly communicate, get married and set up a family."

### Education system

Dubai has again taken the lead in pressing for change here, with Dubai's Chief of Police criticising the existing traditional teaching methods in Arab schools, where children are forced to memorise facts without understanding them. The Arab education system is thought by many to encourage passive thinking, repetition and random thought. This is seen as one of the reasons why it is failing to supply local labour markets with well qualified manpower.

There are currently about fifteen thousand graduates unemployed. One day they will have to replace the expatriate workforce. At present many refuse to take anything except an easy job with managerial status, but such attitudes will eventually change in line with market pressures.

**Literacy increasing**

Adult literacy is now 75%. 19% of the illiterate are over 40. The target is that UAE nationals will fill 30–40% of technical positions by the year 2005. At present the UAE market offers nine thousand technical jobs and local schools produce only 300 technical graduates annually.

Education has been the key for UAE women, and there is a big difference in attitude to studies and work between young men and women. In 1980 female illiteracy was 77%. Now it is 10%. While their brothers often drop out of school and join the army, the sisters go on to university (more women than men now graduate from Emirates universities) and some even go abroad to complete their studies. Regular computer courses are offered by women's clubs and social development centres in the summer holidays. Shaikh Zayed's wife herself, Shaikha

Fatima bint Mubarak al-Nahayan (in Islam, women retain their own names after marriage), has called for women to join the Federal National Council and is keen for UAE women to take a greater part in the political process.

A woman's personality is, without doubt, the single most important factor that allows her to overcome social type-casting. UAE women have come a long way today. Women's associations, social development centres and cultural establishments now exist to allow the UAE woman to play an active role in the cultural life of her country. In the words of one national woman who wears a headscarf and drives her own car, "The more you learn, the more you can contribute to the progress of your country, and it's not that I'm trying to copy the West or the way English people do things. I do things in keeping with my culture, my identity." And another, "The more politically aware a woman is, and this can only come through education, the more a woman can instil a sense of nationalism and patriotism in her children, apart from monitoring their upbringing and their education."

**Encouragement for women**

Since 1972 the number of girls enrolled in educational institutions has increased over 14 times, to reach a number very similar to the male students. Women can even study courses like engineering in the Higher Colleges of Technology, just like men. Most women work in the Ministry of Education, which itself guarantees full equal opportunities to women. Women are being actively encouraged to work, be it at home or outside.

### Religion

Before the advent of Islam to the tribes of this region, they were probably Moon and Star worshippers, though there was also known to be a small Christian community, and Oman had a bishop from the fifth century. The advent of Islam in 632, gradually changed the old tribal ways. Before the battle of Dibba (on the east coast just south of Musandam) established the new religion totally in the area, the people had not known much security and were constantly at war with their neighbours and even each other. The new faith brought with it new laws, a sense of unity in an Islamic society, and for the first time the expectation of life after death. Unlike a religion in the Western sense, Islam dominates the cultural, social, moral, economic, legal and political spheres of life. All Muslims turn to it consciously or unconsciously many times a day for moral, religious and legal authority. The spirit of Islam is totally

**Islam rules** intertwined with the traditions of tribal society and most aspects of the family's domestic structure and its daily routine within the household and the community are all deeply rooted in Islamic beliefs. All matters concerning marriage, divorce, inheritance, property, fraud and theft are dealt with by Sharia law, that is, Islamic law as based on the teaching of the Koran and the Sunna (the recorded deeds and sayings of the Prophet Mohammed). From the 1940s onwards when different types of criminal offences began to rise with the arrival of foreigners – such as traffic offences, labour and contractual disputes which were clearly not covered by Sharia law – such offences were referred to the political authorities, both the local ruler and the British. In pre-Islamic times compulsory revenge was the norm for crimes, but Islam introduced the concept of

**Moderation** forgiveness as a praiseworthy act. Islam brought a great improvement in the status of women who in pre-Islamic times in Arabia were considered mere objects for trade. Islam restored their position of honour and respect within the family, and the number of wives was limited to four who all had to be treated equally, whereas before there was no limit at all.

**Friday sermon**
The Friday noon prayer is the major congregational meeting of the week, where the *Imam* (prayer leader) gives a rousing sermon designed to instil religious values and to boost social responsibility. Mosques are central to mobilising public opinion and shaping the direction society takes.

**Eids** *(religious holidays)*
The smaller eid, *Eid al-Fitr* (Feast of breaking the fast) can be regarded as equivalent to our Easter, and follows the end of Ramadan and usually is a public holiday of three days. The major eid, *Eid al-Adha* (Feast of the sacrifice) can be seen as equivalent of our Christmas, and commemorates the willingness of Abraham to sacrifice his son Isaac and is generally a public holiday of four days. During the eids, there used to be a tradition of giving to the needy, but in today's consumer society, the emphasis seems to have shifted to spending money on oneself and buying new clothes.

### Ramadan

This month-long period of abstention from bodily pleasures is one of the five pillars of Islam, during which the Koran stipulates that during daylight hours, no Muslim can eat, drink, smoke or have sexual intercourse. Working hours are reduced during Ramadan and tempers can get frayed, especially in the first few days when the body is adjusting to the fast. The self-denial is regarded as purification of the soul, enhancing closeness to God.

**Period of purification**

The big hotels vie with one another during Ramadan to have the most lavish buffets often set up in special Ramadan tents in the gardens. Most hotel restaurants stay open throughout the day, simply adding special *Iftar* (fast-breaking) menus. More food is consumed in this month of fasting than in any other month of the year, and the hoteliers always report booming business. From sunset onwards – the exact time when the fast may be broken is given each day in the newspapers – eating goes on apace after the abstinence of the daylight hours and often continues well into the small hours. Each year some 50 people are arrested for violating local rules against eating, drinking or smoking in public during the hours of fasting.

### Islamic calendar

This starts from the year 622AD, the year of Muhammad's "*Hijra*" (flight or escape) from Mecca to Medina. This is why Islamic dates all have AH after them, standing for After Hijra. The Islamic year has 12 lunar months, making it about eleven days shorter than the Gregorian year. The fact that the start of each month depends on the sighting of the new Moon introduces a leeway of a day or two into the dates of most Muslim festivals, such as Ramadan which lasts the full duration (30 days) of a lunar month, so its beginning and its end depend on Moon sightings. By contrast the *Eid al-Adha*, Feast of the Sacrifice, falls on the 10th of *Dhu al-Hijja* (the name of the last lunar month in the Islamic calendar), so its date is known from the 1st of *Dhu al-Hijja*.

**Lunar**

### Raffles, lotteries and prize draws

Given Islam's strict condemnation of gambling, one cannot help but marvel at the proliferation of these in all walks of life. Dubai in particular has a severe case of raffle disease, each shopping mall vying with the other to attract purchasers who, **Fabulous prizes** having spent Dh100 on whatever, are rewarded by the chance to win various prizes, with expensive cars usually topping the list. Days where such offers are being promoted make an unedifying sight with all nationalities in the scrum.

**Fabulous prizes**

**Protection from the sun**

---

### DRESS CODE

Many expatriates, especially women, are strangely insensitive to their dress and the offence it causes to local people. Skimpy shorts and T-shirts are worn by a significant number in shops and public places. Bikinis are fine on the beach and by the pool, but toplessness is forbidden. The local style of dress for women and men, long loose robes did not originate because of Islam. Long before that, they discovered that this was the most comfortable and the most protective from the sun. From Shaikh Zayed to the poorest the white *dishdasha* is like a uniform. Underneath they wear shorts or pants, cotton socks and shoes in town, sandals in the country. They are never bare headed. Under the headcloth (*ghutra*) in plain white or red and white cheques, and the black twisted coil (*agaal*), the men wear a skull cap called a *taqia*. Men of importance and wealth wear a black or faun cloak edged with gold (*bisht*) over the *dishdasha*. Wearing the *bisht* well requires a certain bearing. When the temperature rises, they put Western-style jackets on over the *dishdasha*, on the principle of body insulation, unlike Westerners who prefer to strip. Children in *dishdashas* still play football and ride bikes. The beard is kept by all men as a sign of virility and social acceptance. In the old days it was a punishment to have the beard plucked out. Underneath the women's black cloak (*abaya*) they generally wear colourful robes and *sirwal* (pyjama-like loose trousers tight-fitting on the calves), which is what they will walk round in within the privacy of their home. Long loose dresses or skirts and tops are the best choice for foreign women, and are also more suited to the climate, offering greater protection against the sun and skin damage.

*Section 3*
# History & Heritage

Arabia has retained its political and social independence, by-passed by the main stream of history, for the simple reason that no one coveted their land. As Stephen Longrigg put it in his *The Liquid Gold of Arabia* published 1949 "They have enjoyed the safety of the undesired, and have lived lives to which a hundred generations have specialised them, in conditions barely tolerable to others."

**The safety of the undesired**

The geographical nature of the Arabian peninsula, mostly desert with a narrow margin of habitable land round the coast, is such as to encourage periodic migrations, when the population increased beyond what the land could support. From the Arabian peninsula, bounded on three sides by sea, an impassable barrier in those days, and with an inhospitable desert interior, the consistent migration route was up the Western or the Eastern coasts to the fertile river valleys. Through comparative linguistic studies only fairly recently made, the widely held view is now that the Babylonians, Akkadians, Assyrians, Chaldeans, Amorites, Canaanites, Arameans, Hebrews, Arabians and Abyssinians all shared

**Semitic similarities**

striking points of similarity in their language structure (which is Semitic) and even certain vocabulary elements like numbers, parts of the body, blood-kinship nouns and personal pronouns are almost alike. This would indicate that these people shared a common ancestry, a Semitic ancestry originating in the Arabian peninsula, from which successive waves of migration moved northwards, arriving as barbarian nomads and encountering the city-dwelling settlers of the river Valley cultures. The one did not destroy or assimilate the other, rather they fused to the betterment of both, resulting in some of history's most dynamic civilisations.

It is thought likely that the Semites of the Arabian peninsula had, at a very early date, crossed over from East Africa where they had formed a community together with the Hamites. These Hamites had their own migrations and settled in Egypt. The original ancient Egyptian language has been shown to be a Semito-Hamitic type, not of the pure Semitic group.

Apart from these ethnic links to the civilisations to the north, the south east corner of the Arabian peninsula, known as Magan at that time, also had increasing links to supply the wealthy cultures to the north with a highly prized metal,

copper, and certain types of stone for their religious statues. **Copper trade**
The copper was mixed 8:1 or 10:1 with tin to make bronze for
weapons, bowls and decorative items.

## Chronology

*3500BC*

Mesopotamian river culture between the Tigris and Euphrates,
people were Sumerians, who spoke an agglutinating language
(non-Semitic) and developed the first form of writing and **Mesopotamian**
irrigation, lived in complex cities built of mud brick and **links**
established a religious hierarchy for worshipping their gods.

First Semitic migration out from Arabian peninsula up the
western coast to the Nile Valley merges with the existing
Hamitic population to produce the Egyptians of history.
Second Semitic migration out from Arabian peninsula up the
eastern coast to the Tigris Euphrates Valley, merges with
existing Sumerian population to produce the Babylonians,
who invented the wheel and a system of weights and
measures. In the case of both migrations the Semitic language,
with its three root consonants, two tenses and conjugation of
the verb, comes to dominate.

Jebel Hafeet tombs have pots which are known to be
contemporary with Jemdet Nasr culture in Mesopotamia.

*3000BC*

Hili tower and settlements built.
Ancient Egyptians get their copper from Sinai, ancient
Sumerians from Magan (now Oman and the UAE).

*2500BC*

Third wave of Semitic migration from Arabian peninsula into
the Fertile Crescent (Lebanon, Syria, Israel) to mix with the
Canaanites and the Phoenicians, who went on to popularise
the first exclusively alphabetical writing system with 22 signs.
Rise of Indus Valley cities Harappa and Mohenjo Daro. In
Mesopotamia, tombs of Royal Ur and King Sargon. Here,
Umm al-Nar tombs and settlements in Abu Dhabi, Al-Ain,
Hatta and Ras al-Khaimah.

*2000BC*

Fall of Ur. Rise of Babylon. Trading ends with Magan.

*2000–500BC*

Qattara tomb. Shimmel tombs and settlement. Al-Qusais tombs. Fall of Indus civilisation.

*1500–1200BC*

Semitic Hebrews make their way into Syria, Palestine, and the Semitic Arameans into Lebanon and northern Syria. Rise of Assyrians.

*1000BC*

Iron Age villages and tombs throughout Emirates. Fall of Assyrians.

*500BC*

Semitic Nabateans migrate north to modern Jordan, later establishing their mighty rock-carved capital Petra. Persians take Babylon. End of Iron Age villages here.

*326 AD*

**Alexander's legacy**

Alexander the Great conquers all lands east to the Oxus, introducing Greek culture and Mediterranean trade for first time. Here, Hellenistic cities of Maleihah and Ad-Dour flourish in this trade.

*600AD*

Final wave of migration out from Arabian peninsula, under the banner of Islam, to engulf all these Near and Middle Eastern regions which then become Arabic speaking and develop a cohesive culture through their shared religion.

*635AD*

Battle of Dibba (on east coast just south of Musandam) in which Muslims won against unbelievers. Marks completion of Islamic conversion of Arabia.

*6th–7th century*

Jumeirah, Dubai. Caravan staging post built in sixth century in Sassanian (Persian) times and enlarged under the Arab Ummayads in 7th century.

*7th–17th century*

Julfar, Ras Al-Khaimah. Julfar is the major port of the Emirates coastline, trading with countries as far afield as China (blue and white porcelain found in digs at site).

*1498*

Vasco da Gama, Portuguese explorer, makes first known reference to the area, describing Khor Fakkan, Dibba and Ras Al-Khaimah.

*16th–mid 17th century*

Portuguese domination of the region from their base at Julfar but leaves no religious or cultural legacy beyond a few cannon and ruined forts. Are forced out by hostile tribes inland and by British and Dutch from sea.

*18th-19th century*

Clashes of the Qawasim sea-faring tribe (now rulers of Sharjah and Ras Al-Khaimah) with British ships. Area dubbed Pirate Coast by Britain. Area passes into Persia's sphere of influence.

---

### NO COLONIALISM

The tribes of the Gulf have never been colonised or subservient to any power. Their leaders have signed agreements and treaties with foreign powers from time to time, but the people's allegiance was only ever to their tribal leaders and they retained their independence, despite being flanked by powerful neighbours. As a result a political and religious tolerance evolved, which has become a hallmark of the way the UAE is viewed in the outside world, enabling this small country to play a role far greater than its size merits, in regional and Arab politics. It is the only federal state in the Arab world, and having withstood the pressures and strains of the last 25 years many of which, like the Iraq-Iran war, were potentially divisive, the UAE is clearly here to stay.

**Value of moderation**

*1819–1820*

British Navy destroys and captures every Qawasim ship and takes over Qawasim forts at Ras Al-Khaimah and at Lingah in Persia.

*1820*

**Truce leads to Trucial States**

Shaikhs sign the General Treaty of Peace, prescribing perpetual abstention from plunder and piracy by land and sea and from unproclaimed war. Henceforth called Trucial States or Trucial Coast. The shaikhs continued to fight with each other and the British attempted sometimes to arbitrate in the disputes.

*1838,1839 and 1847*

Agreements signed by the shaikhs for the suppression of the slave trade, whereupon, having been banned on the coast, the slave trade moved inland to Buraimi.

*1843*

Maritime truce signed by shaikhs, cancelling their right to wage regular war on each other. Disputes to be referred to political resident. This truce was renewed in perpetuity in 1853.

*1892*

Agreement signed with Trucial shaikhs not to enter any agreement or have any agent resident other than British government. Increased British intervention.

*1902*

Trucial shaikhs undertake to prohibit import and export of arms.

*1911*

Shaikhs undertake not to give pearling or sponge fishing concessions except with prior approval of British government.

*1922*

Shaikhs undertake not to give concessions for oil prospecting except with British Government's approval.

*1930s and 1940s*

Mutual mistrust between Shaikh rulers and British authorities. British draw up boundaries between Emirates and two British diplomats spend months travelling by camel asking tribal leaders and village heads to which Shaikh they owe allegiance.

**Borders attempted**

*1939*

First oil concession signed by Shaikh Shakhbut.

*1945–48*

War between Dubai and Abu Dhabi over competing territorial claims. Dubai loses land.

*1950s*

After World War Two gradual improvement in relationship with Britain helping in distribution of food and medicine. First time Britain was felt to have become involved in the local population. Hopes for oil are the catalyst.

*1951*

Trucial Oman Levies (later Trucial Oman Scouts) established to maintain peace and order in the Trucial States.

*1951–1957*

Trucial States exposed to British judicial system with British legislation and jurisdiction as applied to British colonies.

*1968*

British withdrawal from Gulf as part of worldwide cutbacks.

*1971*

United Arab Emirates formed. Creates own set of laws modelled on Egyptian, Sudanese and Jordanian, where French and British law had already been assimilated with the principles of Sharia law.

**UAE Federation**

## 1979

Shaikh Zayed threatens to resign if other six rulers do not settle remaining border disputes and give up private armies. Compromise reached and Abu Dhabi imposes centralisation of welfare state, police, legal system and telecommunications network. Rashid of Dubai takes title of Prime Minister.

## 1981

Gulf Co-operation Council formed with Saudi Arabia, Bahrain, Qatar, Kuwait, Oman, and United Arab Emirates.

### FORMATION OF THE UAE FEDERATION

**Voice of reason**

The impetus to form the federation of the UAE was the announcement by Britain of its withdrawal from the region as part of its cutbacks following the election of a Labour government committed to spending cuts. This left a security vacuum which the Gulf countries were extremely concerned about. Abu Dhabi and Dubai were the driving forces behind the federation and made most of the running in setting up the meetings to agree upon the terms. Bahrain and Qatar were originally to have been part of the federation but opted out at the last moment. Bahrain declared its independence in 1971 and Qatar followed suit. The withdrawal of these two sophisticated states meant that a large number of experienced civil servants were no longer available to set up and run the federal administration. Iran saw itself as the natural power to fill the vacuum and promptly moved to announce its sovereignty over the three islands in the Straits of Hormuz, Abu Musa, Greater Thumb and Lesser Thumb.

Ras Al-Khaimah did not join at the inception, but changed its mind, joining in February 1972. It was allotted 6 seats at the Assembly, putting it in third place of importance after Dubai and Abu Dhabi's 8. In the rules of the federation the President and his deputy are elected every five years and may both be re-elected. The federation has diplomatic relations with 130 countries, a fact which has helped enormously in placing the UAE on the international map. It joined the United Nations and the Arab League at the earliest possible date. In 1974 Abu Dhabi gave away some 28% of its income in foreign aid, which also helped spread the name of the UAE, and earned it a reputation for financial generosity and political reasonableness.

*1985–1989*

Oil prices collapse and force cutbacks. Sharjah worst hit, left in heavy debt. Brother of Sharjah's ruler, Sheikh Sultan, attempts Palace coup as a result, but is forced to back down by UAE Supreme Council.

*1990–1991*

UAE contributes troops to anti-Iraq coalition, resulting in Western troops being based in UAE, mainly at Jebel Ali, Dubai.

*1991*

Bank of Credit and Commerce International (BCCI) scandal causes much embarrassment to Abu Dhabi, the bank's major shareholder. The bank is closed and Abu Dhabi protects local customers by buying up all UAE branches and turning them into Union National Bank.

*1996*

25 year anniversary of UAE Federation. Great celebrations to commemorate achievements.

**Relations with the British**

Given the extreme poverty of the local resources before the days of oil, and the desert landscape which meant that much effort had to be expended to rise above subsistence level, it is not surprising that the competition between the maritime city states and their shaikhs was extremely fierce, not to say violent. The tribes fought and raided each other to try to gain and retain control of their few assets, frequently forming temporary political alliances to extend their influence and power. The same thing happened at sea, with an incessant series of pirate attacks between commercial rivals, and more ever-changing political alliances depending on how they felt they could best retain domination. In this way at sea the tribal chiefs of the maritime city states sought to dominate Gulf naval commerce, in the same way that the tribes of the interior constantly struggled to dominate the caravan routes, wells and oases.

**Struggle for dominance**

The first step towards ending this traditional system of violent competition was brought about by the British imposing the General Treaty of Peace in 1820 which prescribed a land and maritime truce.

Incidents continued to flare up however, notably when in 1833 Dubai declared itself independent of Abu Dhabi and asked the Qawasim shaikhs of Sharjah for support against Abu Dhabi. Both Dubai and Abu Dhabi suffered badly in the fighting that ensued and then tried to recoup their losses by preying on shipping in the Gulf. The British intervened in 1835 and forced the aggressors, mainly the Abu Dhabi people, to give up the vessels they had captured and to pay compensation. At the same time the British Political Resident suggested that the shaikhs sign a maritime truce between each other during the summer pearling season. From then on the coast was known as the Trucial Coast. In 1853 these progressed to a "Perpetual Maritime Truce" prohibiting the prosecuting of feuds at sea and stipulating too that the British would punish the aggressor.

**Conflicting needs**

Several treaties were signed in the early 1800s by the shaikhs after persuasion by the British to suppress the slave trade, but it continued to flourish nevertheless. The shaikhs did not sympathise with or understand the aims of the anti-slavery movement and felt that the slave trade was simply like any other commerce, and was sanctioned by Islam. It did not end till oil wealth and prosperity made it unnecessary as a source of income.

**Mistrust**

Till the mid-1920s the British relationship with the Trucial States had been designed to secure Britain's seaborne trade and to defend India, as well as to prevent the arms and slave trade and to protect the British Indian merchants in the coastal ports. The establishment of the airbase at Sharjah changed the nature of the relationship and a certain Colonel Dickson, who had been brought in from Kuwait to help conclude the air agreement, noted that the mistrust the shaikhs had of the British originated in their fear that the British would interfere more in their internal affairs and insist on the manumission of the slaves who formed a large majority of their pearl divers. Dickson's report said it would be "hard to find any more uncouth and suspicious Arabs than those of the Trucial Coast, who did not want their country to be opened up". It took a further five years for Shaikh Saeed of Dubai and Shaikh Shakhbut of Abu Dhabi to agree to landings on their territory, even though they were more friendly to the British than the other shaikhs, having regarded them as their shield against Saudi domination since 1925. One of the tribal shaikhs said to the Assistant British Agent from Bahrain in 1938, when he was visiting on an exploratory party in the Buraimi area, "We don't want your oil, we don't want your money, we don't like your cars".

Great difficulty was experienced in negotiating with the tribal shaikhs of the hinterland, who did not want British interference. The British used distribution of tea and sugar in generous quantities to help sweeten their interference and also made themselves popular by setting up desert locust control units. In 1939 they established the first dispensary at Sharjah.

**Sugar and tea**

## The Tribal System and the Shaikh

The tribal chief or shaikh was the all powerful ruler. It was the shaikh who sat in judgement over all disputes within the tribe or between tribes, who decided on appropriate punishment, who looked after the shaikhdoms' finances and charged taxes and tariffs to support the needs of the tribe. He generally owned a number of pearling ships himself. The system of who became shaikh was not entirely a matter of hereditary custom but also a question of who from within the ruling family emerged as the natural leader. Hence in recent times we can see how Shaikh Zayed, with the consent of the rest of the Al-Nahyan family, eased out his elder brother Shaikh Shakhbut in 1966, who was felt by all to be holding back the pace of progress for Abu Dhabi. The current system in Dubai with the ruling Al-Maktoum family is also similar, where of the four brothers the strength of personality of Mohammed makes him the most powerful of them all even though Maktoum the eldest is the nominal ruler.

**Natural leader**

In the early 1900s power was generally achieved through assassination of the rival. Whether or not it was then held on to, depended on the personality of the ruler, the length of their reign, and the size of their purse. The whole region was characterised by chronic insecurity, with the shaikhs vying for the support of Bedouin tribesmen through lavish gifts and hospitality. The Bedouin were never cowed by authority and

**MAJLIS SYSTEM**

From around 1800 onwards the area that is currently the Emirates consisted of three shaikhdoms – Abu Dhabi, Ras Al-Khaimah and Sharjah, each with its ruling Shaikh. Each ran his own *majlis* or Council (literally in Arabic place of sitting) to which any member of the tribe could come with his grievances. These *majlises*, generally held at certain fixed times and days which were known to the tribe, were places where much debate and discussion took place about the issues of the day, but the decision of the ruling Shaikh was always final. This simple but effective system of government had existed throughout the Arabian peninsula and Gulf for centuries and continued here till the 1960s.

**Open to all**

knew perfectly well that the shaikhs would rather retain their friendship than incur their enmity, in case they should need Bedouin support in some future quarrel with other shaikhs. As a result the Bedouin quite openly travelled about through villages they had previously robbed, and were assured of hospitality.

Bedouin raids and counter raids sometimes led to all-out war, such as the Abu Dhabi - Dubai war of 1946 which was preceded by skirmishes that began in 1943 with Dubai looting 150 Abu Dhabi camels.

Greed for oil revenues was another frequent cause of fighting, such as when the Ras Al-Khaimah Shaikh signed an oil concession secretly, then denied it so he could keep the money. The resultant squabbles enabled Shaikh Saqr (the current ruler) to declare himself ruler in 1949. He had been one of the greedy ruler's nephews.

**Bedouin philosophy**

Shaikh Zayed himself, ruler for 30 years, is a tribal leader in classic form. His speeches are rich with Bedouin philosophy and Koranic quotes. His vision and wisdom are questioned by no-one. Concern for the Bedouin has always been key for him, and there are today scores of satellites villages built by the government to settle the Bedouin and provide them with full services. Before they walked miles for water, now they can turn on a tap. Taming a people so unused to laws and settled codes of behaviour was not always straightforward, but in a sense once they were provided with equal housing and funds, the reason for all their raids and skirmishing disappeared.

Since the federation of the seven Emirates in 1971 a major characteristic of the UAE has been its ability to reach consensus agreement, even at times of potential conflict, such as during the Iran Iraq war (1980–1988) or during the Desert Shield operation (1991), when there were mixed feelings about the extent of American involvement in the region. In its role within the Gulf Co-operation Council (established in 1991) , the UAE's approach has again been a conciliatory one, looking for common ground and compromise on potentially thorny issues like shared water resources and electricity.

**Consensus approach**

## Pearling

Nomadic or semi-settled peoples could raise cash to purchase essential supplies like rice and cotton cloth by occasionally selling a famous breed of racing or riding camel, but for the remainder of the population based in the oases or on the coast, pearling provided them with their only means of income.

> ### PEARL OYSTERS
>
> There are three types of oyster which produce pearls in the Gulf and each type has its preferred depth ranging from low tide mark to 36 metres and its preferred conditions of light, currents, type of sea bed and feeding matter. The oyster forms in the pearl after a tiny particle of grit has penetrated the shell, causing the oyster to secrete layer upon layer of Mother of Pearl (scientific name *nacre* from the Arabic *naqqara* for small drum) over the particle of grit. The most perfect pearls were generally found at the greatest depths, so captains with good and experienced divers headed for those.

Most of the pearl banks in the Gulf are closer to the Arabian coastline than to the Persian, and although their locations had been known for centuries, none were claimed as the properties of particular shaikhdoms and so all were open to any boat from the Arab ports. The captains of the pearling boats used to find their way to the pearl bank of their choice with no maps or compasses, using instead aids like the sun, stars, colour and depth of the water. The boats were equipped with sails and oars, so in calm conditions the already exhausted divers had to row from one pearl bank to another. Some captains stayed by a favourite pearl bank most of the season, while others liked to move frequently between banks. The pearling season lasted around 120 days from early June to late September. But if Ramadan fell during the summer, it was sometimes brought forward by a month as diving was prohibited during the fast.

**Exhausted divers**

India was the age-old market for pearls and after they became fashionable in Great Britain and then in the twentieth century in the United States, the result was something of a boom in the pearl market, reaching its peak in 1929. Only exceptionally large or perfect pearls were sold individually and the fortunate diver who found such a pearl would then get well recompensed, but such instances were rare. The remainder were carefully graded by using a series of copper sieves with five different sized holes, and then sold in bulk to a middleman. The middleman, frequently from Dubai, then

**Indian merchants**

sold the pearls on to the Indian pearl merchants who came over, generally from Bombay, for the season. The pearl trade was therefore the first incentive for Hindu families to come and settle on these Arab coasts. They remained aliens however even after several generations because their religion, eating habits, customs and dress marked them as different and their men were not permitted to marry a Muslim girl, though the marriage of a Muslim man to a Hindu girl was considered acceptable.

**Slave divers**

One little known fact is that slaves formed over 80% of the diving population, one reason why the Trucial shaikhs were not keen to implement the slave trade agreements signed with the British. If the divers were liberated, the loss to the coast would be extremely serious. After 1902 the African slave trade declined and was replaced by Beluch slaves from Mekran. The pearling industry depended heavily on slaves and the possession of house-born slaves was firmly established on the coast. Slaves were part of the household and the master of the household legitimately took his share of the dive. The Koran authorised the owning of slaves but made it clear the master was responsible for their well-being and humane treatment.

When the pearling industry collapsed in the 1930s, it became increasingly difficult for households with a number of slaves to provide for them, and many were liberated as a result. Such slaves occasionally rose to important positions as trusted employees of rulers and became fully integrated into the Arab society – except when it came to marriage. Daughters of tribal Arabs were not given to slaves in marriage, though a tribal head of family could legitimately father children by a female slave, who were then brought up with the other children and treated as equals until it came to marriage again.

*Derelict dhows on the creekside*

The hierarchy of the pearling industry was so complex that divers' courts were set up to safeguard the interests of all those involved in the diving community, from the financiers and captains right down to the divers themselves. Even the rulers themselves sometimes became embroiled in disputes, often involving imposition of pearling taxes or changes in the season dates.

### Other Livelihoods and Activities for Men
*Importing*
With the cash generated by the pearling industry there was scope for a certain amount of import of merchandise that was not just for subsistence. Weapons and ammunition became one of the more interesting imports to flourish, with the rifle being every tribal Arab's most coveted possession. Merchants, generally from Dubai, flourished in this booming period where the pearl market was buoyant in the early twentieth century, and the rulers of the shaikhdoms also derived a good source of income from customs duties levied on these imports, usually around 2% of their value.

**Prize possession**

### Boat Building

The major manufacturing industry present in the UAE territories was boat building, making boats of all sizes from pearling boats to larger trading vessels to fishing boats. The wood and rope necessary was usually imported from India or East Africa, while the sail canvas generally came from Kuwait or Bahrain.

### Pottery

Some of the wadis in Ras Al-Khaimah like Wadi Haqil were endowed with the right kind of clay for pottery, so small communities developed producing various household pots and water storage jars.

### Metalwork

Small numbers of coppersmiths and blacksmiths existed to make kitchenware and the ubiquitous brass coffee pots, though the majority of items were imported from Oman, the craft centres of Nizwa and Bahla.

### Carpentry

Wood from local palm or acacia trees was unsuitable for carving, so wood for furniture like cupboards and chests had to be imported. Only a handful of professional carpenters existed in the Emirates.

## Bedouin Life

Bedouin in the Emirates in the pre-oil days, as throughout the Arabian peninsula, are not always clear cut nomads. There are stages of semi- nomadism, in which townsfolk who were once Bedouin still betray their nomadic origin, and others who are settled at certain seasons and nomadic at others. These movements are not like the wanderings of gypsies, but are dictated by conditions on the ground. The Bedouin therefore represent the best adaptation of human life to conditions in the desert. In many ways the Bedouin lifestyle was similar to the pirate, with the desert equating to the sea. The Bedouin like the pirate learnt to survive on very little, and then whenever he could or when his needs demanded, he would conduct a **The sport of** raid on his better-off neighbours to take what he wanted. **raiding** Raiding was a form of national sport, a manly occupation, and much early Arabian literature glorified the techniques. Where such keen competition existed for water and pasturage, the desert population was bound to be split into warring tribes, and as such it formed the base of the economic structure of Bedouin society.

In the UAE, Bedouin would often be a mixture, raising camel and sheep and moving round wherever grazing was best, then returning in winter time to villages in oases where they cultivated date gardens and a few other basic commodities.

The hardship of his lifestyle shows itself in his lean physique. Tenacity and endurance (Arabic *sabr*) are his supreme virtues, mental qualities which enable him to survive where all else would perish. Shaikh Mohammad, Crown Prince of Dubai, has reinstituted the endurance horse races (in which he frequently takes part himself and indeed sometimes wins, but always finishes) which foster such qualities.

**Endurance races**

The very inhospitality of the environment has served as protection, till the discovery of oil, against foreign invaders, for there was before nothing to attract them. In a sense the Bedouin sacred duty of hospitality is a mitigating factor for the raiding. No guest could be refused it in such an inhospitable land, and to harm a guest after taking him in is a grave offence against honour and against God.

Society was organised by clan. Each tent represents a family, an encampment of tents forms a *hayy*, the members of which form a clan (*qawm*). A number of kindred clans grouped together make a tribe (Arabic *qabila*). All members of the tribe consider each other as of one blood and submit to the authority of one chief, the Shaikh. The tent and its few possessions are individual property, but water, pasturage and cultivable land are common property of the tribes.

**Tribal structure**

If murder is committed within the clan, none will defend the murderer. If it is committed outside it becomes a vendetta or blood feud which can last up to 40 years and in which any fellow clan member may have to pay with his life. Blood calls for blood in the primitive law of the desert. Nothing could be worse for a Bedouin than to lose his tribal affiliation. Genealogies are of great importance and the Bedouin takes great pride in his ancestry. He views the civilised man as less happy and far inferior. The Bedouin woman lives in a

**Blood feud**

polygamous family in which the man is master, but she is nevertheless free to choose a husband and leave him if ill-treated. Unlike the western system, she retains her tribal name after marriage, as do all Muslim women.

When early Islam spread beyond the Arabian peninsula, the Bedouin armies were divided into units based on tribal lines, and then settled in the conquered lands in tribes, and gave the new converts to Islam the status of "clients" attached to particular tribes till they were assimilated.

*Camels and 4WDs – part of the same world*

### Distances and the Old Style of Travel

In the days before 4WDs and roads, camelback was the only means of travel. The journey from Abu Dhabi to Al-Ain took seven days for the total distance of 160 kilometres, a journey which now takes 90 minutes on tarmac. From Abu Dhabi to Liwa took five days. In an attempt to shorten the arduous overland section, some people used to travel by boat as far as Ruweis before heading inland to Liwa, though the total journey still took five days.

The routes themselves were frequently plagued by raiding parties and bandits, and so together with the actual hardship of the travelling, it follows that such journeys were not undertaken without good reason, and as infrequently as possible. Camel caravans offered safety in numbers and their routes would sometimes stumble upon Bedouin encampments in the desert. A timeless tradition of hospitality evolved in such circumstances, whereby the caravan became the responsibility of the Bedouin encampment for varying periods. If the caravan was offered coffee, the Bedouin would offer protection to the caravan on its departure till it was out of sight. If the caravan travellers stayed for a meal, they were given safe custody from their departure for one day's camel trekking. And if they stayed overnight the Bedouin took on their protection for three days' journey beyond the encampment. Any attack by raiders during this period was defended and avenged by the Bedouin.

**Rules of hospitality**

### Continuing Bedouin Traditions
Such Bedouin hospitality and the traditions that went with it were the basis of everyday life in the pre-oil days. Each tribe had its own particular customs and practices, and the subtle differences between tribes could be recognised by others. Thus the Bedouin watching the approach of a camel caravan, knowing these differences and with such a small base population anyway, could tell who they were and whether they were friend or foe. The offer of coffee (the unsweetened greenish cardamom variety) would only be made once the Bedouin was certain he wanted to welcome you as a guest.

**Importance of coffee**

Still today this tradition continues and when you visit someone's house or office, you have not been fully welcomed till you have been offered coffee, tea or a soft drink as a sign of acceptance. Only after it has been offered by the host and some drunk by the guest, is the guest free to state his business, problem or need and the host is obliged to listen. Before then, only greetings and pleasantries can be exchanged and it is quite wrong to raise any serious topics until after the coffee. The host must always first have welcomed the guest by supplying the refreshment, thereby signifying he has taken responsibility for the visit. With Arab coffee it is polite to drink one, two or three cups of cardamom flavoured coffee, waggle

**Guest etiquette**

the cup to and fro to signify you have had enough, then hand the empty cup back to the server. If you do not waggle it, you will simply be poured more and more.

Before entering a private home or a mosque, shoes should be removed at the door. Always sit in such a way that the sole of your foot is not visible to your host. Never ask after a man's wife or daughters, only after his family or sons. Traditionally men and women do not eat or socialise together when guests are present.

### Hunting and Falconry

The use of firearms in hunting was not traditional in this part of the world. A rifle was a man's most treasured possession, often ancient and highly decorated and was passed from father to son. In old photographs the head of the household is always carrying his rifle, and wearing his curved dagger (Arabic *khanjar*) if he could afford it. Ammunition was extremely scarce and the price for one shot was far more than the meat value of what it might shoot – a gazelle for instance. The only occasions when precious ammunition was used were perhaps one celebratory shot in a family wedding, or to defend the family. On average therefore only a handful of bullets were fired during the father's entire lifetime, before the gun plus remaining ammunition were passed on to the eldest son.

**Rare ammunition**

It followed therefore that most men were poor shots, never having had the opportunity to practise as precious bullets were not to be wasted trying to hunt wild game. Matters changed of course when earlier this century the value of meat began to outstrip the cost of the ammunition and the first species to be hunted in earnest were oryx and ostrich. By 1940 ostrich were extinct in Arabia and oryx by early 1960s.

The most traditional of hunting methods is of course falconry. The Houbara bustard was the preferred quarry, weighing 2–3 kilograms it was large enough to feed a family, yet too small to risk wasting a precious bullet. It is a measure of Bedouin ingenuity that the method of falconry was devised, a complex business which required much careful preparation.

After achieving the capture of a falcon, the men had a bare two to three weeks to train it before the migrating Houbaras started to pass through. This was achieved by first calming the

---

CATCHING A FALCON

The Houbara migrated from the northern hemisphere every autumn passing through Arabia to Africa for the winter. Before it, the birds of prey migrated across Arabia also on their way to Africa for the winter, and the Bedouin devised various ways of trapping Peregrine and Saqr falcons in transit. One such method was where a Bedouin was buried in the sand with only his head and one hand showing, which was then disguised in a bush. Tied to the bush was a pigeon, whose fluttering attracted the falcon as easy prey. Once close enough the Bedouin could throw a cloth over the falcon's head, whereupon an accomplice would appear from downwind and finish the job and dig out his friend. Complicated traps were sometimes also used in which men sat in hides for days on end waiting, often using other birds as fake prey. Female falcons were preferred, as they were larger.

---

wild bird and getting it used to the falconer's voice and handling. For three days the falcon's eyes were threaded shut using a horse hair through the lower eyelids and throughout this time the bird was kept constantly by its master and was spoken to as much as possible, using a pet name. When the thread was removed the falconer offered the bird its first food, thereby cementing the bond of trust with the master it now saw for the first time. Gradually the falconer would let the falcon fly from his glove (Arabic *mangalah*) for ever increasing distances, whilst still attached to a string, to food specially tethered for it. The falcon was also introduced to the scent of Houbara through wings which the falconer had kept for the purpose from the previous season. Ideally the falconer was then ready when the first Houbaras arrived on their migration, and hunting continued every day throughout the winter months to feed the falconer and his family. The falcon was fed the head and neck, while the body was traditionally cooked by being buried whole, feathers and all, in a glowing fire. When done, the charred feathers and skin were removed to reveal the tasty white meat that had cooked in its own juice. Houbara are nocturnal, spending the day resting under a bush. The Bedouin would therefore search for tracks in the sand at the crack of dawn and trace the tracks to the bush, whereupon the falcon would be released hopefully to complete the job. On occasions when no Houbaras were caught, the children were sent out at night to catch a gerbil or jerboa to feed the falcon, or else efforts were simply redoubled the next day.

**Training technique**

**Juicy meat**

When, come the spring, the Houbaras migrated, the falcon was set free, and the falconer consoled himself with the thought of a new bird the following autumn. They did not keep the falcons from season to season because in the summer months any prey small enough for the falcon to kill would not also feed the falconer's family, so the symbiotic relationship reached its natural end.

**Falconry networking**

In summer months therefore the Bedouin hunted on camelback instead with their Saluki dogs, usually hare, which were much slower in the summer heat and therefore easier to catch. In winter hare were notoriously tricky to hunt. As with the Houbara, the hare was shared by hunter and dog. Such hunting expeditions still give the shaikhs and rulers invaluable occasions to spend uninterrupted time with their own people – a little akin to golf for Westerners as a means of chatting informally to colleagues and networking.

### Egg hunting

The other means of supplementing a meagre staple diet was to track down eggs, mainly birds' eggs, especially the Socotra cormorant eggs and turtle eggs which would be found by following the tracks of the female to her nesting hole. They could be kept for several weeks in a shaded spot before going off, because they were freshly laid. Eggs from the huge Socotra cormorant colonies were collected by the bucketful but the impact on the cormorant population was negligible as only the fresh eggs from the very beginning of the laying season were taken. So early in the season the female cormorant would generally lay a new batch on discovering her first ones missing.

### Mushroom hunting

**Truffle treat**

Early rain sees local people out in droves scouring the ground along the coastal scrub for the coveted subterranean mushroom called *"faqah"*, thought to be related to the truffle. This seems to be an especially popular family activity, involving women and all, at weekends along the coastal stretch between Sharjah and Ras Al-Khaimah.

---

### FALAJ SYSTEM

In every oasis irrigated by *falaj* (channel) system the owners of the date gardens contributed to the maintenance of the channels. In some oases, like Dhaid for example, the date garden owners also paid a tax on the *falaj* water itself. Most *falaj* systems bring the water through an underground tunnel several kilometres long from an area where the water table is higher. No new falajs have been built within living memory – in fact almost all are probably pre-Islamic. Their maintenance and restoration is a dangerous and complex task known to a specialised few in the oases. One trusted person in the oasis had the job of diverting the water from one channel to another, timing the duration of flow to each channel using a sundial by day and the movement of the stars by night. Each date garden owner paid his share according to usage, and the money went towards the upkeep of the *falaj*.

---

### Herbal and Plant Medicines

The Bedouin have developed knowledge over centuries of the various medicinal properties of plants and herbs that grow wild in the desert. The desert squash for example (*citrullus colocynthis*) is used as a cure for diabetes, with four seeds a day said to be enough to control diabetes in the elderly. The poisonous sap of the calotropis procera, Sodom's Apple, was dried and used to fill aching teeth, and the woodier stems were used for charcoal. The leaves were made into poultices to heal rheumatic joints, as well as being used for fertiliser, dug into the roots of ailing palm trees. Some plants were used as a snuff to clear the sinuses (*salsola inbricata*), while others were used to cure fevers or even to dry out burns so that no scar is left behind.

**Leaf remedies**

### Henna and Cosmetics

The best known cosmetic is henna, used to dye the hair and to paint as decoration on hands and feet at *eids* (religious festivals) and special occasions like weddings. The henna paste is made from mixing the crushed dried berries and leaves of the henna bush with medicinal herbs. Poultices of henna plant leaves are also used to appease headaches. Twigs of the *salvadore persica* plant are used as chewing sticks to clean teeth.

### The Arabic language

Arabic in the UAE has now been unofficially named the second language, having been overwhelmed by other languages of non-Arab expatriate workers such as Urdu, Hindi and English. Such is the domination in numbers of the non-Arabic speaking population over the local population that nationals sometimes find themselves unable to communicate in places like hospitals and clinics. Arabic is also being undermined by a kind of pigeon Arabic spoken by sub-continentals like taxi drivers and shop keepers. Shop signs frequently have their written Arabic misspelt, so though the shopkeepers are generally Muslim, they do not understand Arabic, but learn the Koran by rote with no comprehension of the meaning.

**Corrupting influences**

English is widely spoken in all shops and businesses, where 99% of all shop keepers and assistants are Indian. If as an English speaker you wanted a second language here, Hindi would in all honesty be the most useful. Arabic is everywhere on the street signs and adverts, along with English, so you will see it everywhere and get plenty of opportunity to practise your Arabic alphabet. Opportunities to speak it or hear it however are very limited and your best chance of hearing it is on the Arabic TV channels. The police are likely to be the only Arabic speakers you ever encounter whose English is poor. The police have to come by law to the scene of every traffic accident, however minor, to write the accident report for the insurance, and given the frequency of road accidents, this is likely to be your best chance of using Arabic. The written Arabic handwriting of the police report is difficult to read unless you are an experienced Arabic speaker.

**Practise your alphabet**

When not in handwritten form, Arabic script is in fact the easiest thing about the language. Many are daunted by the script and the right to left flow of text, yet the alphabet contains only 29 characters and there are strict rules to determine which characters join on to which. The characters change their shape according to their position within the word but always following the same strict rules. The process of learning the characters and their shapes is therefore purely a memory exercise which can be done easily in three days and thereafter just requires practice. As for the right to left flow of text, it just takes a little time to adjust, rather like driving on the right instead of the left of the road.

**Memory exercise**

Having mastered the script the task begins in earnest. The first conceptually difficult thing you now encounter is that only the consonants are written – you have to supply the vowels yourself. In that case, how do you know which vowels to put where? The answer is that you do not, or at least not until you have a thorough grasp of the intricacies of Arabic grammar and word structure, which takes a good three or four months' study. For this reason all beginners' texts and children's school books are fully annotated with vowel signs added in the form of dashes and dots above and below the line. Getting a student to read an unvowelled text aloud is always an excellent way of assessing his level, as it instantly reveals the depth of his understanding of Arabic grammar.

**Where are the vowels?**

Pronunciation is another area which is not as daunting as it may seem. Of the 29 consonants, 18 have direct phonetic equivalents in English such as b, d, t, l, s. The rest have no direct equivalent and range from emphatic versions of d, s, and t, usually transliterated as D, S and T, to a small handful of sounds which are genuinely difficult for Westerners to pronounce. The gutteral stop, usually represented in transliteration as a reversed comma, is probably the one that gives most trouble, sounding like a vibrating constriction of the larynx.

Like Hebrew, Arabic is a Semitic language with a root system. The root of an idea or concept is represented by a simple verb, usually consisting of three consonants. These verbs are the very basis of the Arabic language, and all variations of meaning around the root idea are expressed by imposing different patterns on the basic root. Hence, in the simplest of examples, from the root K T B (*kataba* when vowelled) which means "he wrote", you can make *maktab* meaning "office", *maktaba* meaning "library" and *kitaab* meaning "book". The vowels are fully conjugated, so *katabnaa* is "we wrote" and *yatabuuna* is "they are writing". Arabic dictionaries list words under their root, so if you cannot identify the root, you cannot look up the word. Hunting for words in the dictionary is something the beginner spends a long time doing.

**Root system**

Arabic is, by the very nature of its structure, an extremely rich language, capable of expressing fine shades of meaning, and this is reflected in the wealth of Arabic literature,

**Rich vocabulary**

especially poetry. The average English tabloid reader is said to have a working vocabulary of 3,000 words, whereas the Arab equivalent is said to have about 10,000.

There are also many interesting features of the language which hint at the nature and attitudes of the Arab mind, notably the existence of only two tenses, perfect and imperfect: there is no future tense. In the Arabic concept of time there is only one distinction that matters: has something been finished or is it still going on? Another curiosity is that the plural of inanimate objects is treated grammatically as feminine singular, a characteristic which invites speculation.

**Differing sense of time**

The written Arabic language together with Islam is one of the few unifying factors in the Arab world. It means that newspapers published in Egypt can be distributed and read from Morocco to Iraq and even down to Yemen. In the spoken language however the 22 countries of the Arab League also express their individuality, to the extent that a Moroccan and an Iraqi speaking their local dialect will understand each other only with difficulty. In order to communicate therefore they have to compromise and speak a form of modern classical Arabic which is understood by educated Arabs everywhere, and it is this middle Arabic which you generally speak as a foreigner. The Arabic spoken in the Gulf is the closest to classical Arabic as you might expect, since the Arabian Peninsula has been least influenced by external factors and has never been colonised by a foreign power. By contrast, the forms of spoken Arabic furthest away from the pure written classical Arabic are Lebanese and Egyptian, since these countries have been most exposed to foreign influences.

**Purest Arabic**

### Useful Arabic Words and Phrases

The only opportunity you may have to use any of these words is whilst travelling in the interior of the Emirates. If you make a trip to neighbouring Oman however, you will often find a chance to practise a little.

### Everyday Arabic

| | |
|---|---|
| Hello, welcome | *marhaba, ahlan* |
| Goodbye | *ma'a as-salaama* |
| Yes | *aiwa, na'am* |
| No | *laa* |

| | |
|---|---|
| Please | *min fadlak* |
| Sorry, excuse me | *'afwan, muta'assif* |
| Hurry up, let's go | *yallah* |
| More, again, also | *kamaan* |
| Is it possible? May I? | *mumkin?* |
| How much (does it cost?) | *bikaam?* |
| Cheap | *rakhees* |
| Expensive | *ghaalee* |
| Money | *fuluus* |
| A lot, much, very | *katheer* |
| No problem | *mush mushkila* |
| Never mind | *ma'a laysh* |
| Shop | *dukkan* |
| Open | *maftuuh* |
| Closed | *mughlag* |
| Bank | *bank, masraf* |
| Post Office | *maktab bareed* |
| Chemist | *saydalia* |
| Diarrhoea | *ishaal* |
| Ill, sick | *mareed* |
| Market | *souq* |
| Museum | *mathaf* |
| Hospital | *mustashfaa* |
| Police | *buulees* |
| Airport | *mataar* |
| Ticket | *tadhkara* |
| Suitcase | *shanta* |
| Hotel | *fundug, ootel* |
| Room | *ghurfa* |
| Toilet, bathroom | *hammam, bait maa* |
| Towel | *manshafa* |
| Soap | *saabuun* |
| Gents | *rijaal* |
| Ladies | *sayyidaat* |
| The bill | *al-hisaab* |
| Restaurant | *mat'am, restoraan* |
| Breakfast | *futoor* |
| Lunch | *ghadaa* |
| Dinner | *'ashaa* |
| Glass | *kubbeyah* |
| Wine | *khamr, nabeedh* |

| | |
|---|---|
| Beer | *beera* |
| Mineral water | *maa ma'daniya* |
| Coffee | *gahwa* |
| Eggs | *bayd* |
| Fish | *samak* |
| Meat | *lahm* |
| Fruit | *fawaakah* |
| Butter | *zabdah* |
| Cheese | *jubnah* |
| Yoghurt | *laban* |
| Jam | *murabbah* |
| Honey | *'asl* |
| Bread | *khubz* |
| Sugar | *sukkar* |
| Vegetables | *khudra* |
| Today | *al-yawm* |
| Tomorrow | *bukra* (in keeping with the Arab sense of time, this can mean any point between tomorrow and never) |
| Taxi | *taaksee* |
| Car | *sayyaarah* |
| Right | *yameen* |
| Left | *yasaar* |
| Straight on | *dhughri, 'alaa tool* |
| Far | *ba'eed* |
| Near, close by | *gareeb* |
| Petrol | *benzeen* |
| Where? | *wayn?* |
| What? | *shuu?* |
| Forbidden | *mamnoo'* |
| Bus | *bas* |
| Good | *zain* |
| Bad | *mush zain* |
| Hot | *haar* |
| Cold | *baarid* |

## Greetings

On first meeting when travelling in the interior or generally outside the cities, the standard greeting is, *As-salaamoo 'alaykum*, literally meaning "May peace be upon you".

---

### THE ARAB DIET

The traditional Arab breakfast consists of thin Arabic bread, melted butter, honey, dates, omelette, fruit and coffee. The main meal is eaten at lunchtime and is usually lamb, chicken or fish cooked in stews with rice and salad. In the evening a lighter uncooked meal is eaten, with variables such as bread, cheese, yoghurt and fruit, but no rice. Meals were traditionally eaten from a large common tray round which the whole family sat and ate. The right hand only was used. With no cutlery or plates, washing up was minimal, an important consideration where water was scarce.

Today of course the traditional national diet has been supplemented by American-style fast food outlets and convenience food from the supermarkets, leading not only to the occurrence for the first time of various heart diseases, but also to tooth and gum problems of a type not known in this part of the world before.

---

The standard reply is *Wa 'alaykum as-salaam*, meaning "And upon you too".

There are three common phrases you will hear incessantly. *In shaa Allah*, meaning "If God wishes", used all the time in the sense of "hopefully". If you say "See you tomorrow", an Arab will reply "*In shaa Allah*", meaning "Yes, if God permits it and nothing happens to prevent it in the meantime". It can also be a polite way of avoiding a commitment, conveying "Let us hope so..."

**Optimistic God**

*Al-hamdoo lillaah*, meaning "thanks be to God". This is said every time anything works out the way it should have done. It expresses relief, something like "thank God for that!".

*Taffaddal*, meaning "Please go ahead, come in". This is said by your host when you arrive and on entering the house or room, and before eating. It has the sense of "after you", and literally means "Please be so good as to ..."

### Etiquette

In a Muslim country you must accept that different codes of dress and behaviour apply. Muslim men and women alike find it offensive to see too much exposed flesh. However outwardly westernised, the UAE is a deeply conservative society and you will never see an Emirati woman or man showing more than the hands and ankles. Shorts, T-shirts and

**Muslim codes of behaviour**

sleeveless décolleté tops are inappropriate except in the private beach and sports clubs. Such dress is equated with moral loosesness and sexual availability. Too much direct eye contact and an over firm handshake are also misinterpreted. Women should not proffer their hand for shaking first. Public embracing between opposite sexes is taboo, though perfectly acceptable between men greeting each other. Blowing your nose in public is also considered offensive. During the month of Ramadan you should avoid eating, drinking and smoking in public during daylight hours. There are fines for anyone, even non-Muslims, found violating this. Never take

**Permission for photography**

photographs of local people, especially women, without having first asked permission. Some people find it extremely offensive, and others, who might not have minded, will feel that you have taken a liberty. Women when travelling alone should dress as modestly as possible and avoid direct eye contact. Wear a wedding ring, say you are married and have 10 children.

On meetings with business colleagues the custom is to shake hands and exchange business cards. Meetings and negotiations can be held in restaurants over lunch or dinner. Women are rarely involved in such meetings. If your host does not drink alcohol, do not order it for yourself unless he insists. It is rare to be invited to an Emirati home, but if you are, it is polite to take a small gift such as flowers or sweet pastries. *See also pages 57–8.*

*Section 4*
# Environmental Issues

## Climate

For six months of the year (mid-April to mid-October) Colonel Sir Hugh Boustead, long time resident of the UAE and HMG's first Political Agent, appointed in 1961, described the climate **Awful summer** as "bloody awful". The average shade temperature is 35–41 degrees centigrade (100–105 degrees Fahrenheit), with an average 97% humidity or total saturation on the coast. Sea temperatures in summer reach 35 degrees to 40 degrees centigrade, blood temperature, and drop to around 22 degrees centigrade by the end of December. Unheated swimming pools drop to 21–22 degrees centigrade in winter. On the East coast the range in sea temperature is less extreme. Winter days can be delightful, with occasional rain, clear warm days and fresh starry nights. Average temperatures are 15–25 degrees centigrade (57–77 degrees Fahrenheit). Winter humidity average of 78% compares favourably with London's 83%. In winter months an extra layer will be required over light daytime clothing, as the outdoor temperature drops rapidly after dark, and air conditioning in hotels and restaurants can be very cool.

*Average temperatures*

| (degrees centigrade) | Minimum | Maximum |
| --- | --- | --- |
| January | 14 | 24 |
| February | 14 | 25 |
| March | 17 | 28 |
| April | 19 | 32 |
| May | 23 | 37 |
| June | 26 | 39 |
| July | 29 | 41 |
| August | 29 | 41 |
| September | 26 | 39 |
| October | 23 | 37 |
| November | 18 | 30 |
| December | 15 | 26 |

The high humidity in summer saturates clothes after the shortest of walks and the unfortunate wearers of glasses find **Steamy** themselves steamed up the moment they step out of the air **spectacles** conditioning. Inland the air is drier but the heat in summer from May to October is intense and reflects off the sand and the rock of the mountains. The *Shamaal* (North wind) can blow for days at a time, like a choking and oppressive sand storm.

In the days before air conditioning, much of the male population was at sea from May to September during the pearling season, where the sea breezes dissipated the heat to some extent. On land the rest of the population headed inland to oases like Al-Ain, and to their mountain enclaves. Hence the Ajmanis went to Masfout and the Sharjans went to Dhaid and the Dubaians went to Hatta.

*Hatta Reservoir*

These days oil wealth enables the wealthier shaikhs to escape the summer heat by going to Beirut or Europe, and a significant proportion of the UAE national population, including the rulers, are out of the country for upwards of four months a year.

Air-conditioning is still regarded by many as a mixed blessing, and some traditionally minded villagers leave their air-conditioned government houses for *barasti* (palm frond) huts in summer. At least before, acclimatisation was gradual as the summer heat intensified, whereas now people go from one extreme to the other as they move between their homes, cars and offices. Government clinics confirm that a whole range of ailments from colds to rheumatic conditions have increased.

**Mixed blessing**

Six thousand years ago Arabia was a wet climate and there were even lakes in the Empty Quarter (*Al-Rub' Al-Khaali*). Huge underground reserves of water accumulated, the water which has been tapped in more recent times for wells and is now getting lower, while the climate is getting steadily drier. The greenification and afforestation projects in Abu Dhabi are thought to have reduced temperatures by one or two degrees centigrade. There is speculation that by increasing condensation this will stimulate extra rainfall.

It was in the earlier wet times that the wadis were cut through the mountains, making the huge channels that we see today. This explains how what we see today as a small trickle of water or occasional flood could have created such huge water courses. Sharjah and its ruler publicly pray for rain when it is needed.

### Self-sufficiency

Before oil wealth this part of the world had no environmental problems and the indigenous population had a symbiotic relationship with nature. Since the late 1960s the huge increase in prosperity has brought with it consumerism, the environments' biggest enemy. The key environmental problems in the region are marine pollution from dumping and oil spills, proliferation of waste materials, and the depletion of water resources. Fortunately the campaign groups which have set themselves up are influencing public opinion, thereby creating pressure for the government to take initiatives, something it is now starting to do.

The Arabian peninsula's population is expected to more than double from 43 million in 1995 to 92 million by 2025 which would cause a rapid increase in food imports. A co-operative project with the rest of the Arabian peninsula has been launched by the UAE, on how to increase agricultural output using the limited natural resources available. In dairy products, poultry, fruit, vegetables and animal fodder the UAE has achieved 90 percent self-sufficiency in 1996. The size of the average farm in the UAE is only 2–3 hectares, making them manageable as family-run units. It is the proliferation of these that has formed the basis of the country's steadily increasing food production, transforming over 100 thousand hectares of desert into cultivated land. Whilst this concept of food security and self-suffiency is laudable in theory, in practice the amount of money ploughed into sustaining such projects and the cost of irrigation in a desert country with little rainfall is ultimately a barrier to economic growth. Desalinated water already meets 60–70% of total water demand at the moment and will continue to rise. Agriculture accounts for 80% of total UAE

**Cultivating the desert**

water use, 11% for domestic use, 9% for industry. The World Bank argues that such proportions do not make economic sense, since agriculture contributes less than 15% of GDP.

### Recycling

A massive programme has begun to create awareness among young people above all, and as a result children are causing less pollution than their elders and being more careful not to litter the streets. Sharjah in particular has had a major drive towards pollution control and has set up an Islamic body to help preserve the environment. More than 110 thousand metric tonnes of plastic material is produced in UAE factories, working out at a massive 42 kilograms per person annually. In other developed countries it is less than a quarter of this.

*The famous Fujairah plastic bag tree*

The omnipresent plastic bag is the worst culprit and some Emirates, notably Fujairah and Sharjah, have begun serious campaigns to educate people about the environmental pollution they cause and to find an alternative like paper or cloth bags.

The Emirates Environmental Group based in Dubai was set up in 1991 and regularly organises beach clean-ups and recycling drives. Major hotels like the Ramada, the Marriott, Holiday Inn Crown Plaza and the Forte Grand Dubai offer meeting rooms and refreshments free of charge for the regular gatherings.

**Free rooms**

73

### Pollution control

The Environment Research and Wildlife Development Agency (ERWDA) is a government body set up in 1997 specifically to examine the state of Abu Dhabi's environment including desert ecology, the marine environment and air quality. It gathers data on computer which is then forwarded to the relevant bodies who have the power to implement conservation strategies. Dubai has its own body which monitors any smog, effluent or waste disposal, and checks up on factories to ensure they meet environmental and safety requirements.

### Water

Although water covers 70% of the earth's surface only 3% of it is fresh and 75% of that 3% is trapped in the ice caps of the North and South Poles. Worldwide water consumption has increased threefold in 40 years. Tap water is not recommended in the UAE because although chlorinated, the cleanliness of the pipes and tank cannot be guaranteed. Most people therefore drink the various bottled mineral waters which are cheaply available, or the purified water containers which are delivered to homes each week.

In the UAE, water and electricity consumption are increasing dramatically, on average by 25% per year. In Abu Dhabi the five existing desalination plants produce 220 million gallons of water daily. The cost is colossal, but is highly subsidised to the consumers, to the tune of 35% in the poorer Emirates, and up to 80% in Abu Dhabi. All new buildings in Abu Dhabi are now fitted with water meters in an attempt to limit consumption which has been profligate in the culture of extravagance that has reigned till now.

**Expensive desalination**

Ground water supplies are being used up at an alarming rate, and wells are having to be dug ever deeper to meet the demand for irrigation in areas like Liwa and Al-Ain. In Al-Ain demand has already outstripped supply and water has to be piped in from Abu Dhabi's desalination plants. In the light of this there has to be a serious question mark over the sustainability of the greenification policy so enthusiastically being followed by all the Emirates and by Abu Dhabi in particular.

The UAE has a per capita consumption of 500 litres a day,

the highest in the world. Britain consumes 330 litres per capita per day, France 215 and Jordan 150. Desalination plants are massively expensive and fuel hungry, running on oil. In the UAE as a whole, the cost is a staggering Dh1.08 million a day for a mere 2 million people.

**Highest consumption in the world**

A conservation drive has begun in the light of these statistics and more and more hotels and businesses are installing water saving devices to regulate flow, such as more efficient taps and toilet flushes. Villas also account for huge consumption for garden watering and new devices are being encouraged for drip and bubble irrigation, which though more costly to install, save greatly on water usage. Unfortunately because the cost of the installation falls to the local landlord, many go for the cheaper short term option of hoses and sprinklers and then make the tenant pay the higher water bill.

The water that comes out of the tap in the UAE is desalinated water blended with good quality water from aquifers. The rough estimates say that groundwater recharge provides 130 million cubic metres per year, while desalination plants produce 730 million cubic metres, and sewage treatment plants provide 110 million cubic metres for use in agriculture and landscaping projects.

Satellites have recently been used with some success in locating new aquifers, but ultimately such reserves are finite and ways must be found of replenishing them. During seasonal rains in the mountains there is a massive amount of wadi run-off and so by the construction of carefully sited dams, the plan is to trap the water and allow it to seep back down into the underground reserves. Sometimes though, as at the Wadi Bih dam, the clay-like soil does not permit the water to filter through and huge amounts are simply lost to evaporation.

Water pollution is another issue which has only just started to be addressed. Increased use of chemicals in agriculture, inadequate sewage treatment and seepage from landfill are all direct consequences of the urban boom of the last 30 years. However much the rulers want to see their Emirates turn green, the viability of such low-return agricultural production long-term has been questioned by water conservation experts.

**Is green best?**

All the Gulf countries have water problems on a greater or lesser scale. Fifty percent of the world's desalination plants are concentrated here. At current consumption rates the crunch will come somewhere between 2010 and 2020, which is why efforts are starting now to awaken public awareness to the need to recognise water as the world's most valuable commodity. As one of the delegates at a recent UN conference on Water for Thirsty Cities posed: "If this water were managed by an oil company, wouldn't the shareholders be shocked to learn that 30 to 50 percent of their oil was lost?".

*Flooding after freak summer rain in the mountains*

Traditional farming methods with open channels and basins which lose much to evaporation are also being targeted, with farmers being encouraged to invest at half price subsidies in the use of modern irrigation techniques like bubble or drip methods which would cut consumption by up to 60 percent.

The current desalination plants use the Multi-Stage Flash process which consumes large amounts of expensive oil and electricity. A new wind-powered desalination plant has been pioneered by a German firm which, if successful, could provide the answer to the UAE's water needs, and indeed the whole Gulf region.

### Off-Roading

Any off-roading (i.e., off tarmac) driving should be conducted in a spirit of responsibility, respecting the environment and the local people's traditions and property. With increasing numbers of expatriates and nationals heading for the dunes and the mountains for sport, there has been an increase in complaints from local tribespeople about the behaviour of visitors. It is worth recalling that the Shihuh tribes of the Musandam have lived more than five hundred years in isolation till the tracks were graded in the 1980s. To them the 4WD tribe constitutes an invasion. Some come to mountain villages which have been left by the inhabitants for the summer when the mountain water runs short. When they return in the winter, they are upset to find their few material possessions upturned and interfered with or even stolen or

## THE DATE PALM

One of the diet staples in the Arabian peninsula is dates, on average 70 percent sugar excluding the stones, which prevents the growth of bacteria and enables it to stay edible for long periods in a hostile climate unlike any other tropical fruit. It was therefore an essential item at sea during the pearling season along with limes and fish. Apart from its food value the branches, leaves, fibre and trunk have formed the basic building material for houses, shelters, sacks, bags and matting, for fish traps in the days before metal and nylon, and even for fans and toys. The Prophet Mohamed's first mosque at Medina in 630AD was built with palm trunks for the beams and columns, the branches for roofing and the leaves for prayer mats.

There are male trees and female trees and the farmer carries out pollenation by cutting off flowering branches of the male tree, climbing the female tree and placing the male branches among the female branches. This process is repeated two or three times to make sure it is successful. Arabic has 500 different words to describe the date in its various types and conditions, giving some measure of its importance.

broken. One foreigner was recently thwarted in his attempt to remove the carved window frame from the ruins of the Fujairah Summer Palace in Wadi Hayl. He evidently thought it would look good on his mantlepiece. Local tribespeople also do not like to see women in shorts or otherwise scantily dressed. If you wish to take gifts into remote regions, the advice is do not take sweets and such like, take useful presents like crayons and colouring books for the children.

Also be aware that reckless off-roading damages the environment. Wadi bashing and dune bashing are accurate terms. To minimise the damage, environmentalists urge you to stick to the tracks. That way you destroy less flora and fauna

**Spirit of**
**responsibility**

with your tyres. Avoid picking flowers and breaking branches off trees and try to take your own barbecue fuel rather than collecting the all too rare fire wood, which destroys the fragile ecology. Wear proper footwear so that snakes cannot bite you and neither can scorpions who are attracted by the heat of a camp-fire.

The pools and waterfalls of the mountains flow all year round and village communities survive on this water which has been deposited entirely by rainfall. This rainfall not only collects in pools and streams, but also filters through the grit and stone wadi beds, seeping down into the water table and filling wells and aquifers deep underground. The agricultural development of the mountain villages depends on these water supplies, as does the fragile eco-system of the mountains. Its pollution therefore has colossal repercussions that go well beyond the immediate effects of spoiling the attractiveness of the landscape with litter and debris. Detergents of any sort including soap or washing up liquid should be avoided as this introduces chemicals to the limited supply. Take greasy dishes home with you rather than leaving the greasy residue in the streams. If you meet local people, do not be offended by their gruff way of speaking – this is their normal way. Always wave and greet them politely with "*As-salaamoo alaykum*".

However adventurous you may feel on your travels it is worth recalling Wilfred Thesiger's words in his introduction to *Arabian Sands* (1959):

**Spirit of**
**adventure**

> I went to Southern Arabia only just in time. Others will go to study geology, archaeology, the birds, the plants, the animals, even to study the Arabs themselves; but they will move about in cars and will keep in touch with the outside world by wireless. They will bring back results far more interesting than mine, but they will never know the spirit of the land, nor the greatness of the Arabs.

*Section 5*
# Birds & Wildlife

Some of the earliest information on the wildlife of the Emirates was supplied by Wilfred Thesiger, during his work for the Desert Locust Control unit in the 1950s. After spending a few days on Jebel Hafeet in Al-Ain he was the first European ever to spot the Arabian *tahr*, a goat-like creature with short stubby horns and long reddish-brown hair. He also noted the presence of wolves, hyenas and a leopard from their tracks and droppings.

After the Second World War as the oil industry drew more and more foreigners to the country, studies and reports were gradually written up by them, quite independently of the local **First local** knowledge of the inhabitants. It was not till the late Seventies **interest** and early Eighties that the UAE itself developed an interest in its own wildlife and environment and by 1983 a federal law was introduced banning the hunting of all wild birds' eggs, gazelles, hares and *Dhubb* lizards.

---

### NATURE RESERVES

As local awareness has increased, thanks to amateur groups like the Emirates Natural History Group and the Dubai Natural History Group, rulers have been persuaded to create wildlife sanctuaries like the offshore island of Sir Bani Yas where the Arabian oryx and other endangered local species have bred in safety, and the bird sanctuary for flamingos at the end of Khor Dubai. Five other areas are currently being considered for nature reserve status, two coastal, two mountain and one desert. These have yet to gain official status. The coastal ones are at Khor Kalba (Sharjah) covering 10 square kilometres and at Khor Al-Beidah (Umm Al-Quwain) covering 80 square kilometres, both special for their mangrove swamps; the mountain ones are at Wadi Wurrayah (Fujairah) and Wadi Zikkat, (Ras Al-Khaimah) on the Ru'us Al-Jibaal-Musandam border, and the desert one is at Jebel Ali (Dubai) covering 500 square kilometres where a herd of Arabian gazelles are currently threatened by the expansion of the new airport. Most Arabian mammals have suffered dramatic declines over the last 50 years due to man with his firearms, vehicles and destruction of the desert habitat.

---

Creatures that were always native to the Arabian peninsula are the reptiles, the *Dhubb* lizard and desert monitor. Most mammals like oryx, gazelle, desert cat and ostrich came across from the African Continent geological eons ago when Arabia was joined on to Africa before the Red Sea appeared. The Arabian leopard, ibex, tahr, wild goat and sheep all came from the Indian sub-continent.

*Rock strata in the Ru'us Al-Jibaal (Heads of the Mountains), Musandam*

*The parasitic Desert Hyacinth appears after rain*

*River bank erosion caused by flash floods*

Above: *In the
construction of
modern mosques,
decoration is
bought in bulk
and applied to
the facades*

Right: *The
purple flower of
Sodom's Apple*

Left & below:
*The modern ghost town of Al-Jazira Al-Hamra, Ras Al-Khaimah*

Above: *In the
mountainous region
at Hadf, crops are
irrigated using
pumps to extract
ground water*

Right: *Hobbled
camel grazing*

## Birds

The increased greenery since oil wealth in the 1960s has led to marked increases in the number of birds and insects.There are now over two hundred species of bees and wasps in the UAE and over four hundred species of birds have been recorded.

Of these birds some 90 are resident breeds while the rest are migrants and winter visitors. The UAE lies on a migration crossroads, north to south from Europe to Africa, and east to west between India and the Near East. Autumn and spring are therefore the seasons of greatest activity, with October and

**Migration crossroads**

*An escaped Peregrine falcon in the Liwa dunes*

March the busiest. Monthly averages of species to be seen are about two hundred in the winter months dropping to about one hundred in the summer months. For keen birdwatchers a visit of eight to 12 days is generally enough to see the residents and the most interesting of the migrants. Such trips are on offer courtesy of Colin Richardson birdwatching tours, individually tailored to the season and to the specific ornithological interest. (Tel/fax: 313378).

**Bird watching**

Of the seabirds the most significant in ornithological terms are the Socotra cormorants, the current UAE population of which – 200,000 – is some 25% of the estimated world total. Endangered anyway, it is curiously the only species of bird which may be hunted under UAE law, due to a misperception that it is a threat to fish stocks.

The Sooty falcon also has a large breeding population here. Its nests however are on offshore islands which are now being developed and are therefore under threat, and the numbers of birds going on to winter in Madagascar are dropping each year.

At the mangrove creeks of Khor Kalba, are the only 44 pairs remaining of White-Collared Kingfisher in the country. For most bird watchers visiting the UAE, the easiest and frequently most productive areas to visit are the artificially created habitats like the golf courses, city parks and agricultural areas where the advantageous conditions and permanent water supply has meant that many migrant birds stop here which would not otherwise do so. In Abu Dhabi the favoured areas are Bateen Gardens, Mushref Palace Gardens and the Khalidiya spit at the western end of the corniche. In Dubai the best spots are Safa Park, Creekside Park, the Emirates Golf Course and the fish ponds behind Shaikh Mohammed's Palace. The camel race tracks of Abu Dhabi at Al-Ain and Al-Wathba are grassed and irrigated inside the perimeter, drawing many hungry migrants.

### Arabian Oryx

Pronounced extinct in the early 1960s, captive breeding programmes are now doing well with several herds, which it is hoped will eventually be able to reintroduce some species to the wild. They are the largest species of Arabian antelope and are perfectly adapted to the desert, able to live without the shade of trees or a permanent water source. They get their moisture from the food they eat and can conserve water by a special characteristic of their kidneys. Their twin horns can be seen as one in profile, giving rise to the legend of the one-horned unicorn. These horns are used as sharp deadly weapons in fighting for a female and for dominance in a herd. The female has only one calf at a time.

**Unicorn in profile**

Still found in small numbers in the wild are the Arabian gazelle and the Arabian tahr. The hare still survives in small numbers. If you spot any rabbit-like creature it will be a hare for rabbits do not exist in the wild in Arabia.

There are also foxes, sand cats, hedgehogs, bats, jerboas, gerbils and mice.

### The Houbara bustard

The Environmental Research and Wildlife Development Agency (ERWDA) now incorporates the Abu Dhabi-based National Avian Research Centre which has been enforcing a UAE-wide ban on hunting gazelles, hares, *Dhubb* lizards, wild cows and Houbara bustards. The Houbara is a secretive bird that comes to the UAE for the winter months and has been hunted to near extinction, as it is the favourite prey of the trained peregrine falcons. The wealthy currently have to go to Pakistan and Iran to hunt the Houbara, so the concern to have it reintroduced is largely that it can be hunted locally again, but at least under controlled conditions. The number of wild Houbara that currently visit the UAE in winter is thought to be as low as two hundred. Their movements are tracked by Desert Rangers during their stay, so that they can devise effective conservation strategies.

### The Arabian leopard

Thanks to the GP turned animal-conservationist, Dr Marycke Jongbloed, the Arabian Leopard Trust has received great publicity and has mobilised concern over this endangered animal at the highest level. Her own ardent hope is that the work of the trust be taken over by some federal agency for conservation and be put on a professional footing with UAE involvement – this is essential if real progress is to be made. A move in this direction has recently been made by the Dubai Crown Prince, Shaikh Muhammad loaning his own wild-caught male leopard to the Trust for mating with the female currently on loan from the Omani government. If this succeeds, the Trust will have a start for its captive breeding programme.

**Breeding potential**

The Arabian leopard has been hunted to near extinction by farmers who see it as a threat to their livestock. As recently as 1986 the Ras Al-Khaimah shaikhs gave a Dh50,000 reward for the skin of a leopard shot by a tribesmen. In 1996 they refused a skin – a significant measure of Jongbloed's success. From the work carried out so far, it has been found that leopards are not in the high mountains but in the lower lying areas. There have been sightings at the Hatta Pools and Wadi Shawka. Leopards are always on the go, ranging over wide areas. One animal is thought to require a territory of 140 square kilometres to sustain it. None are thought to be actually resident breeding here. This they do in Oman and then enter the UAE's on their roamings. In the wild a leopard's lifespan is eight years, in captivity 12 years (the oldest lion in captivity is 18 years old). Their mating which is very vocal takes place over about five days during which time mating occurs many times.

**8-year lifespan**

### Butterflies

The four most attractive butterflies of the UAE have recently been featured on a series of stamps. The Swallowtail is the largest and most spectacular with its dramatic yellow and black markings, often to be found in gardens and plantations. The next biggest is the orange and black Tiger butterfly found both in the desert and city gardens. It feeds on the poisonous milkweed plants and the poison transfers itself to the caterpillar and butterfly, meaning that birds leave it well alone.

Next comes the delightful Blue Pansy with its dark fore wings and blue underwings with red "eyes". Living in wadis and plantations it feeds on fallen dates and basks in the sun on flowering desert plants.

Loew's Blue is the smallest, and therefore there are six different species of Little Blues in the UAE. This is one of the commonest, found in wadis where its favourite food grows.

**Tricky flight**   Their darting flight makes them difficult to catch, and when resting on a plant they have their wings closed for camouflage, showing only their silvery underside.

### Desert Habitat

In order to survive the extreme heat of the desert, the creatures that live here have adopted techniques like burrowing, aestivating (the opposite of hibernating), or only coming out at night. Most birds cope by migrating, and many birds including the Houbara bustard, migrate to the UAE for the winter months escaping the cold winters of Iran and Central Asia.

Desert animals like the oryx, the wolf, the striped hyena, the jackal and the honey badger are all close to extinction, under pressure from increased human interference in the desert. The proliferation of vehicle tracks bears witness to the increased disturbance, from rebuilding, digging of well boreholes, agricultural projects, drilling and surveys for oil and gas, desert plantations, and recreational dune driving. Since oil wealth the numbers of camel and goats have increased enormously. They are owned by local people living in cities but looked after by subcontinental workers in the desert. At great financial cost, water is brought to them by tanker and 4WD trucks bringing in subsidised fodder.

**Camel camps**   Artificial " Bedouin camps" are therefore established in the

*Goat numbers have increased dramatically in recent years*

desert which the national owner visits frequently to maintain the link with his past and to spot any potential racing camels.

The triangle formed by the Abu Dhabi-Dubai road, the Dubai-Al-Ain road and the Al-Hayer, Sweihan-Shahama road is designated the Public Hunting Triangle. Desert Rangers in 4WD vehicles equipped with the latest radio and telephone equipment are employed by the Abu Dhabi ruling family to monitor above all the numbers of Houbara bustard. When enough are present, generally around October to November, the falconry season begins. The Desert Rangers' other job is to check enforcement of the 1983 decree banning the shooting of birds, gazelles or hares. The penalties for those caught are severe with heavy fines and prison sentences. Controlled hunting, managed on an ecologically sustainable basis, has a beneficial effect on the desert ecology by establishing the area's preservation as a natural desert habitat, rather than being zoned for development or forestry projects. Thus falconry, and the need to have large reserves where the Houbara is protected, will play a significant role in preserving the UAE's threatened desert eco-system.

**Controlled hunting**

85

### Scorpions

Like most venomous animals, scorpions will only sting when threatened. They have survived virtually unchanged for 450 million years, such is their success. They have one pair of eyes in the normal place and between two and five simple eyes in other places. They live for two to five years, though one species lives to 25. The UAE has 14 species of scorpion. Death from scorpion bite is extremely rare, though young children and the elderly are the most at risk. Whilst there are anti-venom medicines which can be effective if administered early enough, in most cases a painkiller is all that can be given. The

**Bite advice** best first aid advice is to keep the site of the sting up high to stop the poison going to the heart, and to keep it as cold as possible with ice packs. The symptoms after the sharp pain of the sting are generally numbness, drowsiness, itching in the throat, and excessive salivation. In cases where large amounts of poison have entered the blood there can additionally be convulsions, sensitivity to strong light and haemorrhages. The victim is usually out of danger within three hours, but medical supervision is recommended for at least eight hours. The large black scorpions are in fact the least poisonous. The most poisonous are the smaller sand coloured variety. Wearing proper footwear is the best way to ensure never getting bitten. When camping make sure the tent is zipped up, and check shoes before putting them on if they were left outside.

### Camel spiders.

Camel spiders have a nasty bite but no venom. They dislike open sunlight and if you accidentally expose one it will rush frantically for the nearest shade, often at your feet, giving it an undeserved reputation for aggression. They are nocturnal and feed on scorpions, lizards and even mice and birds. Their powerful jaws make this possible. The females are often larger than the males who generally die earlier. Even the females only live a year or so. They are found in sandy undisturbed areas and exist in black or pale creamy versions.

### Spiders

*Arabian Redback/Black Widow Spider*

Native to the UAE and not as commonly thought an import from Australia, this smallish black spider with a red patch on its bulbous back, has large fangs and a potent venom because it feeds primarily on large ground beetles and needs to puncture their armoured shell. They generally live under things such as flower pots and rocks, so special care should be taken when gardening or with children's dens in gardens. The bite can be fatal for a small child or pet. Their webs are usually at ground level, where they are best placed to catch the ground beetles they feed on, and resemble tunnels usually tangled up with dead leaves and looking rather messy. These spiders are remarkably resistant to fumigation, with the ability to close down their breathing apparatus for hours at a time, so do not just spray it and go away – either burn it or crush it to be sure. The female produces 200–400 tiny babies which are dispersed by the wind, the mere thought of which is enough to overcome any instinct you may have to spare it. Painkiller is usually the only treatment administered, though extreme shock may necessitate heart monitoring in hospital.

**Fertile but deadly**

The Orb spider (*Argiope*) has a big yellow body and extremely long legs and spins an extremely tough web. It is often found in abandoned houses and ruins in the desert, and although getting caught up in the web is very nasty, the spider is, mercifully, harmless.

The commonest spider, and the one you will see most often in the house and garden, is the Jumping Spider which has a light stripe on its back. It is completely harmless.

## Ants

As with the scorpion, the bigger and more unpleasant the ant looks the less harmful it is. The only type of biting ant in the UAE is one of the tiny varieties of black ants. Its poison is like that of Poison Ivy, and it can cause a serious allergic reaction which occasionally results in death. The first bite never results in death however, but if you do experience a severe allergic reaction, see your doctor, who will give you emergency medicine – adrenalin and anti-histamine – that you should carry with you at all times in the event of a future bite. The brown ants commonly found in houses and especially in kitchen cupboards with sweet things, are completely harmless, and can easily be deterred with liberal use of Pif-Paf or putting coffee grounds around their holes.

**The bigger, the better**

## Wasps and Hornets

There are over 200 types of bee and wasp in the UAE. The yellow and brown hornet (*vespes orientalis*, Arabic *dibba*) is the chief stinging culprit, especially active in the wadis and mountains. Waspeze spray, anti-histamine pills and painkillers are all worth having along with you on such outings to minimize the painful sting, especially for children.

## Mosquitoes

Mosqitoes are found throughout the UAE but are not malarial because there are no suitable breeding grounds for them and the situation is closely monitored by the relevant authorities. Neighbouring Oman however is malarial and precautions should be taken when visiting there. The normal biting variety are a nuisance in the spring months of March and April and the autumn months of late October/November, but tend to die out in the hot summer months and the colder winter months. Use an insect repellent spray or gel when sitting outside in the evenings to ensure no bites. Most houses are equipped with fly screens so mosquitoes indoors are rarely a problem. Supermarkets sell the electric plug-in devices where you replace the tablet each night, an excellent device to ensure a good night's sleep.

Millipedes and centipedes are poisonous the world over, and the large varieties found in the UAE are especially venomous and should not be touched. Grasshoppers and locusts are abundant but harmless, and used to constitute an important protein element in the local diet before the advent of MacDonalds made them superfluous.

## Snakes

There are many types of snake in the UAE but the only ones to be feared are the vipers which have long tubular fangs in the front of the jaw, linked to poison-producing glands. It is these long teeth which enable the snake to inject large quantities of venom into the victim, be it prey for food or human. The commonest viper is the Saw-Scaled viper, some 50–60 centimetres long, found in the open desert, in the mountains and along the coast. They are nocturnal and do not generally come near towns. They spend the day hiding under bushes or in burrows and will not attack unless threatened. When threatened they run their scales together making a rasping sound reminiscent of a rattle snake. In soft sand they move sideways and are thus also referred to as side-winders, leaving characteristic s-shaped markings behind. Once on firm ground they revert to normal snake motion. The snake is brown/black and cream in colour and is mainly nocturnal, so the chances of being bitten in broad daylight are extremely rare. Its normal prey is geckos and lizards.

As a general rule the long thin snakes which move fast are the most harmless. The shorter fatter ones tend to be the ones to avoid. Those most commonly found in gardens and water-tanks are the harmless long thin racers. If you are bitten you must try to get to a hospital as quickly as possible. Call the emergency services, Ambulance: 998. It is worth identifying the snake that has bitten you, as the type of anti-venom you are given will depend on the snake. The bite will be extremely painful, and you normally have about three hours to get medical attention.

**Beware the short and fat**

The biggest UAE snake is the sand snake at 155 centimetres maximum length which is also active during the day, moving very quickly and gracefully. It is mainly brown with black and white streaks, and is harmless to man because its poisonous fangs are at the rear of the jaw and do not therefore come into contact with the prey till they have started to swallow it. There is also a fake Cobra which behaves when threatened like the venomous Cobra, spreading the skin on its neck and hissing, but it too has its fangs too far back to be a threat to man. There are several other species of snake, like the snake boa, the wadi racer and the attractive diadem snake all of which are completely harmless to man. On the whole the chances of being bitten by a snake are very small. No snake will attack you without provocation, so simply leave any poisonous creature, be it snake, scorpion or whatever, well alone.

## Lizards

There are many species of lizards endemic to the area, all essentially harmless. The larger types like the spiny-tailed lizard (local *Dhubb*) and the monitor use their tails in a whip-like manner in self-defence if cornered. Although quite dragon-like in appearance they are not naturally aggressive and will always choose to flee rather than attack. Lizard meat

**Barbecued lizard** was prized by Bedouin as a source of protein and the Prophet Mohamed was quoted in Islamic traditions as enjoying its flesh cooked over a fire. Its strong skin was also used for leather. It is unique among lizards as being vegetarian. Other lizards feed on insects and small rodents. It also never drinks water, obtaining all the moisture it needs from shrubs.

The other striking lizard of the UAE is the blue-headed *agama* common in the wadis, and growing to about 18 centimetres long. The head of the male goes bright blue when sexually aroused or angry. Feeding on small insects, it is not shy and permits quite close approach.

There are many types of gecko, some living in sandy, some on rocky terrain. The best known is of course the yellow-bellied house gecko found in houses and flats everywhere and **Mosquito diet** much valued in its contribution to stemming the nocturnal insect life in the house, especially mosquitoes. They make a faint bark-like call which is only audible to those with sensitive ears. During the day they find somewhere dark like behind a wall hanging or picture to hide and sleep and digest the night's catch.

### Toads

The Arabian toad (*Bufo Arabica*) is very common in the wadis of the UAE, feeding on insects and even on small wadi fish when the pools dry out in summer. There are no frogs in the UAE so any frog-like creature you spot will be a toad and completely harmless.

*Section 6*
# Shells & Marine Life

### Beachcombing

One of the simplest and cheapest entertainments the Emirates has to offer, beachcombing can provide endless hours of distraction. The range you may encounter is vast, some of it human in origin, but much of it native to the sea. The sandy beaches are themselves composed of millions of crushed shells from eons ago. The booty from your sorties can be used to decorate bathrooms, gardens or ponds or simply to form collections. On sandy beaches the place to look is all along the high tide mark, especially after spring storms. High and low tides are given in the local newspapers, along with sunrise and sunset times.

### Shells

Cowries are common but varying in size and patterning greatly, and the larger "kitten cowries" are prized by collectors. The name "cowrie" is thought to come from the Hindi language and the shells were even traded as currency in the Indian sub-continent. The tabby coloured kitten cowrie is

Left: *a kitten cowrie shell*

Right: *an assortment of shells to be found on the beaches of the UAE*

unique to Oman and the UAE. Spiny murex shells are also common, though they tend to have their spines broken. High spring tides offer the best chances of finding a paper nautilus, not a shell at all, but a highly delicate egg case of the squid-like argonaut fish. The 40 day *Shamaal* (local strong wind) that runs from 6 June to 16 July is a time when water sports drop to a minimum and if you go beachcombing early morning, you may well be surprised by some exciting discoveries. Seahorses are very occasionally found washed up on the beach, but are now so rare that you should report your find to the local natural history group. A dead one was recently found on the beach near Dubai Offshore Sailing Club, and live ones have been seen in the northern sea grass beds of Khor Al-Beidah in Umm Al-Quwain. Although the seahorse is classed as a fish it has many peculiarities which set it apart. For example it is the male seahorse which gives birth after the female lays the eggs in his pouch. He delivers about 200 over a two-day period.

**Daddy is Mummy**

Different types of shore yield different finds and apart from the sand, there are *fasht* coastlines, flat rocky slabs of dead coral, rich in crabs, sea stars and chitons. The best places for shells are usually sandy beaches near shallow coral reefs. Breakwaters and jetties are also places of high concentrations of sea life, as are rocky beaches with rock pools.

To preserve your shell collection a thorough wash-off is recommended, then after drying, a light coating of baby oil. If you leave it too long the shells will spoil, losing their colours and sheen. Any shells still alive will soon let you know by their revolting decaying smell, and these need to be boiled to make sure all perishable matter inside is gone. Before collecting, try to check if the shell is still alive and if so put it back in the sea.

**Wash and oil**

### Snorkelling
The best spot for snorkelling in the UAE is thought to be Snoopy Island off the Sandy Beach Motel in Fujairah. At low tide you can walk out to the island, even right round it at exceptionally low tides, and watch the sea life left behind in the rock pools.

### Edible fish
The commonest fish found in supermarkets is King Fish, Red Snapper and Hammour, a white fish similar to cod. Other types of local edible fish found at the fish market are: *Safi*, Dorade, local crab, local lobster, sea scallops, mussels, squid, *Sigaali*, goat fish, red mullet, *Saafi*, parrot fish, sardines, seabream, Golden Trevally, Sultan Ibrahim, Emperor, Bourri, Pomfret, *Sheri'i*, and *Zreidy*, an excellent fish with yellow fins and vertical black stripes. It is best to experiment, buying small quantities of several types from the fish market, where prices are considerably lower than the supermarket.

## Marine Mammals

In the course of evolution some mammals returned to the sea, where their ancestors had lived. They adjusted completely to life underwater, eating, sleeping and giving birth in the water.

## Dugong

**Hairless mermaid**

**Elephant ancestors**

These sea cows are now near extinct in the waters of the Gulf, numbering some five thousand. They belong to the family known as *Sirenia* because seamen and sailors used to mistake them for mermaids or sirens. Apart from the dugong the only other types of Sirenia are manatees, found off the coast of America. Sirenia are known as sea cows because they are the only herbivorous marine mammals, feeding on seaweed and other plants in shallow waters. They are known in Arabic as Bride of the Sea (*Arous Al-Bahr*). They grow to about 4 metres and have heavy but streamlined bodies weighing 500 kilograms. They share a common ancestry with elephants who are also herbivores. Dugong are shallow water grazers, and they lack air spaces in their bones, allowing them to sink effortlessly and remain submerged. The flexible overhanging upperlip is used to uproot clumps of seaweed and the males have tusks for their incisor teeth, another throwback to the elephant heritage. The body is hairless but the muzzle is covered in thick stiff whiskers. The dugong is mainly a solitary creature, unlike its American counterpart the manatee which is gregarious and gathers in herds. They are found mainly round offshore islands to the west of Abu Dhabi and are most readily spotted between April and August. Calves suckle for up to 18 months and swim close to their mothers for that long. Accidental net capture by fishermen is the biggest threat to the dugong and its meat is still highly prized in the Gulf.

## Dolphins

Though superficially like fish with beaked snouts, the internal bones and organs of dolpins closely resemble those of mammals. Their front paddles are in fact modified fore limbs, and like all mammals they breathe by taking in oxygen from the air, and so have to return to the surface at intervals to breathe. The hind limbs have disappeared and instead the tail has evolved a horizontally flattened section called a fluke which is the means of propulsion by moving up and down (hence our "dolphin kick" in swimming strokes like butterfly). Fish on the other hand propel themselves by moving their tails from side to side. Dolphins have enormous numbers of teeth – 260 is the maximum yet discovered in one mouth – a record for any mammal. They feed on fish, octopus and squid and detect the prey using a form of ultraviolet sonar (similar to bats) emitting high-pitched squeaks and clicks to gauge the position of surrounding objects. They are very gregarious, sometimes forming schools of over a hundred with a well developed social hierarchy. They grow to 2.5–4 metres long, and like all mammals they produce a single calf, born tail first, which is then helped to the surface to take its first breath.

**Toothiest mammals**

Dolphins are being used increasingly to assess the indications of other environmental pollutants. Hydrocarbon oils accumulate in their blubber and so, by analysing the blubber of dead dolphins, the levels of oil pollutants can be measured. Dolphins themselves are known to die of diseases like pneumonia, and are then often washed up on shore where the exact cause of death can be investigated. The best times to look out for them at sea is early mornings and evenings. Numbers are high and schools are large (5–35) so they are readily spotted by the special boats, on the Musandam for example, which head out in search of them. Such dolphin tours are offered by Khasab Travel and Tours tel: 00 968 830464. There are several different species of dolphins found in the UAE of which the most normally encountered is the inquisitive bottle-nosed dolphin.

**Environmental pointer**

### Sea Turtles

Under threat now from urban and industrial development which has interfered with its nesting beaches, the green turtle, measuring up to 1.2 metres long and weighing up to 200 kilograms, used to be the commonest. There are seven species of marine turtle in the world, and four of them are found in UAE waters – the green turtle, the hawksbill turtle (80 centimetres up to 1 meter, weighing 50 kilograms), the loggerhead (100cm and 160 kilograms) and the gigantic leatherback turtle (3 metres long, up to 1000 kilograms weight!). The Environmental Research and Wildlife Development Agency is conducting an extensive marine programme to study the turtles of the UAE so that effective conservation measures can be implemented to protect them. Tel: 03-747555, fax: 03-747607. Green and hawksbill are the ones most seen by divers and snorkellers. They are thought to sleep underwater in a state of semi-hibernation for weeks or even months, achieved through slowing the heartbeat to a bare minimum. They feed on sea grass beds in shallow off shore waters and are entirely herbivorous unlike the other species which feed on goldfish as well as algae. While the males spend their entire life at sea, the females come to land only once – for egg-laying in summer. The most important beaches for this are thought to be in Ras Al-Khaimah and on the offshore islands of Abu Dhabi. Such beaches should never be driven on as this crushes the eggs. They reach breeding age somewhere between 25 and 50 years and are thought to return to nest on the same beach where they themselves hatched so long ago. How they "remember" the beach of their birth is not known but they are thought to invoke a sense of smell and even magnetic and celestial influences. The female digs a pit of up to a metre deep and green turtles lay about 110 eggs per batch, each the size of a golf ball. The whole process takes her about an hour and if she is disturbed at any point during it, she will return to the sea. She will then return every two to four years to lay on the same beach till she is over the age of 70, but the young hatchlings will never know her. They hatch after some 55 days in the warm sand, their gender determined entirely by the temperature of incubation. Females are produced by warmer temperatures, males by cooler ones.

The hatchlings dig their way out of the nest at dawn, drawn to the sea as the lightest horizon. Flood lighting on beaches at night has been shown to interfere with this instinct and attract the hatchlings to head inland where they soon perish. They are on their own from the start and if they make it to the sea before foxes, cats, dogs, seagulls, and crabs get them, they swim further out for days, drifting on ocean currents. As few as two or three in every ten thousand are estimated to survive to adulthood. Fishing nets alone are thought to kill tens of thousands each year. They are directly hunted also for their decorative shells and for their meat, considered to have medicinal properties in some parts of the world. Male turtles establish their mating territories around the nesting beaches, as the females generally lay three or more times at intervals of

**Males never land**

**Homing instinct**

**Lonely start**

two weeks or so after being fertilised by the males. The cheap blue plastic bags all local supermarkets use are also frequently mistaken by the turtles for blue jellyfish and eaten, causing a horrible death.

## Sea Snakes

Not naturally aggressive, sea snakes will attack if threatened or if handled. They are quite often found washed up helpless on the beach where they wait for the next tide to take them back to the sea, so you should never pick such a snake up. Their highly toxic venom disables their prey of fish, crabs and squid, and aids digestion. One drop of sea snake venom is said to have the power to kill five men, but in practice very few are bitten, both because they are avoided as dangerous and also because their small mouths do not open wide enough for them to get hold of anything except an appendage such as a finger. They move slowly and calmly through the water and are generally yellow and black, measuring 100–200 centimetres long. They are thought to be inquisitive and have been known to raise their heads out of the water to observe passing boats.

**Feigning dead**

**Fingers and toes only**

## Sharks

There are at least 10 different species of shark in the Arabian Gulf, but attack on humans is very rare. The pearl divers used to consider barracuda to be much more of a threat than sharks. The tiger shark, considered among the most dangerous, very rarely comes close enough to shore to encounter swimmers. The common reef sharks are harmless to humans. They feed on sea turtles and even dolphins.

## Sting Rays

Preferring the sea bottom, ideally soft mud or sand, rays bury themselves and can then inflict a nasty wound if a hapless swimmer should inadvertently stand on the venomous spines of its tail. Stories are told, but in practice stings are rare. Electric rays can give a powerful shock when stepped on, but there are few in UAE's waters.

## Lion Fish and Stone Fish

These are the most likely species of dangerous fish to be encountered by swimmers and snorkellers, commonly found on coral reefs and rocky shores. Mottled brown and white with sharp venomous fin spines, they like shaded spots and grow to about 40 centimetres. They are not aggressive but their fins will give a nasty sting if inadvertently touched. Painkillers and anti-histamines are the best treatment.

### Jellyfish

Jellyfish are commonest in late summer and their season lasts till April. The small blue variety is found in large numbers off the beach in spring, but their stings are very slight. Some types of jellyfish stings are extremely painful and the best first aid is to pour white vinegar on the affected skin. A jellyfish sting spray can be bought at most pharmacies, and is worth keeping in your beach bag. Pain killers and anti-histamine tablets are also very effective. The best precaution however, as always, is prevention, so simply stay out of the water once you notice jellyfish there. If you must swim, wearing a T-shirt protects the chest and back, a good idea since these are the most serious places to be stung.

**White vinegar**

**T-shirt protection**

### Poisonous Shells and other Dangers

Cone shells are the only poisonous shells in the UAE, and one in particular, the textile cone should not be picked up on the shoreline, in case it is still alive, in which case it may give an intensely painful sting. It is mottled brown and white and medium sized.

The fire worm, a small spiny caterpillar-like creature coloured orange and white, should also be avoided, as if touched, the bristles detach and stay stuck in the skin, causing irritation rather like fibreglass.

The sharp black spines of the sea urchin found on rocks near the shore should be avoided, as the spikes can give a nasty wound.

Although it may appear from this summary that the sea is brimming with dangerous creatures, the risks in practice remain low. As a local doctor said, "You are far more likely to have an accident on the way to the beach than you are in the water yet no one thinks twice about the risks of driving."

**Keep it in proportion**

*Section 7*
# Geology and Plantlife

## Geology

Ninety to seventy million years ago, just before the time the dinosaurs became extinct, eruptions drove the ocean floor upwards to form the Hajar mountains which straddle the UAE and Oman. Geologists get extremely excited about this, for it means that this is one of the very few places in the world **Exploring the** where you can study the ocean crust easily on land. That these **sea bed** mountains were once under the sea is evidenced by the many fossils to be found a long way inland, as in Fossil Valley (Jebel Huwayyah) near Al-Ain, where the natural basin collected the skeletons of millions of tiny sea creatures, including rudists (large solitary coral-like bivalve), echinoids (sea urchins and sand dollars) and gastropods (snails). Fossils from this period can also be found  at Jebel Buheis and Jebel Rawdah.

The Jebel Hafeet Rock at Al-Ain was formed 50–30 million years ago. Because of its structure like an elongated dome, known to geologists as an anticline, it drew much interest in the hunt for oil, as this geological formation is often associated with oil deposits. The foot of Jebel Hafeet, especially where the road from the cement factory passes through a man-made gorge, has numerous fossils to be seen, including corals, **Fossil clues for** oysters, gastropods and sea urchins. Fossils give important **oil** clues to the possible hydrocarbon wealth hidden under the surface.

The Musandam group of rocks range from 97–200 million years ago and are limestone formations which evolved more gently and gradually than the volcanic harder mountains. The valley that divides the Hajar range from the Musandam range **Wetter climate** is called the Dibba fault. The climate was a great deal wetter then, and huge rivers cut out the deep wadis and canyons that we have today such as Siji, Ham, Jizzi and Hatta.

Then there are the sand dunes that are being blown slowly south eastwards by the prevailing north westerly winds. The sand colours range from white to cream to deep red-brown. The desert between Abu Dhabi and Dubai is thoroughly unprepossessing – a drab neutral, with grey green camel scrub criss-crossed with vehicle tracks and ugly with abandoned debris and cans. But as you proceed inland it improves, becoming golden and warmer, and as you approach Al-Ain it becomes a fine deep red, particularly magnificent at sunset. This redness is, for those who like their romance analysed, explained by the presence of iron oxide, a feature of the arid climate. There are many types of sand and one fun souvenir of the Emirates is a little picture frame filled with seven different colour sands from the seven Emirates. There are numerous types of sand, classed according to the shape and fineness of the grains. Abu Dhabi sand is mostly rounded, whereas ironically the best building sand is angular for greater strength. The whole Arabian peninsula has rather coarse grains, whereas glass for example needs fine grains. Absurdly therefore Saudi Arabia imports sand from Finland for glass manufacture.

*The romance of sand*

At the end of the last Ice Age some 15, 000 years ago, most of what is now desert was grassland. As a result of this great climatic change archaeologists have discovered ancient sites which are now 10 miles (16 km) inland that lay on the sea shore a mere 3000 years ago.

*Changing shorelines*

### Fossils

The UAE has the most diverse fossil heritage of any country in the Arabian peninsula, and ranging in age from a mere 8 million years to 300 million years. Apart from the volcanic eruption that resulted in the seabed thrusting upwards to form the Hajar mountains and the areas rich in marine life fossils already mentioned above, around 23 million years ago a second major geological event took place. This was the creation for the first time of a land bridge to Asia, thought to be somewhere between Qatar and the Fars region of Iran, which enabled animals to move across the continents. A land bridge from Arabia to Africa had already existed for some time, allowing dispersal of African animals to and from Africa and Asia using Arabia as a bridge. This geological phenomenon accounts for the discovery of 16 million year old horse teeth, primitive giraffes, hippos and elephants.

*Bridges to Africa and Asia*

### Parasitic Plants

The UAE has three parasitic plants and all are of interest. The Desert Hyacinth with its striking yellow flowers flecked with maroon is a parasite of salt-tolerant plants and is often to be found in the scrubland behind sandy beaches. After heavy rains it can emerge from its host's roots almost overnight. The other parasitic plant is the aptly named Red Thumb which the

Bedouin regard as a delicacy. The third plant is the edible mushroom known as *faqah* to be found in spring after rains along the flat grassy landscapes between the creeks from Sharjah northwards to Ras Al-Khaimah. Local families emerge in droves to seek out this delicacy, accompanied by the women of the household, who sometimes stray surprising distances from the 4WDs in its quest.

**Hunt the mushroom**

## Trees

One of the commonest trees to be found all over wadi beds is the flat-topped umbrella-like *Acacia Tortilis* with its tough thorny branches. Also in the wadis are the Morenga, pink flowering almond trees, wispy and graceful. Growing wild in the wadis too is the sidr (*Ziziphus spina-christi*) tree, recognised by its ovate leaves each with three almost parallel veins. Belonging to the Buckthorn family, it has sharp thorns and red cherry-sized edible fruits, tasting a little like apple. It is related to the jujube tree.

Inland of the high sand dunes of Ras Al-Khaimah are impressive ghaf forests, the *ghaf* (*Prosopis Cineria*), one of Arabia's biggest and most graceful trees with hanging almost weeping – willow like branches. They are grazed by camels to have a uniform bottom branch line, giving them all the same hairstyle.

**Camel haircut**

## Sodom's Apple

This extraordinary two to five metre-high bush is easily the most prolific and noticeable plant growing wild in the Emirates. It frequently lines the roadside of the highways leading inland from Dubai and Sharjah, and is incredibly tough. The distinctive silvery grey leaves grow along upwardly curving stems, usually topped with delicate purple five-leafed flowers. Belonging to the Milkweed family, it has a toxic white sap that bleeds copiously when cut. Local people traditionally used the sap to treat camel mange, and the leaves as fertiliser. Its bark when burned was used to make the finest charcoal for gunpowder.

**Toxic**

*Section 8*
**What to see**

# Abu Dhabi

Area: 64,750 square kilometres
Population: 1,065,000

## Overview

In 1960 there was nothing but a sorry collection of huts where now the Manhattan-style skyline dominates the coast. Nowhere has the dramatic change of lifestyle for the Emirati people been so marked as in Abu Dhabi. The shaikhdom of Abu Dhabi has always been the largest of the shaikhdoms that now comprise the UAE, and today it represents 80% of the total area. First Among Equals describes its position within the Emirates well. As capital city with colossal oil wealth and reserves estimated to last another 100 years, it controls the oil and financial wealth of the country and has the self-assured feel that goes with such a position. Only Dubai stands a little apart from dependence on Abu Dhabi, since it earns so much of its revenue from non-oil sources.

**First among equals**

Abu Dhabi is bordered by Oman and Dubai (which was part of Abu Dhabi till 1833) to the east, by Qatar to the west and by Saudi Arabia to the south and west. Within its territory there were in pre-oil days only three areas that could support life. Of these the two main ones were the inland oases of Al-Ain and Liwa, where there was year-round fresh water and shade from the sun. The island of Abu Dhabi, where the skyscraper city of that name and capital of the UAE now stands, was one of the bleakest spots imaginable, shadeless, barren and with only brackish water supplies. The well was discovered accidentally by a hunting party from Liwa in 1761, when it tracked a gazelle along the coast. Following the gazelle they crossed a narrow waterway at low tide onto the flat island and found the gazelle drinking at the spring. The name Abu Dhabi, Father or Homeland of the Gazelle, comes from this, and the shaikhs of Liwa ordered a settlement to be established there. In 1793 the shaikh's son and successor built a fort round the spring, the origins of today's Qasr Al-Husn. The brackish well supported a meagre village in the winter for fishing or in the spring in preparation for the four months' summer pearling season, which was the local population's only means of earning money. In the heat of the summer, it was evacuated in favour of Al-Ain or Liwa.

**Father of the gazelle**

In all three settlements the inhabitants belonged to the Bani Yas tribe. Dubai was also part of this until 1833 when the Al-Bu Flasah tribe headed by the Al-Maktoum family split away from Abu Dhabi to become independent in Dubai.

## Pearling

Pearling is thought to date back some 2000 years in the Gulf region, and by the nineteenth century had become the chief means of livelihood for the inhabitants of these lands where only the most meagre form of subsistence living was possible.

Viewed from afar the pearling trade has traditionally carried a certain mystique, the idea of diving for these valuable and exquisitely beautiful treasures conjuring up romantic pictures. For those actually engaged in the trade the reality was quite different and the advent of each pearling season was viewed with much dread. The summer was chosen in preference to winter as the hotter sea temperatures made it safer, sharks and other large predatory fish preferring the cooler water of the winter months. The boats would set out in May or early June, returning in late September, thus separating the men from their families for at least four months at a stretch. The only event which interrupted these long seasons was if the ruling Shaikh called back the ships to take up arms against a neighbouring territory, a dispute of some sort having arisen which he felt could only be settled by war.

**Dangers of diving**

At the end of the nineteenth century Abu Dhabi had over 400 boats, the largest pearling fleet in the Trucial States. Sharjah had 360, Dubai 335, Umm Al-Quwain 70, Ras Al-Khaimah 57 and Ajman 40. The boats were small, geared for six to seven people, but at the start of the season they crammed up to 20 people on board together with provisions to last for several weeks till a supply boat would stock them up. With the diving gear, food and water, there was barely space to sit, let alone sleep, amongst all the provisions. There were on average 8 divers, 10 haulers for pulling the divers up by rope, one apprentice who had to catch fish, cook it, serve coffee and scrub the deck. Some of the bigger boats also had a *mutawaa* who led prayers and led the rhythmically chants often used to help in a communal task like rowing between the pearl banks. The captain was responsible for deciding the location of the dive and sale of the catch, but the actual dates for setting off and returning at the start and end of the season were set by an admiral-like figure who ran the pearling fleet, and was appointed at each port by the ruling Shaikh.

**Cramped conditions**

Most divers had a white cotton garment with long legs and sleeves to protect against jellyfish and other stings, a clip made

---

## PROVERBS OF ARABIA

To understand a people, acquaint yourself with their proverbs.

Every falcon dies with his eye fixed on his prey.

Climb like a cucumber, fall like an aubergine.

He licked the sky with his tongue.

In this world only three things dispel anxiety: women, horses and books.

An Arab's intelligence is in his eyes.

The arrogant man has no friends.

It is a lazy man who becomes an astrologer.

100 years of tyranny is preferable to one night of anarchy.

If you wish to be obeyed, do not ask the impossible.

Though he wears a crown, one man's needs are the same as another's.

Better than beauty is a Camel.

The fortunes of the Arabs who wear sandals have been eaten by the Arabs who wear slippers. (a slur on townsfolk).

After 40 years the Bedouin took revenge and said: I have been quick about it!

---

of goat horn for the nose, and a rope tied round the waist for his partner to pull him up by. His dive was speeded up by a heavy stone tied to his foot which was pulled up by the assistant once he reached the bottom. Diving began at dawn, each dive lasting some two minutes, long enough to harvest about a dozen oysters from the sand bank some 20 metres below and gather them in a basket attached to his waist. Pauses between dives were extremely brief, just a few minutes, and diving continued till light faded some 12 hours later. They only ate in the evening because it was impossible to dive on a full stomach. Their survival diet of dates, rice and fish meant they were under nourished, many losing all their teeth, and the extensive diving caused many painful and debilitating skin and eye diseases, as well as ear damage if they surfaced too quickly. It was also the diver's job to open all the oysters to hunt for pearls, a task which was done in the evening or early morning before diving began, under the careful supervision of the captain, who registered all finds in his book. Work

**Survival diet**

**Rigorous regime**

continued day after day with no break for the length of the season, with supply boats bringing extra provisions of brackish water and food periodically. Even the toughest of men were worn down and exhausted by this process, returning home at the end of the season enfeebled and weak, needing to be nursed back to strength by the rest of the family over the winter months to recover in time for the next season.

Their reward for these exertions was alas pathetic recompense. Middlemen took the lion's share of the season's harvest. The ship owner got 10%, and 20% went to pay for the supplies. The remaining 70% was divided up between the captain, who got 3 shares, the divers and helpers who got one share each and the ruling shaikhs who got one diver's share from each boat in the fleet.

When they received their pay at the end of the season, most barely had enough to pay their debts, and some became trapped in a spiral of debt, from year to year. In order to help family finances, boys were sent off to dive as young as 12. There was little alternative, since the agriculture which the land could sustain was not enough to guarantee self-sufficiency even for those families engaged in it, so some source of cash was necessary to buy essential supplies like rice and clothing.

### Orientation and Approach

**Grid system**

The most common approach to Abu Dhabi is from Dubai and is extremely impressive. Immaculate 4-lane highways lead in all directions, lined with trees and palms, all beautifully landscaped. The grid system should make finding your way round easy, but in practice it is very disorienting for a newcomer because every street, every junction and traffic light all look so similar. It is almost worth having a compass in the car to help keep your bearings and sense of direction. The road from Dubai crosses over Maqta bridge onto the main Abu Dhabi island, which is some 17km long and 6km wide. A little white watchtower guards the bridge from a tiny island. The current bridge will be widened to three lanes for incoming traffic only and a twin replica has been approved for three lanes of outgoing traffic, to ease congestion. A second bridge exists at Mussaffah to the west and a third is planned in line with the planned expansion in the economy and population.

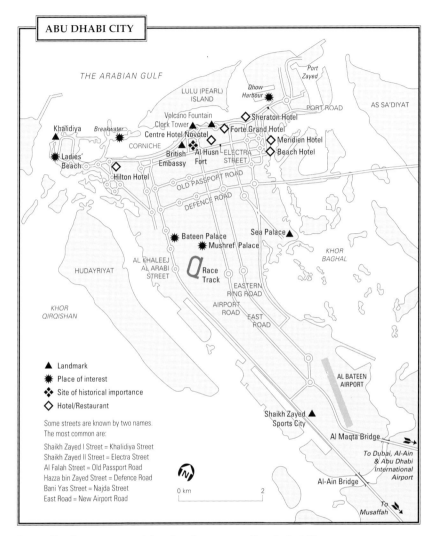

## ABU DHABI CITY

THE ARABIAN GULF

Port Zayed

LULU (PEARL) ISLAND

Dhow Harbour

AS SA'DIYAT

PORT ROAD

Volcano Fountain
Clock Tower
Centre Hotel Novotel
Sheraton Hotel
Forte Grand Hotel

Khalidiya    Breakwater

CORNICHE

Meridien Hotel

Ladies'
Beach

British
Embassy

Al Husn
Fort

ELECTRA
STREET

Beach Hotel

Hilton Hotel

OLD PASSPORT ROAD

DEFENCE ROAD

Bateen Palace

Sea Palace

Mushref Palace

KHOR
BAGHAL

AL KHALEEJ
AL ARABI
STREET

Race
Track

HUDAYRIYAT

EASTERN
RING ROAD

AIRPORT
ROAD

KHOR
QIRQISHAN

EAST
ROAD

AL BATEEN
AIRPORT

▲ Landmark

✳ Place of interest

✤ Site of historical importance

◇ Hotel/Restaurant

Some streets are known by two names.
The most common are:

Shaikh Zayed I Street = Khalidiya Street
Shaikh Zayed II Street = Electra Street
Al Falah Street = Old Passport Road
Hazza bin Zayed Street = Defence Road
Bani Yas Street = Najda Street
East Road = New Airport Road

Shaikh Zayed ▲
Sports City

Al Maqta Bridge

To Dubai, Al-Ain
& Abu Dhabi
International
Airport

Al-Ain Bridge

To
Musaffah

0 km                    2

Immediately on your right the fancy crenellated fort-like building is the private Falcon Club. For the most impressive approach take the Eastern Road signpost which leads along the amazing corniche, passing endless compounds of new palaces. The little islands opposite are covered in green, indicating they are all mangrove swamps with the accompanying protected marine and bird life. The streets all have numbers as well as names though there is much

**Official Names and Common Names**

confusion about the names, as some have common names like Airport Road, even though the official name is Shaikh Rashid bin Saeed Al-Maktoum Street. Many people live here for years, including taxi drivers, and still don't know the official or common names anyway. Distances are much bigger than they appear from the map as you would soon discover if you tried walking about on foot. Even by car the corniche approach seems endless, lined with elaborate picnic pavilions mainly in use by Indians. After the Meridien Hotel a sign points right to Port Zayed which enables you to get your bearings from the map, and shortly afterwards, the brown Sheraton Hotel looking more like a factory than a luxury hotel, signals your arrival on the main corniche at the far end of the island.

### Dhow Harbour

Taking the signpost off to the right towards Port Zayed you will come to a roundabout at which you turn left to reach the Dhow Harbour, visible on your left. Impressive still for its size, the Dhow harbour is very much in use, and the government **Spectacular races** sponsors dhow sailing races to keep the sailing tradition of the city alive. These races make attractive spectator sports. The island off shore which protects the harbour is called Lulu Island (Pearl Island).

### The Main Corniche and Breakwater

Following the main corniche, after passing the Sheraton Hotel, your landmarks are now the Volcano Fountain, an extraordinary apparition on the sea edge of exactly what it says, then the Clock Roundabout. You then pass a whole series of luxury skyscraper hotels, each more bizarrely modern than the last, till you reach the roundabout by the Hilton, at which you fork out on to the breakwater. Although these skyscrapers seem incongruous at first in a place where there is no shortage of land, they do of course offer the best commercial return for **The virtues of skyscrapers** the owner/developer, and the other practical benefit is that they cast a lot of shade. In the absence of hills, they do offer a view. The white sandy beach has been generously planted with palm trees for shade, but on a Friday especially the beach and pavements appear full of subcontinentals, all male, with barely a local family among them. A western expatriate would feel rather out of place using the beach here. On the break-water itself everything is an eating experience. The first area is a compound of barasti fencing and huts inside known as Heritage Park, designed as a cafeteria and restaurant with a few stalls selling artefacts. It was opened in time for the December 1996 Silver Jubilee celebrations. A little further on are a pair of amazing carved wooden house boats, equipped as seafood restaurants, and right at the end, dhows run as transportation between the breakwater and the Dhow Harbour, doing 30 minute trips.

**Houseboat restaurants**

**Cultural Foundation and Al-Husn Palace** (White Fort)
Sunday to Wednesday 7.30–1.30, 4–10pm. Thursday
7.30–12.00, 4–9pm, closed Friday and Saturday.
Free admission. Tel: 02-215300.
This whole complex covers an area of 14 hectares set in landscaped gardens and represents Abu Dhabi's, or to be precise, Shaikh Zayed's determination to promote and preserve the heritage of the Emirates. The modern buildings house the National Library, the Institution of Culture and Art, the Arts Workshop, theatre, lecture rooms and the exhibition halls, which are frequently used to exhibit the works of local and foreign artists. Throughout the year it offers a busy calendar of concerts, art exhibitions, films and lectures, as well as art workshops for adults and children. Environmental groups like the Emirates Natural History Group and the Flower and Garden Group hold their regular monthly meetings here. The amateur dramatic groups, choral society and orchestra all hold their performances here.

**Cultural fort**

The only building of any age (the oldest part dates back to 1793) is the Al-Husn Palace or White Fort, used today as home to the National Archives, with an attractive courtyard. Its whitewashed walls stand out incongruously against the backdrop of colourful skyscrapers. Originally built on the site of the only well in the area, in the nineteenth century by the first Shaikh of the Al-Nahyan dynasty, it has been restored many times since then and served throughout as the residence of the ruling Shaikh. The fort is open mornings only at the times given above for the Cultural Foundation, and displays old documents relevant to the heritage of the country. Even its enclosing fence has mini castles in white at intervals, and at night it is festooned in coloured lights.

**Abu Dhabi's oldest building**

### Heritage Village

On the Al-Khaleej Al-Arabi Road adjacent to the Abu Dhabi International Exhibition Centre on the the city outskirts, is Abu **Friday's best** Dhabi's main Heritage Village. On Fridays it is at its most lively, when a bazaar is held with stall holders selling traditional handiwork and popular local foods. Falconry skills are sometimes displayed by local handlers. The village recreates nomadic Bedouin life with goat hair tents, barasti houses, camel and horse stables, and irrigated plots round a well. Bear in mind that such villages are not designed primarily as tourist attractions for expatriates. They are for local Emiratis, for the older generation to be able to show the younger generation how they all lived in the pre-oil era, surviving the extraordinarily harsh climate and environment as best they could.

---

**DAILY CHORES**

While the men were off fishing in the winter months or pearling in the summer months, the women, in addition to rearing their children, had a list of chores to complete which was enough to make the hardiest blanch. They had to fetch water from the wells twice daily in goatskin bags slung over their back or in clay urns balanced on the head. The communal wells were located about one kilometre from the town and had to be constantly re-dug as they were always refilling with sand. They had to tend the livestock, milk the sheep and camels. In the oases they climbed the palms to gather dates each day, tended the farms, ploughed, sowed, watered and harvested. Before cooking they had to gather firewood or buy it from the Bedouin who brought it from the desert scrub.

---

The diet was mainly rice, fish, yoghurt and dates. The rice **Fruit and veg** was imported from India via Dubai. Fresh fruit and vegetables **treats** were great rarities and treats. With no refrigeration, fish had to be eaten at lunchtime as by the evening it was off. For this reason the inhabitants of Liwa and Al-Ain, the inland oases, never ate fresh fish, only the dried very salty variety. Clothing was scarce, each person having but a single dishdasha which was washed and worn over and over, and everyone was barefoot. Any form of footwear was useless in the sand, it simply got lost and buried within a few steps. At the Heritage Village there is a traditional pearling boat on display, fully equipped as it would have been throughout those 300 years in which pearling was the mainstay of the local economy, till the takeover of the Japanese cultured pearl in the international pearl market.

### Women's Craft Centre
Located five kilometres south of central Abu Dhabi on the Airport Road, it is well signposted. It is a government-run centre selling traditional weavings and other crafts.

### Shopping
Shopping is a national pastime, and Abu Dhabi has numerous modern shopping malls and department stores selling the latest high fashion accessories, jewellery, electronic and electrical goods. A new blue and white Central Souq has been opened offering traditional style shopping with over 400 shops, post office, bank and cafeteria in the comfort of air-conditioned corridors. It is located on East Road near the Central Post Office. Al-Nasr Street has memorabilia shops selling Bedouin jewellry, coffee pots, wooden chests and *khanjars* (curved daggers).

**Favourite pastime**

*In camel racing, the correct 'seat' is a long way back*

### Camel Races
In winter from October to April camel races are held all over the Emirates and Abu Dhabi's track is at Al-Wathba 40 kilometres east of Abu Dhabi city on the Al-Ain road. These races tend to be held every Friday morning and Thursday afternoons and offer a rare opportunity, not simply to watch the races, but to see local society close at hand, the poor and the rich rubbing shoulders.

### Falconry

October to March is also the falconry season and anyone who can afford it buys a *Saqr* or Peregrine falcon and trains it to answer their voice. Less so these days but in the season it was quite common to see hooded falcons on their masters' forearms in the car or at the shops. The sport had its origin in necessity, as the Bedouin trained the falcons to hunt and kill the Houbara bustard or other edible fowl. Since Shaikh Zayed declared the whole of Abu Dhabi emirate a conservation area – the Houbara is on the verge of extinction having been literally hunted to death – hunting is now the province of the wealthy, who have to go to Pakistan and Iran for hunting expeditions.

**Unusual passengers**

### Parks and Gardens

In line with Shaikh Zayed's vision of a green city, Abu Dhabi has over 25 parks and gardens and the number is being constantly added to. Many of them have some theme or other, like the new Heritage Park on the Airport Road with its giant statues of a threatening canon, a coffee pot, fort, incense burner and other reminders of the pre-oil period. Abu Dhabi Municipality must have the largest town council budget of any in the world, and if it contributes to the greater greenery of the city, then money is no object. The lush greenery has led to a huge increase in the birdlife of the capital.

**No expense spared**

### Futaisi Island

A short 12 minute boat ride from Abu Dhabi, Al- Futaisi Island has been developed as a nature reserve cum holiday resort, an environmentally protected National Park/Golf and Country Club. The project has been masterminded by a German imaginatively referred to by all the workers as "the German". A replica of an Arabian mud brick fort is being used as a hostel, while traditional Arabian tents provide facilities for camping. It is open to members or organised tours only. (Golf and Country Club Tel: 02-668846). There is a beach club with diving and canoe facilities to view the coral life, stabling for 22 Arabian horses, and a sand golf-course with 18 holes. There is coral just offshore, and a large enclosure houses three giant Seychelles tortoises. No noisy electronic gadgetry will be permitted here, and as a result it offers total tranquillity not

**Peaceful retreat**

only to the wildlife but also to the visitors, a welcome escape from the City and its traffic. It is sometimes nicknamed Fantasy Island.

## Coastline and Reclamation

The bulk of Abu Dhabi emirate's coastline is *sabkha*, salt flats, which glisten white and shimmer dazzlingly in the sun, especially the stretch from Abu Dhabi west to Ruweis. There are some mangrove swamps on the islands close to the capital, introduced for habitat creation. The three peninsulas in the far west near the Qatar border have some unique cliff structures which dominate the coastline, but they are a four hour drive from Abu Dhabi city and reaching them from the tarmac is not easy. Further east, Jebel Dhanna and Ruweis are the centres for the oil and petrochemical industry, unattractive to the casual visitor by any standards.

A programme of reclamation of some of the islands has been initiated in recent years with causeways being built to join islands that are within a few kilometres of the mainland. Part of the thinking behind this is thought to be avoidance of territorial disputes with Iran and to claim islands irrevocably as Abu Dhabi land. These always then alter the tidal effects and patterns and consequently the marine life in ways which have not been fully thought through. In many areas here the tidal zone, that is, the difference between high and low tide, can be as much as half a kilometre. Nearer Abu Dhabi the series of barrier islands face the prevailing wind, sheltering inland lagoons. Eight thousand years ago the sea level was much higher everywhere and the old coastline is still visible in the western area of the Abu Dhabi peninsula.

**Cause and effect**

## Sir Bani Yas Island

Known as a nature reserve for the highly protected Arabian oryx along with giraffes, emus, leopard and other endangered species like the Houbara, Sir Bani Yas has also yielded the surprising discovery by archaeologists of a unique monastery and church site thought to be a Nestorian Christian community dated to 400AD, 200 years before the advent of Islam, the site measures 30 by 30 metres, and so far 9 domestic courtyard houses have been revealed around a central courtyard containing the monastery. The monks would have

**Unique church**

been Arabs of the Eastern Church in Syria, who gradually spread across the Arabian Peninsula. This is the best preserved such site in the region, as the other similar site off the coast of Kuwait is now too dangerous to dig because of land mines following the Gulf War. There is no evidence of violence or weapons on the site, so the Christians are thought to have left peacefully after the advent of Islam. The island can only be visited by special permission from the Abu Dhabi Islands Archaeological Survey and can only be approached by helicopter or by boat. In the early days Shaikh Zayed chose Sir Bani Yas as his island retreat with his family in the summer months, to enjoy the relative cool of the sea breezes. The idea of gradually introducing more and more species was entirely his.

**Special permission**

## Conservation and Afforestation

Few rulers have spent so much of the country's wealth on the beautification of the landscape as Shaikh Zayed. It has been a lifelong dream of his to greenify the desert and even on his appointment as a young man as Governor in Al-Ain in 1946, one of his first tasks was to have the ancient *falaj* channels cleaned and repaired. A tree planting programme then began which has resulted in Al-Ain being known as the Garden City.

**Shaikh Zayed's vision**

### CONSERVATION AWARD

Shaikh Zayed has set up many agencies and bodies for protecting the environment and the desert wildlife as well as the bird and marine life. For these efforts, he received in 1997 a world conservation award from Prince Philip, President of the World Wildlife Fund, making him the first ever head of state to receive such an award. Together with the wildlife and conservation aspects, there is also the agricultural potential which Shaikh Zayed has encouraged. In 1972 there were only five thousand farms in the Emirates, while now there are over twenty thousand and in the last 20 years the area of farmed land has increased fivefold, making the UAE 90% self- sufficient in milk, 43% in vegetables and 40% in eggs.

Al-Ain used to have the groundwater reserves to cope with the irrigation of of all the newly planted vegetation, but in recent years the wells have run dry and 35 dams have been built in the area to collect rainwater to supplement the desalinated water which is now piped in from Abu Dhabi city. The afforestation projects around Abu Dhabi city and Liwa also require extra desalinated water to supplement the recycled sewage water currently used and the increased areas of greenery are thought to have contributed to a climatic change, a drop in temperature of one or two degrees, as well as attracting many more migrant birds to visit the area.

## The Future

The pace of development of Abu Dhabi's economy and population shows no sign of slowing down. Each year more and more luxury hotels open, confident that there will be ever increasing numbers of visitors – tourists and businessmen alike. The current drive is to promote Abu Dhabi as a major leisure centre to encourage businessmen to stop over for a few days of relaxation and sport. Huge sums of money are being spent on further improving an already excellent road and transport network, paralleled by spending on more and more Heritage schemes, intended not to lose sight totally of the Emirate's humble origins, as well as to persuade visitors that there is some cultural interest on offer here. Heritage Festivals abound, often initiated by the big hotels, which give residents and tourists the bizarre experience of watching traditional Arab dance and music, complete with authentic Arabic food and drink in the setting of a Bedouin tent set in the landscaped gardens of a five star hotel. In Ramadan, the holy month of fasting, the big hotels vie with one another in offering tantalising *Iftar* (breaking of the fast) menus each evening, and more food is consumed in Ramadan than in any other month of the year. Tourism is seen as a good income earner, but such events, as witnessed by the existence of the Abu Dhabi-based UAE Heritage Revival Society, also serve to remind local people of their roots, roots which are fast disappearing under a sea of skyscrapers. But some habits die hard. In the old days the seasonal migrations from coast to inland oases were a way of life. Now, even though there is no longer any need to leave the coast in summer, many families migrate by 4WD to Al-Ain or Liwa where they now own splendid country mansions whose gardens are tended by Pakistanis. The wealthiest of all, of course, simply migrate to Europe or the United States for the summer.

**Heritage in abundance**

**Continuing migrations**

The heritage theme continues even into the field of religion, and construction has now begun on the region's largest mosque, Zayed bin Sultan II Mosque, and on Shaikh Zayed's instructions it will incorporate a museum for Islamic heritage, along with its four 107 metre high minarets. It will be faced with white marble and located at the entrance to Abu Dhabi island between the Mussaffah and Maqta bridges and will cost Dh1.5 billion, built by an Italian company.

Preserving the domain of women and their right to privacy is also something that is moving ahead with the times. Single Russian women have been banned from making bookings in hotels, for fear that the prostitute image which has somewhat tarnished Sharjah and Dubai may tarnish Abu Dhabi's image. Following Sharjah's lead, Abu Dhabi has also recently opened an all-women's Beach Club at the newly reclaimed Ras Al-Akhdar, linked to the Ladies' Beach by an overhead tube bridge to ensure privacy. The Club boasts all the usual gym, health, sport and eating facilities and is open to nationals and expatriates alike at a fraction of the cost of hotel clubs with similar facilities. Children are allowed, but boys must be under 10.

From a place which in the 1960s had no modern schools or hospitals, no piped water or electricity and no proper roads, Abu Dhabi has become in the space of a few years an excellent **Local** place to be a national. The Class 1 National, that is whose **privileges** parents were both born in the Emirates and of Bedouin origin, is guaranteed a standard of welfare and medical support unrivalled anywhere in the world. Here it pays simply to be a local.

### Abu Dhabi Airport Archaeological Site

In summer 1995 whilst working on an extension to the Airport, a large Late Stone Age site was discovered with many flint tools. Excavations continue whilst flights take off all around, and the site is not open to the public at present.

### Umm Al-Nar

Known today as the site of a new Beach Park 10 kilometres east of the city, the Umm Al-Nar island was also the site of Abu Dhabi's oldest civilisation, and the first archaeological site discovered in the UAE. With the findings of copper daggers in the tombs and traces of copper working in the settlement, the archaeologists were able to conclude this city based its wealth on copper exported to Mesopotamia and the Indus Valley. Some two dozen ancient stone-built houses were unearthed here, one of which was a 300 square foot 7-roomed residence, pointing to an astonishing level of affluence and sophistication. Excavations were first carried out by Danes from 1959–65, and by Iraqis and the Al-Ain Department of Antiquities in 1975 and 1979. It was Shaikh Zayed himself, then governor of Al-Ain, who after visiting the Danes' excavations in the early 1960s, told them of similar mounds around the oasis of Al-Ain, which indeed turned out to be the settlements of Hili and Qarn Bint Sa'oud. The pottery finds, now on display in Al-Ain Museum, have dated the Umm Al-Nar site to 2, 700BC and the culture is known to have links to the Indus Valley, now Pakistan, and the Sumerian culture in Mesopotamia (Iraq). A study of the bones on the site revealed that the people ate dugong (sea cow, the origin of the mermaid myth), raised camels, spun, wove, grew corn and fished. Their lifestyle indicated that their community lived in a different climate to today's – a climate of far greater rainfall. The circular rock-crafted communal tombs, some 50 in all, are the trademark of such settlements, and this style of tomb has given its name to similar settlements throughout the Emirates and Oman. Some of the tombs bear reliefs showing camels, oryx, ox and a serpent. The name itself, meaning Mother of Fire, is scarcely sufficient explanation of why this, out of all Abu Dhabi's 200 islands, should have been chosen in 1973 as site for an oil refinery, thereby making the ancient settlement out of bounds to visitors, unless they obtain a special permit from the Antiquities Department. This may not be such a great loss however for as Michael Tomkinson wrote in 1975, the spot was "scarcely scenic even before the refinery bulldozers arrived in 1973 to disfigure it entirely."

**Shaikh Zayed's eagle eye**

**Mother of Fire**

## Liwa Oases
*The approach from Abu Dhabi*
The drive from Abu Dhabi to the centre of the arc of 40–60 village-oases called Liwa takes three hours today along largely empty roads, or five hours from Dubai. Before 1960 the journey took five days of gruelling hardship. The drive today

**From five days to three hours**

is not exactly riveting, and the scenery along the coast west of Abu Dhabi to reach the turn-off just past Tarif is a monotonous expanse of salt marsh, gleaming dazzling white in the sun. The causeway off to the island of Abu Al-Abyadh shimmers like a mirage. There is a petrol station just before the turn-off at Tarif, the first for a long time. There is then more petrol at Madinat Zayed and at Liwa.

Once you are on the Liwa turn-off itself, a large range rises to your right, which you can easily reach in 4WD and picnic on, one of the few places where you can get away from the road easily.

Beyond the ridge an unattractive landscape greets you of man imposing technology on the scrub-like desert. A gigantic gas processing factory dominates the higher ground where the road divides between Madinat Zayed and Bu Hasa, with tall towers firing off the gas. Telegraph poles, radio masts and gas pipelines run in all directions as far as the eye can see. Whole communities of expatriate workers seem to live beside this godforsaken landscape, even with a school.

**Forest plantations**

As the road approaches Madinat Zayed you begin to see large plots of forest, calling themselves plantations, lining the roadside. Each plantation generally has its mosque and a few corrugated iron huts for the labourers who live here tending the trees.

Entry to Madinat Zayed is heralded by a huge palm-lined dual carriageway, and the government Resthouse is set up on an elevation opposite the petrol station. You pass a fine new sports stadium and as you reach the town centre, there are grass meadows under the palm trees and abundant flowers. Outside the school is a huge model of a book and pen, the pen the size of a cannon. On the outskirts of town on the Liwa side is an enormous public garden with modern forts and children's playgrounds to explore.

After Madinat Zayed the road is flanked with huge fields of wheat and fodder, a bizarre and quite unreal sight in the midst of the desert. The smell of manure is pervasive. The labourers for these fields are almost entirely Pakistani, with hardly any Indians. Shaikh Zayed gives huge quantities of aid to his fellow-Muslim country Pakistan, and has a special relationship with it, going on hunting trips there.

The point where the road meets the arc of the Liwa itself is a place called Mizaira'a. From the roundabout here the tarmac dual carriageway now extends west as far as Aradah and east as far as Hamim. Turning right (west) you will notice, within one kilometre of the roundabout, a 3-towered fort set down in the date palms about 500 metres to your right. On the high hill immediately above it a colossal structure is nearing completion, Shaikh Zayed's new Liwa Palace, and on the slightly lower hillside opposite (south of the road) the new Liwa Hotel is being built, a privately owned hotel that will be more luxurious and more expensive than the Resthouse. You can approach the fort by choosing one of the tracks through the date plantation. This would be tricky without 4WD, but if in doubt, it is close enough to the tarmac road to walk anyway. It has clearly been recently restored, but then allowed to fall into neglect again, so the illumination lights have been smashed and inside a load of rubbish and debris has accumulated, with graffiti on the walls. Nearby is a breeze block and corrugated iron village of shacks lived in by the Pakistani labourers. Some are even equipped with air-conditioning and satellite dishes. In the fields around tomatoes and cabbages are being grown.

**Old fort among the palms**

Continuing on the western side of the arc you pass, again on your right, one of the very few old-style houses left in Liwa, built of mud bricks, its windows set high up in the walls. Almost immediately past this, just after the Police Station, the blue sign points off to the Resthouse on your left. Continuing on towards Qatouf, there is another single-towered fort, derelict again, beside an old mosque. Surrounded by goat pens and a Beluch shanty town, the fort's role rather sadly is now to guard the tomato fields. It clearly means nothing to the neighbouring villagers.

**Qatouf Fort**

For a general exploration of the Liwa, the best option, having seen the two old forts of the western arc, is to turn round and drive along the eastern arc. The Resthouse offers an alternative to camping, and, bearing in mind the distances, two nights are required to make the whole experience worthwhile, especially if you are coming from Dubai. 4WD is essential if you are going to get any sense of the real desert in Liwa.

No archaeological site has yet been discovered in Liwa, so apart from the two forts already mentioned, there is nothing of historical interest to see. What Liwa is therefore all about is scenery and sand. The sense of oases and fertility and the contrast with the sudden sand immediately beyond has been marred somewhat in the name of progress by the newly planted crops creeping up the sides of the dunes, diluting the impression of oases. Barasti (palm-frond) fencing is used as a hedge to protect fields of corn. Ten years ago there were 300–400 farms, while now there are 15,000 and rising. Groundwater supplies are still managing to cope, but will obviously not last indefinitely. Chemicals are used on the crops and certainly the quantities must be rather adrift because the tomatoes become huge and tasteless, many being simply dumped as there is no market for them.

**Multiplying farms**

All original Abu Dhabi Bedouin have their ancestral roots either in Liwa or Al-Ain. All have been given land here by Shaikh Zayed which they then farm using Beluch or Pakistani labour. No Emiratis apart from Abu Dhabians are allowed to have land here. It is difficult travelling in this terrain today to gain a feel for the old lifestyle as you drive along the dual carriageway with palm trees planted in its central reservation. By the time you reach Wadhail, the irrigated plots are beginning to thin out, and you approach one of the few tracks which, as a single 4WD vehicle you can still take. This is the wide track that heads south towards the Saudi border, and those who are in a group and sufficiently well-equipped, (bearing in mind there is no water en route), can continue on this track to skirt the Saudi border and head across to Al-Ain, thereby making a huge triangle out of the drive. This requires one night's camping between Liwa and Al-Ain, and several police posts are encountered at which you need to have passports and all relevant vehicle docu-mentation. The drive is gruelling but exhilarating, taking you through an interesting range of desert scenery.

**Gruelling drive**

This track to the Saudi border begins exactly 60 kilometres from the Mizaira'a roundabout, the central point of the Liwa arc, some 3 kilometres before Hamim, and turns right in front of a high red and white radio mast. The track is wide and quite badly rutted in parts and it is only after the first few kilometres that you finally shed the last telegraph poles and wires. Tracks lead off to a few isolated farms on the way, giving a much clearer idea of how life must have been in pre-oil times. Along the main wide track you can stop wherever you like and just experience the total silence of the true desert. In all directions you are surrounded by a scenery that is constantly changing in form, but never in substance. Every single feature, be it steep escarpments, high plateaux or low flat plains, is composed of sand alone. Many dunes are over 30 metres high, and sitting in the midst of it, surrounded by it on all sides, you can examine the minute detail of each dune surface, the ridges and ripples that change constantly in the wind, the delicate trail of each tiny insect's footprints. To the untrained western eye, sand deserts can seem tedious expanses of monotonous scenery. Yet the Bedouin, for whom this is their world, have evolved a complex and exhaustive vocabulary to describe the numerous aspects of sand formation and wind action.

**Desert experience**

The prevailing winds of Abu Dhabi are north, northwesterly which ensures that sand is incessantly swept up the slope then down a smooth steep escarpment. Whole mountains of sand here are therefore constantly changing and on the move, averaging 20 metres per year. Rain, when it comes, then transforms everything in a flash. But a few hours spent here, or even a night's camping, will be the closest you can get in today's world, to the sensation of life in the Empty Quarter, untroubled by man's modern inventions, exposed, if only for a moment, to nature in its raw form.

**Raw nature**

### Ruweis/Jebel Dhanna

This is the centre for the gas and petroleum oil industries, a new city 240 kilometres west of Abu Dhabi, first built in 1978. Jebel Dhanna is the export terminal for all Abu Dhabi's crude oil and has been since 1963. A permit is required to enter the industrial precinct, which has high security.

The young Mohammed Al-Fahim experienced what he called "Heaven on Earth" at the Das Island terminal in 1961. Compared to his primitive home in Abu Dhabi, it was another world. "I stayed with my uncle", he wrote, "in a room which had an electric lamp and a fan, an experience in modernisation beyond my wildest dreams... They had piped water, showers and towels. I had never owned a towel; here there were towels for everyone, an unbelievable luxury."

**Height of luxury**

## ABU DHABI PRACTICAL INFORMATION

### Airport
30 kilometres from the centre of town, back on the mainland. First opened 1982, set in landscaped gardens, French-designed in curve-shaped terminal building. Takes 20–30 minutes into city centre.

### Taxis
These are white and gold all over the Abu Dhabi emirate, including Al-Ain and Liwa. They are metered and reasonably priced. There are always plenty at the airport and about town.

### Limousines
Tel: 02-447787. A little more expensive, radio controlled minicabs, Al-Ghazal Taxis operate 24 hours.

### Government Resthouses
The government runs a series of Resthouses offering good simple accommodation at very reasonable prices throughout the Abu Dhabi emirate at Liwa (tel: 08-822075, 21 rooms), Ain Al-Faydah, just outside Al-Ain (tel: 03-838333), Sweihan (tel: 03-747333), Madinat Zayed (tel: 08-846281), and Ramah (tel: 03-772400). Madinat Zayed is on the way to Liwa, and Sweihan and Ramah are both on the Al-Ain road from Abu Dhabi. All the Resthouses have a simple but adequate restaurant.

### Hotels
All the top names are here, with Hilton, Le Meridien, InterContinental, Sheraton, Forte Grand and Holiday Inn Crowne Plaza, the most recent addition with a Roman-style swimming pool. Al-Shatie Palace Hotel on a man-made hill between Abu Dhabi and Dubai, was originally built as a shaikh's palace, beside the Jazira Beach Resort and Hotel.

The main four and five star hotels are as follows: (code for Abu Dhabi from abroad: 009712)

*Abu Dhabi Gulf Hotel*, P O Box 3766, tel: 414777, fax: 414537.

*Abu Dhabi Hilton*, P O Box 877, tel: 661900, fax: 669696.

*Beach Hotel*, P O Box 45200, tel: 743000 fax: 742111.

*Corniche Residence Hilton*, P O Box 6677, tel: 211200 fax: 344596.
*Forte Grand Abu Dhabi*, P O Box 45505, tel: 742020 fax: 742552.
*Holiday Inn Crowne Plaza*, P O Box 3541, tel 210000 fax: 217444.
*Hotel InterContinental*, P O Box 4171, tel: 666888 fax: 669153.
*Jazira Beach Resort and Hotel*, P O Box 26268, tel: 5629100 fax: 5629035.
*Khaldia Palace Hotel*, P O Box 4010, tel: 662470 fax: 660411.
*Le Meridien Abu Dhabi*, P O Box 46066, tel: 776666 fax: 729315.
*Sheraton Resort and Towers*, P O Box 640, tel: 773333 fax: 725149.

## Diving
Scuba Serena at InterContinental.

## Riding
Abu Dhabi Equestrian Club, one of the finest racing centres in the Middle East. Racing season November–April, with lessons for all ages mornings and evenings. As in Dubai there is no betting, but a form of lottery where spectators 'forecast' the winners and win thousands.

## Tours
Blue Dolphin for cruises along the corniche tel: 669392.
Sunshine Tours for desert safaris and sand skiing.
Tel: 02-449914.

## Restaurants
The floating restaurants of Al-Safina and Al-Sufun on the Breakwater have the most authentic ambiance with good Arabic food. For dinner on the move the Forte Grand's dhow *Al-Mansour* with wood fittings offers 5 star cuisine during its two-hour sail, setting off at 9pm daily. Bookings via the Forte Grand Hotel tel: 02-742020.

*Centre Hotel Novotel – Le Rabelais*, excellent French cuisine, lunch and dinner.
*Beach Hotel – Come Prima* for Italian food .
*Al-Dhafa Restaurant* in Mina Free Port Area is a floating ship that does a full dinner voyage for groups.

*Abu Tafesh Floating Restaurant* close to the InterContinental offers live entertainment at weekends.

Ethnic restaurants abound from Indian, Chinese, Lebanese, Filipino and Italian. Only the hotel restaurants are licensed.

## Food Shopping

Abu Dhabi does not have the colossal range of Dubai, but it has all the major supermarkets like Spinneys, Choithrams and Union Co-op, which between them stock virtually anything you might want. Al-Ain has supermarkets like Choithram and Co-op for picnic shopping, but Liwa is much more limited, with simple Indian-run general stores, so you need to come well-equipped yourself. Mineral water and soft drinks are always readily available at even the simplest places, though try never to let your stocks get low when you're off tarmac.

## Climate

Air-conditioning is needed 8 months of the year from April to November.

## Embassies

British Embassy tel: 02-326600 7.30am–2pm daily, shut Friday and Saturday.
USA Embassy tel: 02-336691.

## Liwa

Resthouse. Government owned, located between Mizaira'a and Mariyah just west of entry point to Liwa. Signposted. 21 spacious rooms and four suites, each with private bathroom and refridgerator. Roughly half the cost of a four star hotel. Surprisingly large building for 21 rooms, lots of corridors with traditional plasterboard screening instead of windows for added coolness. Large dining room. Set in large semi-landscaped grounds. Room service. Curious absence of fresh vegetables on the menu considering Liwa produces them. Tel: 08-822075.

# Al-Ain

Al-Ain, set 160 kilometres from Abu Dhabi, inland and surrounded by mountains and bordering Oman, is so different in feel from Abu Dhabi city, that it almost seems like a separate emirate. The population has a high proportion of UAE nationals, giving it a more authentic Arab feel, and English is less widely spoken. Of the expatriates a few are western, but the majority are Pakistani, Beluch and Afghans. Always somewhat apart from the oil boom, though undoubtedly a recipient of much aid from it, Al-Ain has established itself as Abu Dhabi's cultural centre, home to the first UAE University and to the Higher Colleges of Technology. The university has the most advanced medical **Shaikh** facilities in the whole Gulf region. Birthplace to Shaikh Zayed, **Zayed's** the ruler has always had a special affection for Al-Ain, and **birthplace** when his older brother Shakhbut became ruler, Sheikh Zayed was governor of Al-Ain and the Eastern Region and spent his formative years here developing the oasis town into an impressive Municipality with landscaped parks to earn it the epithet the Garden City. Roundabout City would be equally appropriate. Its name means 'the spring' (of water) and Al-Ain has always been blessed with abundant springs and groundwater. At Ain Al-Faydah, now a resort complex just outside Al-Ain, you can still "take the waters" in a modern spa facility.

Archaeologically it is also the heartland of Abu Dhabi and its plentiful water and other attractions were clearly such even in ancient times, that earlier civilisations chose it in preference to any other part of the Emirates.

### Orientation and Approach

Al-Ain's suburbs run into the adjacent town of Buraimi, part of Oman, which can be visited with no visa formalities. The main road into town from Dubai even passes through Buraimi and out again, with no indication other than a roadside sign. **Omani** In fact many of the most attractive excursions from Al-Ain are **excursions** into Omani territory, a large enclave of which is visitable from here, as the border crossings are located further into Oman proper.

The journey to Al-Ain from either Abu Dhabi or Dubai is an easy traffic-free drive along excellent dual carriageway and takes one and a half hours. Before the oil boom it was a five

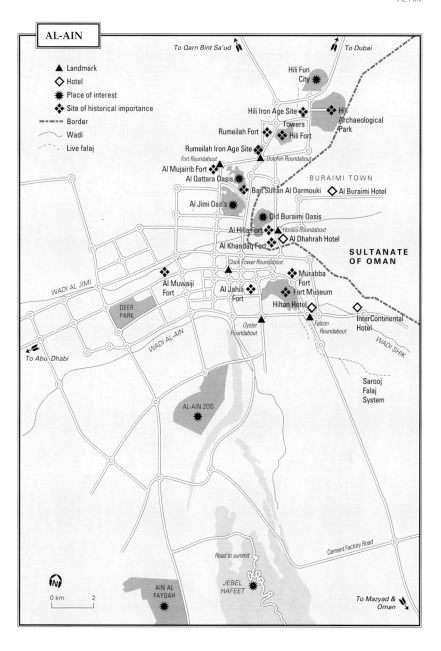

AL-AIN

▲ Landmark
◇ Hotel
✳ Place of interest
❖ Site of historical importance
----- Border
〰 Wadi
---- Live falaj

To Qarn Bint Sa'ud    To Dubai

Hili Fun City ✳

Hili Iron Age Site ❖    ❖ Hili Archaeological Park
Towers ✳
Rumeilah Fort ❖    ✳ Hili Fort
Rumeilah Iron Age Site ❖
Fort Roundabout
Al Mujairib Fort ❖    Dolphin Roundabout
Al Qattara Oasis ❖    BURAIMI TOWN
❖ Bait Sultan Al Darmouki    ◇ Al Buraimi Hotel
Al Jimi Oasis ✳
✳ Old Buraimi Oasis
Al Hilla Fort ❖    Horses Roundabout
Al Khandaq Fort ❖    ◇ Al Dhahrah Hotel
Clock Tower Roundabout    SULTANATE OF OMAN
❖ Murabba Fort
Al Muwaiji Fort ❖    Al Jahili Fort ❖    ✳ Fort Museum
DEER PARK    Hilton Hotel ◇
WADI AL JIMI    ◇ InterContinental Hotel
Oyster Roundabout    Falcon Roundabout
To Abu Dhabi    WADI AL-AIN    WADI SHIK
Sarooj Falaj System

AL-AIN ZOO ✳

Cement Factory Road

Road to summit    JEBEL HAFEET ✳

Ⓝ
0 km    2

AIN AL FAYDAH ✳

To Mazyad & Oman

**Visionary road**

day camel trip. As you approach at night-time, you will be mesmerised by the near biblical vision of a series of yellow lights snaking upwards as if to the heavens. This is the illuminated German-constructed road up Jebel Hafeet, the colossal rock outcrop that dominates the south of Al-Ain. The sprawl of the town appears endless with roundabout upon roundabout linked by identical landscaped dual carriageways and it is easy to become disoriented. A compass is a definite help when navigating about town, as although there are large purple signposts to the sites, they frequently send you on circuitous routes to keep you out of the town centre. The museum can provide you with a good tourist map if you ask.

It takes a full half hour to cross from the north side to reach, say the Hilton or the Inter Continental hotels which both lie on the south side towards Jebel Hafeet. The total area of sprawl is something like 12 kilometres by 16 kilometres. The mingling of the Omani with the Al-Ain territory is one of the major interests here, and the orange and white taxis are Omani, while the UAE ones are gold and white as in Abu Dhabi.

**Buraimi dispute**

The current border was demarcated in 1966, though some 20 years earlier the Saudis laid claim to the whole Buraimi oasis due to a historical link dating to the eighteenth century. The move was prompted by the Saudi-based oil company Aramco's desire to drill for oil here. The Saudis actually occupied part of the Buraimi oasis forcibly in 1952 and after arbitration attempts in Geneva broke down, the British Trucial Oman Scouts and the Al- Nahyan family, led by Shaikh Zayed, took the law into their own hands and drove the Saudis out. The Saudis only formally renounced their claim to Buraimi in 1974. The Al-Nahyan family did not move to Al-Ain until the nineteenth century, long after they founded Abu Dhabi town, and ruled the two oases jointly with Oman till the Saudis interfered in the 1950s.

**Hotter and drier**

The climate of Al-Ain is hotter and drier than the coast, and families from Abu Dhabi used to retreat to the oases for the summer months to escape the coastal humidity. Sightseeing is still possible into the months of May and June as long as energetic excursions are confined to the last few hours of daylight from 5pm onwards.

## Al-Ain Food Souq

Set in the centre of town near the Grand Mosque, Thursday morning is the busiest time at Al-Ain's bustling souq. The inner covered section has meat and vegetables, and the outer section is where the fish, fruit and dates are sold. The first buyers arrive at 6am to catch the freshest produce and 70% of market trade is over by 9am. At weekends people come from Abu Dhabi, Dibba and from Oman. By 11am when western expatriates tend to hit the scene, most of the trade is over, and the souq has lost much of its hustle and bustle.

**Early start**

## Al-Ain Museum

Tel: 03-641595. Open winter ( from 1 November) 8am–1pm, 3.30–5.30pm daily except Saturday. Friday 9am–11.30am. Summer (from 1 May) 8am–1pm, 4.30–6.30pm daily except Saturday. Friday as in winter. Ramadan 9am–1pm only, closed afternoons. No shop or refreshments are available. Nominal entry fee.
*Allow about 2 hours including the Eastern Fort.*

This museum was the first to be established in the Emirates back in 1971, opened on the instructions of Shaikh Zayed, true to his saying "a country without a past has neither a present nor a future". Most of the earliest excavations in the Emirates were conducted by Al-Ain's Department of Antiquities on Shaikh Zayed's instructions, and so Al-Ain Museum is in the unusual position of having displays from digs it conducted in Sharjah, Dubai, Umm Al-Quwain, Fujairah and Ras Al-Khaimah. Nowadays all digs within an emirate are conducted by the emirate's own Department of Antiquities, so each museum generally has displays only of its own local antiquities.

**First ever museum**

The museum is located in the town centre, just off the Pouring Coffee Pot roundabout, beside the modern livestock souq which is very confusingly disguised to look like a fort. The museum itself is housed in a modern building within the precinct of the Eastern Fort, the old 3-towered fort built by Sheikh Sultan, Zayed's father, in 1910 (1328AH). The fort is open mornings daily except Friday and Saturday, so mornings are the best choice for your museum visit. On hot days you may wish to visit the fort first, so you can escape to the air conditioning of the museum before the sun gets too strong. The fort was rebuilt in 1969 and restored in 1991. A pair of fine cannon flank the entrance. The fort gives a vivid idea of how simply life was lived in pre-oil times and it is worth remembering that it was Sheikh Zayed's birthplace and home throughout his formative years. It was in this courtyard that a

**Early cinema** film projector used to be rigged up by Shaikh Zayed, connected to the first palace generator, projected against the palace wall, and then the one film he possessed, an Egyptian film called *The Black Knight*, was shown again and again and again to the enthralled town inhabitants. "Shaikh Zayed was always somewhere in our midst", recalled Mohammed Al-Fahim. "Not one of us cared that we only had one film, which we knew by heart after several showings."

The barasti huts within the fort's courtyard are the summer houses, with open walls to allow the breeze to run through. The tower in the far corner was used as a jail. The well, now dry, was a real luxury, alleviating the need to walk long distances to collect water. The raised-up wooden platform in front was a summer *majlis* area for evening sitting or sometimes even sleeping. The room to the left of the gatehouse was the indoor *majlis* and the room to the right was for the guards. The walls of the inner rooms are covered in interesting old photos, depicting life in times gone by. Access to the stairs up to the battlements and towers is kept locked. Like all such defensive forts, there are no windows to the outside, only small holes high up on the battlements for rifles to be poked through.

## Museum
*Ethnography Section*
The museum divides roughly half and half between ethnographic and archaeological exhibits and the ethnography section is entered first. The exhibits chart the course of a child

**From birth to manhood** in the pre-oil era from birth to manhood, starting with the old cradle that used to be hung from the roof and covered in a mosquito net. Shell milk feeders are displayed, such as have been in use for 5000 years.

Circumcision happened between the ages of five and 10 and the accompanying tools are displayed. These days all boys are still circumcised, but in hospital, and the accompanying ceremonies have virtually died out.

Education was the next stage, and small boys were taught to read and write entirely from the Koran. The teacher's blackboard was an animal shoulder bone, from which the ink could easily be washed off and the bone re-used. The ink was made from the bark of the acacia tree which had to be burnt, powdered and mixed with water and gum. Pens were made from reeds. The first non-Koranic School in Al-Ain opened in the early 1960s.

**Bone as blackboard**

---

### MARIA THERESA DOLLAR

These striking solid silver coins so often found in Bedouin jewellry were first minted in Austria in 1773. They were also later minted in many other European cities including London, Milan, Venice and Rome, but by the time they became popular currency in the Middle East, where they were preferred to paper money and base metal coins, the date on the coin was always 1780, the date of Maria Theresa's death. The lady herself was Empress of Austria at the time of the Hapsburg empire and married at 23 the Grand Duke of Tuscany. From this marriage she produced 16 children, the 15th of whom was Marie Antoinette, born in 1755, later to marry Louis XVI of France and meet her grizzly end. Maria Theresa herself was known to be a happy, vivacious and intelligent woman, living life to the full and loving art, music, riding and gambling, as well as skilfully handling her political rivals, so that the empire under her enjoyed great prosperity and stability.

---

The women's section displays the typical silver jewellery which women from here and Oman have worn for over 4000 years. The Maria Theresa dollar (stamped 1780) used to be the currency of southern Arabia and was therefore widely used in necklaces which also formed part of the dowry. These dollars were often melted down to make jewellery, and Nizwa, 275 kilometres to the southeast in Oman was the main silver production centre. Gold was generally imported from India. One exhibit shows a life-size model of a bride decked in her costume and surrounded by her cosmetics and perfume bottles.

The agricultural display is centred round a real well, 15 metres deep, that used to serve the barasti huts around the fort. It is of course now dry, since the water table level has dropped sharply in the last 30 years due to increased irrigation needs. There is a fine display of wooden chests made from teak and generally imported from India or maybe Zanzibar and a few were also made in Oman. They are called *mandous* and served as wardrobes in which all the clothes were folded up in the chest section, and all the precious objects and jewellery were kept in the three drawers at the bottom.

An interesting herbal medicine chest is also on display showing the various herbs and spices many of which are still used to cure ailments. Ginger is still used for coughs, and black cumin for headaches.

**Ginger for coughs**

A fine display of weapons follows, with swords, bows and arrows, shields of rhino skin, rifles and *khanjars* (curved daggers). The khanjar, worn round the waist on a belt, was originally defensive and worn by all men in the Arabian Peninsula, but today it is worn as an ornamental object. In Oman it is part of the national dress.

The hunting displays show an eagle catching a rabbit, a bustard and a falcon. All the falconry accessories with the eerie black leather hood for the bird's head are shown. Falconry continues to thrive as a sport today and falcons are traded, each species having different characteristics and strengths. Pearling accessories are also shown, together with the drums and musical instruments considered essential on board the bigger boats.

*Archaeology Section*

Arranged chronologically and starting with the Stone Age 5500BC and later, the first signs of man's occupation are the primitive flint arrowheads, found in abundance in today's sand deserts, suggesting that the terrain was once more hospitable to settlement.

**Hafeet Graves**

Far more interesting though are the next finds, all from the Jebel Hafeet family graves, 5,000 years old, and dating from 3200–2700BC. This was a massive burial site for a whole community, with hundreds of stone cairns set along the northern and eastern fort of the bare mountain. The dead were buried with such belongings as bits of copper, stone beads, and pottery. No weapons were found. No settlement contemporary with these graves has yet been found in the

**Earliest-known graves**

Emirates but the sophisticated painted pottery had its origins in Mesopotamia and enabled archaeologists to date the graves and to infer that these ancient settlers clearly had trade links with Mesopotamia. The key to this trade was copper, the newly discovered precious metal which existed in the Hajar mountains of Oman, known in ancient times as Magan. Mesopotamian cuneiform texts detail how boats loaded with copper came from Magan via Dilmun (modern Bahrain) to the ports of Akkad and Ur in Mesopotamia (modern Iraq), so the existence of this relatively wealthy community in Al-Ain was entirely based on the copper trade.

**Wealth from copper**

### Bronze Age Sites 3000–2000BC

The earliest actual settlements found in the UAE are known as the Umm Al-Nar sites, named after the island near Abu Dhabi city where the first such site in the UAE was discovered back in 1958. The objects unearthed from the tombs there are exhibited, along with a dugong task. The archaeologists have been able to deduce from their findings that the dugong, now near extinct, was the main diet of the Umm Al-Nar people 4,500 years ago, together with wheat, barley, sorghum and dates, all of which they cultivated. Copper and gold were the main metals of the Bronze Age (bronze is an alloy of copper mixed with a little tin).

**Dugong diet**

Contemporary with the Umm Al-Nar site but better preserved are the Bronze Age sites at Hili, in and around the Hili Archaeological Park in the north-east of Al-Ain on the road out to Dubai. The museum shows a reconstruction of the striking Grand Hili Garden Tomb and its reliefs of people and animals. These sites and their significance are discussed in detail later in the Al-Ain excursions section. The finds, including pottery and jewellery from these sites, are on display, together with some fine chlorite (a kind of soapstone) boxes, beakers and bowls, decorated with patterns carved out of the soft stone. Magan was well known for stone vessels such as these and other examples have been found in Mesopotamia and other parts of the Gulf.

**Reconstructed tomb**

Also contemporary with the Umm Al-Nar and Hili sites are the Ajman tombs found by accident in 1986 and the finds from those tombs are on display here too.

### Second Millennium BC

The most eye-catching displays and the richest finds from any grave in the Emirates are those from Qattara, now a district of Al-Ain. In this long rectangular grave, the only one of its type dating to the second millennium BC, these delicate and beautifully worked pieces of ornamental jewellery were found depicting double animals, lions, goats or bulls, joined at the rear end, like Dr Dolittle's Pushmi-Pullyu. Gold in colour, the pendants are in fact made of electrum, gold and silver mixed. **Stunning jewellery** The quality of workmanship for something nearly 4,000 years old is staggering. Such dress ornaments were worn by powerful individuals to display status and the more important the person the more bronze weapons and gold jewellery he would have owned and had buried with him.

### Iron Age 1000BC–0

Finds from the Iron Age were quite different to the Bronze Age, and far more settlements were found, whole villages which are surprisingly well preserved, and the exhibits give a clear picture of daily life, with soapstone bowls and pourers, bronze axes, pottery incense burners, pottery storage jars and copper tweezers. Sites of this period are Hili 2, Rumeilah and Qarn Bint Sa'oud in the Al-Ain area, Qusais in Dubai. The **Delayed Iron Age** term Iron Age is slightly misapplied to Oman and the UAE, since iron objects were not in use here till a few centuries later, but the term has been used by archaeologists since these are the dates where iron was first used in the world at large, notably in Mesopotamia and Syria. The first iron objects actually found in the UAE date from a few centuries later. Next to the Iron Age displays is a large coin collection all items purchased or donated by local people, ranging from Greek to Byzantine and Islamic times.

### Hellenistic Periods

This is the culture that resulted after Alexander the Great's conquests in the Middle East, from the mingling of the Greek and the Near Eastern cultures. The sites of this period in the Emirates are at Maleihah in Sharjah and Ad-Dur in Umm Al-Quwain, but Al-Ain has exhibits from the early excavations in the 1960s from both these sites. The later discoveries are exhibited in the museums of the Emirates concerned.

## Islamic Period

When Islam began in the mid-7th century AD in the heart of Arabia, the people of the UAE and Oman were the first to adopt the new religion after Yemen. A big battle took place at Dibba, the northernmost point of the UAE's East coast, soon after the Prophet Mohamed's death, and the eerie gravestones can still be seen covering a large area to the northwest of the town. The museum here has displays too from the area called Darbahaniyah from the 15th and 16th century site of Julfar, the ancient Islamic sea trading port. Digs still continue there and the finds are displayed at Ras Al-Khaimah Museum.

## Gift Section

This is an interesting collection of gifts to Shaikh Zayed by kings and presidents from round the world. The collection of Islamic pottery and tiles from Hafez Al-Asad, President of Syria, is especially fine.

## The Majlis

Just by the exit to the Museum, do not miss a chance to rest your feet in the atmospheric Bedouin tent. Draped and decorated in authentic items from Bedouin everyday life, the majlis is a welcome spot to loll back on the cushions and digest your surroundings a little. The exhibits on display in the entire Museum are but a fraction of what the Department of Antiquities has in its stores and a new building is in the offing for expansion.

**Bedouin relaxation**

## Murabba' Fort (Old Prison)

*Allow 15 minutes.*

Before returning to the Pouring Coffee Pot roundabout where the Old Prison stands, take a few minutes to look at the livestock souq just beyond the Museum. Here if your stomach is hardy, you can watch sheep, goats, cows and chickens being traded. Watching them being loaded into the backs of trucks can be quite a spectacle, in which the women often take part, clucking and shrieking at the confused creatures to get them up the ramp. Be warned that the whole process may turn you vegetarian.

**Comic**

The Murabba' Fort (Arabic Square Fort) is an impressive building, slightly forbidding with its high walls and windowless exterior. It is marked on old maps as the Police Headquarters, but in recent years that function has moved elsewhere and the fort has been left to its own devices with a guardian. Though theoretically open, the writer has failed on any of numerous visits to Al-Ain, ever to find its door unlocked. Inside there is said to be little, beyond the courtyard and a few empty rooms. But the views from the roof must be interesting. The Camel Market which till March 1997 nestled picturesquely against the northern wall of the fort, has now unfortunately moved to the eastern industrial area of Hili, to the south of the Hili Archaeological Park.

*Old Camel Market at Al-Ain, formerly beside the Murabba' Fort*

### Al-Jahili Fort
*Allow 30 minutes.*

The next most central fort is Al-Jahili (Arabic, the ignorant or unknown) and certainly very little is known about it. Marked by a purple sign, it stands beside, though not in, a small public garden which is curiously wrapped round its circular fort tower. Unlike the garden which is subject to the usual curious opening hours, the fort is open all the time. Older maps show only the four square towers set to the rear of the site as the original fort, so the buildings you have to pass through with their courtyards and endless rows of corridors must be later additions. Stairs lead up to the battlements and are fun for children to explore. Downstairs notice the elegant decorative window screens and the fine old door with its fierce metal spikes. The inside of the round tower, the former Trucial Oman Scouts fort, is generally kept locked. A group of Pakistani workers lives in the more modern courtyard rooms beside it.

A visit to Al-Jahili can be combined with a visit to the Al-Ain zoo, or with a trip to Al-Muwaiji Fort and the Deer Park.

**Al-Ain Zoo**

*Half day*

Open daily from 7am–5.30pm including Fridays and public holidays, with a small admission charge.

The Al-Ain Zoo nestles in the north-east lee of Jebel Hafeet and the vultures from the mountain regularly come and help themselves to the meat thrown out for the antelope in the open paddocks at the back of the zoo. The roundabout that lies at the entrance to the zoo is charmingly decorated with near life-size models of giraffes and zebra. The zoo is the largest in the Middle East, so large in fact that a couple of electric trains run people round on tours free of charge, in recognition of the fact that most people are not prepared to walk the five or six kilometres required just to see the basics. There is also an extensive aquarium with penguins and a lone seal and many other types of indigenous fish. The indigenous visitors are evidently unused to zoos, and notices on the enclosures and even the back of the entry ticket itself, find it necessary to request people not to throw stones at the animals and not to climb their fences.

**Biggest in the Middle East**

The zoo was originally set up by the Bularts, a father and son team, Otto and Hans. Hans Bulart had built the Dubai Zoo in 1969 to house his private collection of animals and fish, and he then set up the aquarium in Al-Ain Zoo. Otto, a construction engineer and designer, built the Al-Ain Zoo in 1972, and together he and Hans, an aquaculturist and marine biologist, ran the zoos till the local Municipality took over in the mid- Eighties. Hans and his wife hunted for sharks for the zoo and caught 6, none of which survived after his departure. The running of the zoo has in recent years been a disaster, culminating in press stories about elephants with overgrown toenails, gorillas with open sores and wounds, and limping leopards. The aquarium has been allowed to run down woefully and the water is dirty and smelly.

**Hunting for sharks**

In response to public outcry and complaints from western expatriate animal lovers in horror stories publicised in the *Gulf News* over the last five years, Al-Ain Zoo closed for a time and has now announced a major overhaul of its facilities. Appalling cross-breeding mistakes were allowed to happen, thereby diluting the gene pool of Arabian oryx, which had been declared extinct in 1972. Incorrect feeding programmes

**Tragic death**

led to the death of a hundred Saudi gazelles who are supposed to be part of a breeding programme. They were fed fresh alfafa and pellets all year round, whereas in winter they do not need so much protein and the imbalance caused a bacterial infection in the intestinal tract which led to their death.

### Al-Mujairib Fort and Garden *(1hour)*

Usual park opening hours of 4–10pm weekdays, 10am–10pm Fridays. In practice there is generally someone at the gatehouse and they do not seem too concerned about letting you in.

This fort up in the north-west corner of Al-Ain is set well back from the road inside park gardens with a playground. The park is alive with Indian gardeners for whom your visit is the highpoint of the day. There are three separate sections of the fort, a round watchtower with flying buttresses, a nearby small L-shaped fort, and a larger square tower at the back of the park. With the exception of the round watchtower, all can be entered and clambered over, much to the delight of children. A torch would be handy for the darker recesses of the downstairs room.

### Al-Muwaiji Fort and the Deer Park *(1 hour)*

The fort at Al-Muwaiji is open all the time and so can fit into your itinerary at any stage that is convenient. The fort itself is announced by a purple sign and parking is just by the entry gate, since you will probably be the only visitor anyway. A 10-pillared mosque with courtyard and minaret has just been restored and slightly enlarged by the entrance. This mosque is an elegant and interesting building, the only one of its kind to stand beside any of the forts in Al-Ain or elsewhere in the Emirates. At the time of the writer's visit there was an enormous bee's nest near the top of the minaret tower which discouraged further ascent.

**Unusual mosque**

The fort itself is large and set within its courtyard is a very attractive and lush palm plantation, still tended by the Pakistani labourers. The fort was restored around 1980 and because, in the usual pattern of renovation with these mud brick forts, they are restored and then not maintained, parts of it are becoming unsafe and rickety, especially on the stairs and upper levels. In the north-west tower on the first floor is one of the lovliest majlis rooms of any of the UAE forts, an L-shaped room with shuttered windows banging in the breeze giving onto tranquil date groves beyond. Pigeons and doves of course are convinced that these forts with their high defence holes, have been constructed as fine dovecotes. Apart from a few dead pigeons, the rooms of these forts frequently also have decaying cats and dogs inside.

**Splendid majlis**

Continuing out west on the old Abu Dhabi road beyond the Diwan to the left of the road you come after about three kilometres to the Deer Park, an area of 2–3 square kilometres, where a bit of careful peering through the fence (binoculars help) reveals Arabian gazelles in plenty. Further east along the same road you come to the Al-Ain camel race track, where the fodder fields make an excellent spot for bird watching in early morning, especially larks, pipits and wheatear.

### Al-Khandaq Fort and Buraimi Oasis (2 hours)

There are no border formalities to cross into Buraimi, just a signpost welcoming you to one country and bidding you farewell from the other. The Oman/Abu Dhabi border was only formally demarcated in 1966, and Saudi Arabia continued to try to lay claim to Buraimi till as recently as 1974. You can enter from the north having come from Dubai, or from the south having come from Al-Ain centre. One of the first differences you notice is the Omani orange and white taxi. One interesting shop is a free-standing antiques shop called Majan selling pots, old brass and knick-knacks, silver and weaving at reasonable prices in Dh or Omani riyals. The old souq in pre-oil days here used to import goods from Sharjah, Dubai, Abu Dhabi and Sohar, and was the most important place for the inland communities both settled and nomadic to buy supplies like coffee, rice, sugar, pulses and cotton cloth. At the Horse roundabout where the modern Wali's (governor's) fort stands, the road forks off to the Al-Khandaq Fort, now newly renovated and open free of charge, except when the guardian has gone walkabout. Inside you can explore its fine battlements and towers, climbing the primitive ladder rungs sunk into the walls to reach the roof. From there you have fine views over the old oasis to the West, with its picturesquely decaying mud brick houses. Drive over afterwards and have a walk in the palm gardens, where the attractive alleys wind

**Fine battlements**

between plantations tended nowadays by Beluch and Pakistanis who live in huts round the edges of the oasis.

### Rumeilah Fort *(15 minutes)*

In this very rich archaeological north-east corner of Al-Ain stands the last little fort, Rumeilah, all by itself in an open sandy space. The blind guardian sits outside listening to Koranic recitations on his radio, and hands you the key to let yourself in. No tip is permitted for this service, as the Municipality pays him a wage. Inside, the upper staircase is starting to collapse, but light-footed visitors can still proceed to emerge on the roof.

**Blind guardian**

### Rumeilah and Hili Iron Age Villages *(1¹/₂ hours together)*

To find the Iron Age village of Rumeilah from the Rumeilah fort, proceed to the road behind it (west of it) that runs south for half a kilometre. Just at the point where the road bends to the left to rejoin the main dual carriageway, take the sandy track that leads you to a fenced area and a gate built in a new concrete wall. This gate, just 50 metres from the tarmac road, is generally open, because some storehouses and flats for the archaeologists are still being built at the top of the site. The excavated area is small so far, compared to the size of the fenced area, and the foundations of several houses have been dug out. Among the articles found in these houses, now displayed at the Al-Ain Museum, are pottery jars, one with a coiled snake on it, several elaborately decorated soapstone containers, and some bronze tools like hoes, axes and daggers. Earliest excavations here took place in the 1960s under the Danes, then a small local team worked here in the 1970s. During the early 1980s the French carried out extensive excavations to reveal the mud-brick houses dating to the first half of the first millennium BC making them at least 2,500 years old.

**Mud brick houses**

The Iron Age village of Hili (pronounced Healey), known to archaeologists as Hili 2, is far better preserved, or more excavated (it is difficult for the layman to tell which), and more impressive to the untrained eye. The site lies 2–3 kilometres north-east of Rumeilah, on the way to the Hili suburb and is set in a residential district within a large wall of sandy colour, topped with crenellations. You reach it by turning east from

Dolphin roundabout just by the Qattara Sports Club and continue past a filling station and two little watchtowers on your right to the next roundabout at which you continue straight. Before the road rejoins the main dual carriageway T-junction to Hili, look for a tarmac road on your left that heads in through the houses. Keep looking left till you see the crenellated walls and the gateway in it. This gate is also generally open, since the site guardian lives inside in the archaeologist's huts.

Impressive for their size and height, these 3,000 year old houses must have been relatively luxurious. At one point a blocked-up doorway can be seen, showing that even in ancient times people made alterations to their houses. One building near the centre, has column bases and appears to be an outdoor majlis-like structure for sitting out in the hot season to catch the breezes. The columns would have supported a palm frond roof. Excavations here have been carried out by the Al-Ain Department of Antiquities since 1976. Originally just a large mound, the archaeologists painstakingly dug it out to reveal the village almost intact. The walls still stand to two metres high, only the roofs have fallen in. Smoke blackening is still detectable against some of the outside walls, where cooking must have taken place. The village seems to have been abandoned round 500BC, for no obvious reason as there are no signs of a violent end. In sites such as these, archaeologists can deduce the functions of rooms or spaces from the original position of objects such as pottery, and determine whether they were used for industrial, ceremonial or domestic purposes.

**Intact village**

Already sand is going back in between the houses and each rainstorm washes away a little more of the ancient mud brick now that it is exposed.

**Hili Archaeological Park** *(1¹/₂–2 hours)*
These public gardens containing the UAE's most spectacular and best preserved Umm Al-Nar style tomb are open 4–10pm daily and 10am–10pm Fridays like all the Al-Ain parks.
They are well signposted, in the north-east of Al-Ain on the road out to Dubai. There is a small admission fee and inside there are extensive playground areas so you can examine the archaeology in depth while the children romp. Simple

refreshments are available in the park.

This Park in effect represents the centrepiece of the Bronze Age settlements, as, apart from the buildings inside, there are further excavated areas outside the park which will be described later. The Grand Garden Tomb which you cannot miss 100 metres straight on from the park entrance, is the largest ancient monument in the UAE, 12 metres in diameter and a projected height of five metres. The quality of stonework is unrivalled by any other tomb of the same period, each huge stone perfectly shaped to fit its neighbour. It was first excavated by the Danes in 1964–67 and reconstructed by the Al-Ain Department of Antiquities in 1974. Shaikh Zayed himself first alerted the Danes to the site at Hili. Having visited their excavations at Umm Al-Nar, he told them that at Al-Ain, where he was governor at that stage, there were similar ancient mounds, so the Danes made the five day journey across the sand to see for themselves. The Hili site appeared at that time to be a mound with a strange stone circle poking out, and round about were a series of other mounds with pottery scattered on the surface. The tomb has two porthole-like entrances and on each are the striking 5,000 year old stone carvings. These entrances would initially have been blocked off by three small doorstones, one of which had a handle, each decorated with lively animal scenes. The southern entrance has two human figures standing in between two oryx recognisable by their horns, and the northern entrance has two figures embracing each other, while another figure rides a donkey. Behind the donkey is a further figure holding a stick, and below the entrance are two cheetah-like animals devouring a gazelle. Inside, the partition walls would once have supported a corbelled stone roof. No bones were found inside this tomb, only many fragments of shattered pottery, prompting speculation that it may not even have been a grave, but a temple, the clay vessels containing offerings to the dead or to their gods. To add to the mystery, in one tomb at Hili, some 20 skeletons were discovered by the French, the only ones to be found undisturbed, lying in a neat row side by side. From sites such as this where skeletons are found in their original positions, much can be deduced about the age and sex-structure of the population, congenital disorders, famine, weather conditions, blood types and diseases. These people,

**Grand Garden Tomb**

**Mysterious skeletons**

Above: *Abu Dhabi's corniche skyline with a motorised dhow in the foreground*

Left: *Lush greenery in the Buraimi Oasis*

Above:
*Mizaira'a Fort,
Liwa*

Right:
*Madabbah
waterfall*

*Fort at Wadi Sharm, near Al-Ain*

*Barasti wind-tower at the Heritage Park Café on the Breakwater, Abu Dhabi*

*The dune wilderness of the Liwa*

from their bones, had died young, around 40, and had been pretty disease-free. Another mystery though was the strange cuts that some of them had in their bones, apparently inflicted at the time of death. All the skeletons appeared to have been buried simultaneously, but the most curious thing was their size, tall well-built people, far taller than the current inhabitants of Al-Ain, men averaging 1.78 metres (5 ft 10 inches), women 1.72 metres (5 ft 8 inches), suggesting they were not Semites at all. These people produced better pottery and were better able to craft stone than those who came 2000 years later. The stone to build these monuments must have been somehow transported from the mountains 2 kilometres away, a feat requiring considerable social organisation. Examination of their refuse pits revealed evidence of their diet, which apart from meat of local animals, included wheat, barley, sorghum, dates, melon and jujube. Knowledge of their trading patterns from the pottery found and designs used has enabled the archaeologists to deduce that this superior race was creating its wealth from exploitation of the copper mines in the nearby hills. Many ancient mines have been identified, most of them still in use in the tenth century, and again in the seventeenth century. In some of these mines, as at Wadi Safarfir, *(see Ras Al-Khaimah section)* traces of much earlier mining activities dating to the third millennium BC can be distinguished underneath the Islamic remains. Since the only strikingly tall races came from Africa rather than from the East, it is tempting to speculate that these people came to Al-Ain from Africa via Oman. Ethnic minorities have throughout history frequently been the dominant traders and craftsmen in the countries where they settled. The fact that such a skilled civilisation should have died out without trace and without signs of violent struggle, suggests that when the trade route waned and their income began to decline, they moved on elsewhere, to where conditions were more favourable. Environmental and climatic changes were also at work, a fact deduced by careful study of seeds, pollen counts, insects, geology and original water table levels and well depths. Geologists think that climatic drying at this time led to a drop in the water table, meaning that wells had to be dug ever deeper, and sand dunes blown by the prevailing northwesterly winds began to encroach across the land from the coast, blocking off the trade routes to the sea.

**Taller and more advanced**

**Superior miners**

**African origins?**

Complex
society

The civilisation on which these early Al-Ain inhabitants had depended from 3000–2000BC was the brilliant Sumerian culture of Mesopotamia, modern day Iraq, the world's first real civilisation. Mesopotamia means in Greek "land of two rivers" and the culture grew up based round the Tigris and Euphrates and the fertility their annual flooding brought to the land. They invented the wheel and the alphabet and the art of writing and developed the first cohesive city life based on agriculture. Mesopotamian farmers had to build complex canals, dykes and reservoirs to control the annual floods and this demanded much organisation and co-operation. Social classes evolved through this process, as different levels of soil fertility led to increased wealth for some, who because of their food surpluses, were able to become merchants, craftsmen or administrators. A need for centralised decision-making evolved and hence the beginnings of urban civilisation. What they lacked were raw materials like metal and stones, so to obtain these they established trade routes. Statues from Ur in Mesopotamia were found to be of diorite from the Hajar mountains of Oman and UAE and their copper came from here in shipments, transported to the coast near Umm Al-Nar (modern Abu Dhabi) by camel, and this is thought to be the

Domestication
of the camel

earliest known domestication of the camel, for how else could the copper have been transported across the desert from Al-Ain? The metal was then shipped up the Gulf making stops at Dilmun (modern Bahrain) where there was plentiful fresh water for the ships to re-stock before unloading at the cities of Ur and Akkad in the south of Mesopotamia. The other contemporary culture was the ancient Egyptian, the earliest Pharoanic dynasty starting around 3100BC, continuing with the Step Pyramid of Pharoah Zoser and Saqqara circa 2700BC, to the building of the Great Pyramids at Giza ending in 2134BC.

A further area of excavation in the park, enclosed by a small fence, is an unusually large watchtower which was both defensive and residential with a group of mud brick houses round it. It was excavated by the Danes in 1976–1978.

### Hili 8

As you leave the park, if you take the track that forks to the left to skirt the wall you will reach on the south-west corner of the park the foundations of the large mud brick watchtower surrounded by a moat, that is known as Hili 8. Excavated by the French from 1977–83, the various habitation layers extend over 1000 years ranging from 3000–2000BC. The tower originally had a well in the centre. The site is unfenced and is approachable at any time. Nearby are remains of more Umm Al-Nar stone-built tombs excavated by Al-Ain Department of Antiquities from 1970 onwards.

Also nearby are Iron Age stone-lined falajes (channels) for water supply and irrigation, showing how this skill for mastering water dates back 2,500 years.

---

### IRON AGE FALAJ CHANNELS

These channels are thought to have been fed by underground tunnels (known as qanat in Persia and elsewhere), examples of which have been found still in Al-Ain. The longest known such underground falaj runs for 9.5 kilometres from its "mother well" at the foot of the mountains to bring water by gravity to where it is needed. The mining and tunnelling skills required for such an exercise are known to have been acquired by the inhabitants of the third millennium BC, from their mining activities. After the original mother well hole, they sank further shafts at intervals, to lead the channel, always inclined just enough to allow the water to flow freely downwards to emerge at the final point desired. From there, the water was channelled off above ground to irrigate fields, with a series of sluice gates to control the direction of flow around the date plantations. The construction shafts along the length of the tunnel later permitted easy maintenance.

---

### Hili 17

At the start of the road leading to Hili Park is a Heritage Revival Association, a collection of barasti huts selling clay pots and other crafts. Beside it, enclosed by a red and white posted fence is a further area of excavations from the Iron Age known as Hili 17. The gate is locked, but it is possible to walk inside through holes in the fence.

### Bayt Sultan Al-Darmouki, Jimi and Qattara oases *(2 hours)*

Within little over one kilometre as the crow flies from the Mujairib fort on the other side of the Qattara oasis, stands the impressive mansion, currently under restoration, of Sultan Al-Darmouki, father of the current mayor of Al-Ain and local dignitary. It is interesting to see a private house for a change, rather than a walled fort. The Palace falls into two parts

**Fine mansion**

separated by an open courtyard, and down at the edge of the fields is the tiny family mud brick mosque. The grander northern part, its roof decorated with toadstool-like structures in the corners, has a fine double majlis room on the first floor. From the roof you can look west across the oases to see the two towers rising above the date palms that you are shortly to visit.

From the mansion continue down Al-Qattara Street southwards a little till you reach the purple sign pointing right into the Jimi and Qattara oases. This road is an experience in itself, one of the very few winding roads in Al-Ain, and within the space of a few hundred metres you feel you have left the **Old village** City behind and are in an old village oasis. The crumbling fort **atmosphere** of Qattara stands to the right of the road and a little further on to the right you can park beside an old souq and walk into the oasis itself through a large gateway and work your way towards the second large fort that rises up in the centre of the Qattara oasis. Traversing falaj systems and passing little reservoirs gives you a good idea about how the irrigation system still works in these oases.

### Qattara Tomb *(30 minutes)*

If you are curious to see the tomb in which so many of the rich finds in Al-Ain Museum were discovered you can return to Al-Qattara Street and head north up the dual carriageway. Look out for a 2-storey parade of shops on your right and take the track that leads behind them into a farm. The gate is generally open and the farmer does not mind people visiting the long thin grave.

### Hili Fun Park and Ice Rink *(Half day)*

Open daily 4–10pm. Fridays and holidays 9am–10pm. Closed Saturday and Sunday. Tuesday and Wednesday women and children only.

Located at the beginning of the Dubai road in the north of Al-Ain, the Hili Fun Park is one of the largest amusement parks in the Gulf, with over 500,000 visitors a year. During the Al-Ain Festival held annually in February, crowds of over 7,000 a **Water and fair** day come. The high admission fee covers rides on all the water **rides** and fair rides, and there are several fast food outlets set within the landscaped gardens.

### Qarn Bint Sa'oud (1¹/₂ hours)

Whilst in this northern part of Al-Ain, as a complete contrast you could take the opportunity to drive out to the 800 metre long and 50 metre high rocky outcrop known as Qarn Bint Sa'oud that lies 12 kilometres to the north. Here you will find 40 or so tombs dating some to the third millennium BC, contemporary with those of Jebel Hafeet, and some to the Iron Age in the first millennium BC. The tombs cover the top and the slopes, though the top ones have now been destroyed. Some 18 have been excavated by the Danes from 1970–1972 and by the Al-Ain Department of Antiquities from 1973–1974.

The drive itself, starting from the roundabout just west of the Hili Fun Park, leads through a charming landscape along a winding road, back to nature after the regular dual carriageway grid network of Al-Ain city. At one stage to your left is a fenced area clearly awaiting excavation, several tempting-looking mounds still concealing their treasures. The road leads on through red dune country to end finally at the unmistakable rock outcrop itself with a winding track to its summit.

**Back to nature**

There are a few huts nearby, but no actual settlements. To the west, if you follow a graded track along the line of the pylons you will see after about 1.5 kilometres, a recently excavated Islamic site to your right. It appears to be a mosque of sorts, maybe used seasonally by caravans, and there is some interesting red stonework in places. The desert scenery is very evocative especially at sunset.

**Islamic desert site**

### Jebel Hafeet summit and Ain Al-Faydah Resort (3 hours)

No trip to Al-Ain is complete without a drive to the summit of Jebel Hafeet, preferably at sunset. The spectacular dual carriageway built by the Germans snakes up to the 1240 metre summit for about 15 kilometres of hairpin bends, surprisingly demanding on petrol consumption, so make sure you set off at least with half a tank. The drive out from the centre is well signposted to Ain Al-Faydah and Jebel Hafeet, taking you round the western side of the outcrop. Forking off to the left a little before Ain Al-Faydah, the road approaches the hill and a track branches off to the right to reach a series of springs tucked at the foot of the mountains with men's and women's bathing pools. This area, called Mubazzara, appeared newly in

1996. A few facilities for visitors have now been built around it, including a small resthouse.

As the road up the mountain begins to climb, you can start to examine the amazing limestone rock structure of the mountain. Its slabs of limestone lay on the sea bed geological eons ago, and were thrust upwards in an undersea eruption to stand near vertical. If you get a chance to look closely at the rock you will see tiny white flecks which are fossilised marine creatures from the days when it was all underwater. You may also spot some larger types of shellfish which, because of their hard exterior, fossilise well. Some of these species still exist today, some died out long ago. They have been dated to 38 **Young fossils** million years ago, making them relatively young in the life of a fossil, most of which in the UAE date to between 70 and 135 million years.

On the ascent the flora begins to change above the 500 metre mark. The name Jebel Hafeet means Bare Mountain in Arabic, but as you climb up, a few caper bushes can be seen breaking the barrenness as they cling to the steep rock. In April and May many species of flowering plants can be identified on the higher reaches. Egyptian vultures may be seen wheeling round the steep crags in the updraughts. Humes Wheatears and the rarer Hooded Wheatear are resident on the mountain. On the summit itself there are many Brown-Necked Raven. **Less peaceful** Eagles and vultures used to breed here on this once peaceful **summit** mountain top but the advent of construction machinery both for the road itself, for the Palace already constructed and the 5-storey, pyramid-shaped 300 room hotel which is nearing completion, has severely disrupted their breeding in recent years. At the time of writing there were no refreshment facilities on the summit. It is usually quite windy at the top, where the road ends in a massive car park.

Returning to the main road out towards Wegan at the foot of the mountain you very soon reach the fork left to Ain Al-Faydah, extensively developed now as a resort garden based around the spring waters. The resort offers chalet-style accommodation of varying sizes, restaurants of the fast food variety, and a number of parks with children's playgrounds, some just for women and children. The central pool with a bridge over, offers pedalo rides which, at the right time of year and day, can be a very pleasant way of taking some exercise and enjoying the view towards Jebel Hafeet dominating the horizon. Tucked at the back of the developed areas of the resort to the left of the last small roundabout, you can find the old bath house, a covered but partly open structure where the waters could be taken by going down the steps. Somewhat run down now, with defunct lavatories, the pool of water is alive with fish who seem very grateful that someone has so thoughtfully built a shelter over them. Further to the left are more reed pools which occur naturally here, ringed with Tamarisk trees. Approaching silently you will spot many varieties of birdlife here.

### Jebel Hafeet Cairn Tombs and Mazyad Fort *(Half day)*

The stone-built burial cairns that line the eastern fort hills of Jebel Hafeet are the earliest signs of human construction yet discovered in the UAE. More used to exist on the northern slopes but have now disappeared under the urban sprawl of Al-Ain city. Dating from 3200–2800BC they fall into the early Bronze Age era and there are 500–600 in total, some 100 of which have been excavated first by the Danes, Iraqis and French, and then by the Al-Ain Department of Antiquities from 1962 onwards.

To reach them you drive out towards Mazyad, south of Al-Ain, virtually at the Omani border post. Just before the petrol station on the right hand side of the road, within half a kilometre of the border, a sandy track leads off towards the mountain and brings you within 2 kilometres to a high grey concrete wall with a gateway which is always open. 4WD is preferable as there are parts of the track that can be tricky for saloon cars, with softish sand, and later rocky patches. This wall encloses a huge area which is the private farm and stables of Shaikh Zayed and, as currently configured, this is what you will return to when you visit the Mazyad fort. It is hardly surprising that Shaikh Zayed knew the mounds and told the Danes digging at Umm Al-Nar: "If you are interested in mounds like these you should come to Al-Ain. We have hundreds of them there." When they did make the five day trek across in 1962, Shaikh Zayed drove them over to the mounds himself.

Continuing past the gateway to the south and skirting round the edge of the wall, the track leads on to Mazyad fort

Shaikh Zayed's farm

now claimed in the corner of Shaikh Zayed's farm. It may well be that when restoration is complete, access from here will be possible rather than having to enter from inside the farm, but at the time of writing the gateway to the fort that is outside the farm is kept locked. Following the track on towards the mountains that tower above, the dramatic geological strata of the limestone outcrop are almost hypnotic in their fascination. The track is lined with metal posts set in concrete bases and these will lead you after 1–2 kilometres to within sight of the burial cairns. If the weather allows it (the best time to visit is late afternoon when the whole area is cast into an eerie shade as the sun sets on the other side of the Jebel), leave your car here and walk to climb around these strange mounds. The more you look the more you will notice, some clustered together, some set apart. On the excavated ones, the double ring walls are apparent. They are thought to have been built over a period of 400 years or so, as a huge cemetery for the community which lived here about 5,000 years ago. The items of painted pottery found in the excavated graves, now on display in Al-Ain Museum, were recognised by archaeologists as being of the same style as pots from Mesopotamia dating to 3200–3000BC, indicating that trading links must have been well established with the Sumerian civilisation of that time in Mesopotamia. Inside, the graves had one round or oval chamber, roofed by a corbelled stone dome. The entrance was almost always on the south side and had a large lintel. Being so conspicuous, they were inevitably robbed of most of their contents in ancient times.

**Fascinating geology**

Returning along the same track to Mazyad fort you can enter if possible from the eastern gate. If this is locked you must follow the concrete wall and enter Shaikh Zayed's farm to reach it. Once inside, you pass almost immediately on your right, the bungalow where Colonel Sir Hugh Boustead lived till his death. Trusted adviser to Shaikh Zayed and HMG's first Political Agent, he was a likeably direct character who described the climate in the UAE as "bloody awful for six months of the year."

**Boustead's bungalow**

Beyond this on your left you pass Shaikh Zayed's stables, where the Pakistani and Beluch workers will gladly show you round. Finally you arrive at the gateway to the fort, just beside a mosque and simple collection of huts. The gate is sometimes locked, but the workmen will happily open it for you and give you a tour of the fort and its towers and battlements. Restoration is in progress and the courtyard is used as a date palm grove.

From Mazyad an alternative route back to Al-Ain centre, or if you are going on to the summit of Jebel Hafeet, Ain Al-Faydah or the Zoo, you can look out for the road marked Truck Route for Cement Factory, which forks off towards the northern base of the mountain and leads through some weird eerie moonscape-like foothills. You can then return to the centre by forking right towards the area called Sina'iya, meaning industrial in Arabic, where Al-Ain factories to process dates and surplus food produce can be found.

**Moonscape**

### One Day Excursions

Although these excursions assume a starting point of Al-Ain, they can also be completed by the energetic in a long day from Abu Dhabi or Dubai, with a departure time of 7 or 8am, returning around 8pm.

### Hanging Gardens and Fossil Valley

This one day excursion is for the energetic, and is possible with a carefully-driven saloon car. All the excursions described here are into Omani territory where no visa is required, and the way to begin is the same for each trip. From Al-Ain City centre, take the road north to Oman, passing Al-Khandaq Fort and arriving at the roundabout with model horses by the modern Wali's fort. Turn right here following signs to Sa'raa. At the second roundabout with the model gazelles, follow the sign to Al-Khadra'a Al-Jadida. The third roundabout with the model oryx is known as Buraimi Hospital roundabout and at this one, you continue straight on, following Al-Jizi and Sohar. The turn-off left towards Mahdah comes shortly after the Buraimi Hotel, also on your left, 1.8 kilometres from the Buraimi Hospital roundabout. If you are coming from Dubai, the quickest way is to approach from the Hatta road, where shortly after the Madam roundabout, a wide graded track forks right towards Mahdah, passing turn-offs to As-Sumaini and Juwayf. This is an easy track, fine for saloon cars and rejoins the tarmac just before Mahdah.

**Route into Oman**

From Buraimi the turn-off into Fossil Valley is 8.2

**Fossil Valley**

kilometres from the Mahdah turn-off just by a triangle roadsign of camel crossing the road. The valley is a flat wide plain about 2 kilometres by 3 kilometres ringed in a sort of horseshoe by Jebel Huwayyah to the south and other low hills. Behind it a little to the east is the unmistakable flat tabletop of Jebel Qattar, 786 metres, with its sheer cliffs. Fossils are in great abundance in this valley because when it was under the sea geological millions of years ago, the shallow waters trapped sea creatures here because of the encircling ring of mountains. On Fridays and public holidays the spot gets quite crowded.

The so-called Hanging Gardens are the more exciting part of the trip, but involve some rocky climbing, so is only for the active and sure-footed. The spot is an exceptionally rich patch of trees and plants set in a sheltered crevass of Jebel Qattar and **Shattered** partly hanging from the rock where springs and waterfalls **crevass** emanate from the rockface. The track to it leads off the Mahdah road 16.6 kilometres from the Mahdah turn-off in Buraimi, or 8.4 kilometres after the turn-off to Fossil Valley. The track is on the right just after a blue sign with oryx on it, exhorting preservation of the environment. You have come too far if you reach the patch of green grass on the right with two plastic gazelles and a sign in Arabic announcing Wilayat Mahdah Greets You.

The track leads 4.6 kilometres to a dead end where you can park beside a huge rock at the start of the wadi, tucked at the foot of Jebel Qattar. Make sure you have plenty of water with you at hot times of year as the climb is strenuous, taking a good 40 minutes to reach the gardens. Good strong shoes are recommended. Begin by walking upstream in between the clumps of reeds and oleander. The amount of water in the wadi varies considerably with the season. After about 150 metres choose a spot to start the climb up the loose rocks to the **Steep** right, a scramble rather than a walk, with no path to follow. **scramble** Once at the top of the steep ridge you can pick up a path of sorts, from which a steep ascent leads to Bat Cave, clearly visible at the base of the Jebel Qattar cliffs. Views from the cave are dramatic, but apart from the droppings there is no sign of the bats in any of the cave recesses. The path on to the Hanging Gardens is easy, flat walking after the rocky scramble. The pond below the cascading plantlife is often dry, disappointingly, so there is nothing to refresh yourself in. There are two waterfalls here, but depending on the season, they may just be trickling down. The spot is beautifully peaceful, with only the sound of birds as they drink merrily from the dripping falls. As well as the smaller birds like the Yellow Vented Bulbul, Desert Lark and Red-tailed and Humes Wheatear, Scrub Warbler and the House Bunting, the larger local residents are Lappet-faced Vulture and Barbary Falcon.

You can return the same way or attempt to do a circle, supposedly a longer but less steep way of descending to the original wadi bed. The writer and family have thus far failed to find this easier route, and have ended up getting stuck down one false wadi exit after another, each appearing to be the right one, but then becoming impassable due to sheer drops or high rocks, and the route therefore turned out to be both longer and more difficult. However, according to other reliable sources, there is a circuit where you continue past the pond away from the cliff face, then cross a steep valley and shortly arrive at a small plain where a few stone built graves and some scant fortifications indicate that the water must once have been permanent enough to allow habitation. From here it is meant to be an easy downhill walk.

**Elusive route**

### Wadi Sharm and Wadi Khudayrah *(4WDs only)*

The approach to these wadis can, like the Hanging Gardens expedition, be either from Al-Ain via Buraimi, or from Dubai via the Hatta-Mahdah track that turns off the Dubai-Hatta road after the Madam roundabout. On arrival at Mahdah, some 25 kilometres from the Buraimi turn-off, take the sign left to Mahdah Municipality. At the roundabout at the back of the town, follow Al-Juwayf to the right. See the beginning of the Hanging Gardens trip for the exact description of how to get on the Mahdah road from Al-Ain city centre.

The tarmac road towards Al-Juwayf from Mahdah runs for 11 kilometres till you reach the point where three wadis converge on the road in a slight dip. The first one, leading slightly backwards to the left, leads for 3 kilometres up the wide loose gravel wadi to Sharm fort which you spot with some relief on the left side of the wadi, rising above the palm groves. There is usually some water in the wadi and it is a popular place with local families for picnics on Fridays in the shade of the lush vegetation that lines the wadi. The fort itself is quite ruinous but still strong enough to be clambered over. Around the fort are the abandoned houses of the village that

**Sharm Fort**

was once Sharm, the inhabitants having now moved to new breeze block homes further away, equipped with electricity, TV and air-conditioning. The date plantations are tended by a few Pakistani labourers.

Returning to the main road and the confluence of the three wadis you can now test your nerves with the steep exit to Wadi Khudayrah, generally reckoned to be one of the most demanding pieces of driving in these wadis. The exit is marked by a group of three trees on the right side of the wadi, just where Wadi Khudayrah itself bends to the right. The track is steep and badly rutted and does a near right angle turn in the middle with steep drops to the left. The angles at which the car lurches make it fairly worrying as a passenger, and you may find it preferable to walk up the 20 metres or so of hill instead. The writer and family were begged by a picnicing local family at the bottom under the trees, not to attempt it. "Your car is too weak" they pleaded, "It is too dangerous", thereby turning it into an irresistible challenge.

**Demanding driving**

Once up, you emerge onto an expansive plain, ringed by the Hajar mountains. After about one kilometre you come to the ruins of a stone-built village to the left and right of the track, where the walls in some parts are high enough to cast a little shade for lunchtime picnicking. The plain is virtually treeless otherwise. After 2.6 kilometres from where you exited the wadi up the steep track, before reaching the settlement with its white mosque on ahead, you reach a space where cars have evidently parked before, right at the edge of the wadi drop. From here a little stony path leads down to reach the rock canyon. Below you can lie on flat rocks in the sun or find the place to climb down into the canyon where you can swim in deep pools. Once down inside, you can continue downstream, swimming through narrow chasms to reach the next pool, or upstream to arrive at a 4 metre waterfall. The flat rocks above were the scene in 1986 of a flash flood which swept some people away in the middle of their picnic in the sun. Floods can occur very suddenly in areas even miles away from where the rain is falling, so be alert to any warning signs like distant rumbling or insects and wildlife scuttling out of the wadi in large numbers.

**Deep pools**

**Aboul and Khatwa** *(Saloon car possible)*
You can approach this trip from Al-Ain or from Dubai as described before in the Hanging Gardens trip. The turn-off to Aboul is signposted almost immediately after Mahdah, to the left. Very soon, after a bend, the dirt track leaves the tarmac and heads to the right, and after 8 kilometres of easy driving you come to the new settlement of Aboul with its pretty playground and mosque. Drive straight through the village and out of the walls on the far side, following the track that leads for a further couple of kilometres into the highly scenic dead end valley. The fort rises up to the left of the track to greet you, a delightfully preserved building, its little dark stairs to the towers still intact.

**Delightful fort**

Tread carefully though and don't allow too many people in the towers at a time, because they are becoming increasingly fragile. Bats occasionally roost in the dark rooms. The village, abandoned in the 1960s in favour of the new town, lies a little further on, at the edge of the oasis. The layout and arrangement of the old village gives a clear picture of the lifestyle enjoyed by the villagers, the larger houses with their courtyards. Do not interfere with or remove any items from these houses, as the villagers do return and even occasionally still use the little mosque if they are working in the plantation at prayer times.

From here there are lovely walks out beyond the oasis into the hills, and many shallow pools at the oasis itself where you can wallow hippo-like after lunch in the shade of the palms or the dark green mango trees.

**Wallowing**

From Aboul you return to the main tarmac road at Mahdah and continue for 15 kilometres in a great loop round to the east through the plains surrounded by interesting Omani mountain scenery till you reach the turn-off to Khatwa on your left. This easy track runs for some 5 kilometres or so into the mountains, reaching, at the summit of a high pass, a point from which you have a fabulous view down to the green oasis ringed by mountains in the distance. The track narrows as it reaches the village and there is an open space at the edge to the left of the track where you can park your car. There are even wastebins and notices exhorting respect and care for the falaj system and the environment.

The abandoned houses here can be explored, but left

**Shady oasis walk**

undisturbed, and you then follow the path to the right of the mosque that follows the falaj water channel through the oasis. The attractive shady walk ends where the palm trees stop at the dramatic edge of the gorge, the rocky landscape making an abrupt contrast with the lush oasis.

A concrete bridge has recently been constructed over the narrow deep ravine where before you had to cross a single palm trunk. Further across the flat rocks is another bridge, leading over to the oasis on the far side of the gorge, known as Khabbayh. Several hours could easily be spent here exploring the gorges and finding your way down to the water level. Fridays can be quite busy, as people come from the urban centres in their saloon cars to escape the city.

**Madabbah** (*Fine for saloon cars except for final section*)
This trip makes a very pleasant gentle day's outing from a base of Al-Ain and is really too far as a day trip from Dubai or Abu Dhabi for all but the most energetic prepared to make a very early start, with a two and a half hour drive each way.

Remarkably Madabbah is 40 kilometres within Omani territory, but the route along which it lies has no border post till further on, so there is no need for visas.

Leaving Buraimi on the Sohar road as for the previous expeditions already described, you drive out for 19 kilometres from the Buraimi Hospital roundabout to reach a roundabout which the Al-Ain-Sohar road runs through in a north-south direction. Just before this roundabout your road from Buraimi drives through a dramatic V-cut in the mountains, to the left of which are caves and interesting rock climbs in the stratified rock. A track leads off towards the rockface.

**Caves**

At the roundabout follow the sign to Wadi Agran, and from here the track off to Madabbah is 21.7 kilometres to the left. All the track is easy in a saloon car except the final 2–3 kilometres, so you can do it if you are prepared to walk the final stretch.

At 26 kilometres you look out for a solitary tree set in a gravel triangle, with the Wadi Madabbah down to your right. There is a difficult track down and having reached the wadi floor, head leftish towards the date groves, and you will come within a kilometre to a point where there is no more driveable track, and you can see the pools ahead in the wadi.

From here it is a short but beautiful walk among the rock

pools and lush oleander bushes to the mountains where the water originates. White lime deposits mark many of the rocks and pools, and there is the usual range of fish, toads and insects in abundance. There is an ingenious falaj system built into the hillside by the oasis near where you park the car, and nearby are notices exhorting visitors not to pollute the falaj and the pools by changing engine oil!

**Lush mountain wadi walk**

The pools which await you at the mountain edge are among the prettiest in the UAE, though Fridays are best avoided if you want to enjoy the place in peace. The first large pool is good for swimming, with a charming waterfall about three metres high and one metre wide. Climbing up and over the rock wall to the right of it, you arrive at the site of the highest waterfall as it pours down some 15 metres from a cleft high in the mountains to form a beautiful pool at its foot where more swimming can be enjoyed.

## AL-AIN PRACTICAL INFORMATION

Al-Ain Airport opened 1994.

### Climate
Very hot but less humid than the coast. Dress is more conservative than Abu Dhabi or Dubai. More Arabic is spoken.

### Hotels
*Al-Ain InterContinental* Tel: 03-686686
200 rooms, opened 1982, recently renovated. Three restaurants, two pools, gym, tennis and equestrian centre.

*Al-Ain Hilton* Tel: 03-686666, fax: 03-686888.
Renovated 1993–94. 202 rooms, 48 chalets and villas, landscaped gardens, 9 hole golf course, two pools, one new pool complex with slides and fountains, island and Dhow model, tennis, three restaurants, shops.

A new luxury hotel is opening in 1998 operated by the Rotana Group, with 12 additional chalets and a shopping mall, large ballroom for weddings, fitness centre, swimming pool, several restaurants including Lebanese and Trader Vic's, the French franchise. Reflects the investment in the city's infrastructure by the Abu Dhabi government, which is expanding the airport, the medical facilities and the university.

*Buraimi Hotel*, Oman Tel: 00968-652010, fax: 00968-652011. Express reservations tel from UAE: 050-474954.

*Al-Dhahrah Hotel*, cheapest place in Buraimi, on the right just after crossing the border from Al-Ain city centre.

### Restaurants
Apart from the hotels, the cheap places are concentrated round the Grand Mosque and Clock Tower roundabout. Pizza Hut has opened.
*Falcon Restaurant*, tel: 03-645414, offers a good variety.

### Tours
Al-Ain Camel Safaris, September–June. Tel: 03-688006
Adventures Unlimited Al-Ain (ground floor Al-Ain Inter-Continental Hotel) Tel: 03-687458. Founded by a former SAS soldier, the company specialises in caving, rock-climbing, canoeing, hang-gliding, dune bashing and camel expeditions.

### Walking
The best walking areas from among the places described in the Abu Dhabi section are all in the Al-Ain region:

in and around the Buraimi oasis;

in and around the Jimi and Qattara oases;

Qarn Bint Sa'oud and surrounding desert;

foot of Jebel Hafeet around the cairn graves and Mazyad Fort;

Hanging Gardens and Jebel Qattar;

Wadi Khudayrah, all along the wadi bed;

Aboul, into the hills beyond the oasis;

Khatwa, down into the gorges and up into the surrounding mountains;

Madabbah, along the wadi beds in the surrounding area.

# Dubai

Area: 3,900 square miles
Population: 700,000

Dubai is the most centrally located of the
emirates, with the best road connections, and
therefore if you are prepared to make early
starts and do not mind drives of 2–3 hours
each way, most of the places described in this
book can be reached from Dubai in a day trip.
Listed below are some of the easier ones:

## Overview

Dubai is a phenomenon, a place whose policy of no taxes, no red tape has encouraged staggering expansion and turned it into the businessman and construction engineer's dream. A UAE national said, "Sharjah may be more cultural, but Dubai is more fun", and certainly for nightclubs, restaurants, sports facilities and shopping Dubai tops the bill in the Gulf, and is indeed now actively seeking to position itself as a top destination for the international conference-goer, exhibition-holder, businessman and quality tourist. By setting up high profile annual sporting events in areas like golf, tennis and horse-racing, and providing top prize money, Dubai is succeeding in buying itself global publicity and credibility. A recent survey showed that Germans now see Dubai as in the top 10 of their favoured holiday destinations. Dubai's avowed aim is for tourism to contribute 20% to GNP by the year 2000, compared to 12% in 1996. Alcohol is freely available and a liberal view is taken towards westerners, their habits and their dress. 70% of the UAE's tourists stay in Dubai hotels.

**High profile**

In Dubai anything goes if it makes money. Its policy throughout its recent history has been to maximise all possible means for economic expansion. Many have likened it to a boom town in the Wild West, and the raw commercialism of the place can be not a little shocking to new arrivals. The other fact that strikes newcomers is that the place appears populated by Indians with a few westerners, and hardly an Arab in sight. On stepping out of the airport you are greeted by an endless vista of cranes and construction sites which speaks volumes of the amount of investment in the city's infrastructure. Roads, bridges, hotels, everything must be the best money can buy, the most advanced, with the best technology available. As a result of this approach, the road network is excellent and constantly being improved through flyovers and underpasses; the port facilities are superb at Jebel Ali, the world's largest man-made port and at Port Rashid, and always being extended; the Airport is supremely efficient and so is the national carrier, Emirates Airlines, and a new cargo Airport is planned for Jebel Ali.

**Excellent facilities**

Seeing all this, it is especially difficult to conceive that until well into the 1960s most of the population of Dubai lived in *barasti* (palm frond) houses. The first concrete block was built in 1956. Life expectancy then was 45, now it is 72.

Dubai has oil, around 400,000 barrels a day, compared to Abu Dhabi's 1,900 barrels a day, but current estimates are that the reserves will be exhausted within 25–30 years. The philosophy of the emirate, started by Shaikh Rashid (ruled 1958–1990) and continued by his four ruling sons, has therefore been always to diversify its economic base away from dependency on oil, and to exploit its talents as a merchant entrepreneurial city. Oil provides only 18% of its income and is shrinking. Tourism is predicted to take over from oil within five years. The re-export trade has been its speciality, notably gold to India, which in the old days was smuggled out of India, and was then sold back legally.

Dubai's *raison d'être* throughout its history has been to trade, using its sheltered Creek for safe harbourage, between Iran, India and Pakistan to the east, and central Arabia and Africa to the West. It began as a small trading port in the eighteenth century. In 1822 the commander of the British ship Discovery described it thus: "The town is an assemblage of mud hovels surrounded by a low mud wall." There were about 1000–1200 inhabitants, with 150 black soldiers to guard the town. It was supported by pearling, sending 90 ships to pearl each season. Its small population was then given a boost by the arrival in 1833 of 800 or more Bedouin who left their oases of Liwa and Al-Ain to settle in Dubai and base their livelihood on the sea, with fishing, pearling and trade. They belonged to the Bani Yas tribe, like the Abu Dhabi Bedouin and were known as the Al-Bu Flasah. Up to that point Dubai had been a dependency of Abu Dhabi, but the new Dubai leader, Maktoum bin Butti, ruled till 1852, and thereby established the separate Maktoum dynasty which rules Dubai today. They settled in the area now called Shindagha, around the Shaikh Saeed House/Palace.

Its population of merchants was given a further boost when in 1902, all ports on the Iranian coast put up their customs dues dramatically for imports and exports, so a large group of Iranian merchants from Lingah, the dominant Persian port of the time, moved to Dubai which was directly opposite. Indian merchants had also come across, attracted by the flourishing trade, to set up shops in the souq, and the exodus from Iran continued so that even by the 1930s a quarter of the population

**Trading in the blood**

**Maktoum dynasty**

**Iranian influx**

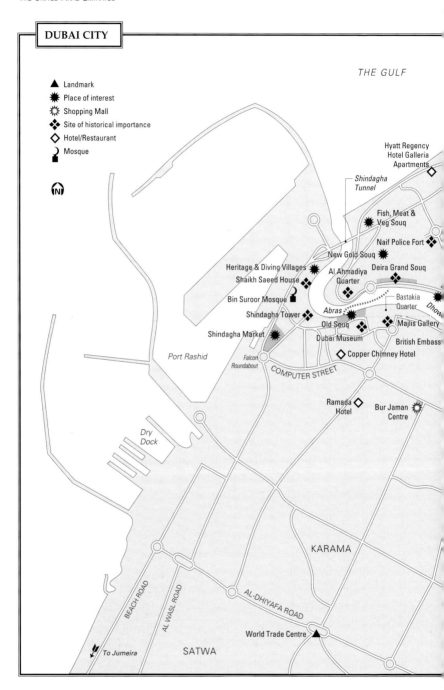

**DUBAI CITY**

THE GULF

▲ Landmark
✹ Place of interest
☀ Shopping Mall
❖ Site of historical importance
◇ Hotel/Restaurant
☾ Mosque

(N)

Hyatt Regency
Hotel Galleria
Apartments ◇

Shindagha
Tunnel

Fish, Meat &
Veg Souq ✹

Naif Police Fort ❖

New Gold Souq ✹

Heritage & Diving Villages ✹         Deira Grand Souq
Shaikh Saeed House ❖    Al Ahmadiya ❖
                        Quarter
Bin Suroor Mosque ☾                     Bastakia
                                        Quarter
                    Abras ✹                          Dhow
Shindagha Tower ❖
                    Old Souq ❖
Shindagha Market ✹  Dubai Museum        Majlis Gallery ❖

                                        British Embassy
Port Rashid    Falcon   ◇ Copper Chimney Hotel
               Roundabout  COMPUTER STREET

                        Ramada ◇
                        Hotel      Bur Jaman ☀
                                   Centre

Dry
Dock

                        KARAMA

         BEACH ROAD
              AL WASL ROAD

                    AL-DHIYAFA ROAD

                    World Trade Centre ▲

⚑ To Jumeira    SATWA

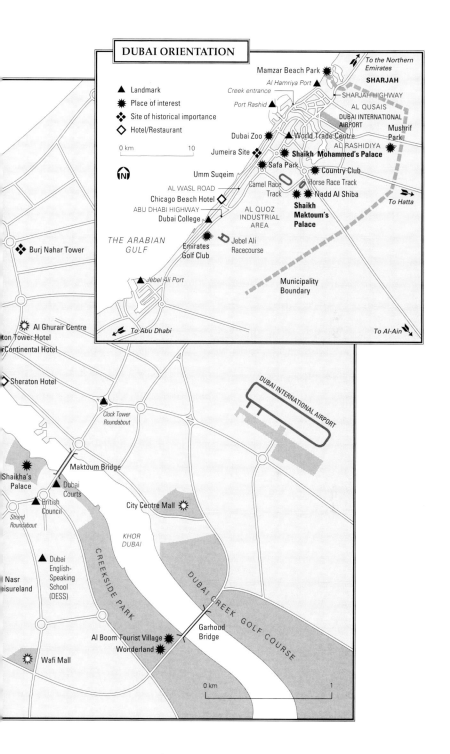

# DUBAI ORIENTATION

▲ Landmark
✹ Place of interest
❖ Site of historical importance
◇ Hotel/Restaurant

0 km           10

Ⓝ

To the Northern Emirates

Mamzar Beach Park ✹

SHARJAH

Al Hamriya Port
Creek entrance
SHARJAH HIGHWAY
Port Rashid ▲
AL QUSAIS

DUBAI INTERNATIONAL AIRPORT

Dubai Zoo ✹
World Trade Centre ▲
AL RASHIDIYA

Mushrif Park

Jumeira Site ❖
Shaikh Mohammed's Palace

Umm Suqeim
Safa Park ✹
Country Club ✹

AL WASL ROAD
Camel Race Track
Horse Race Track

Chicago Beach Hotel ◇
Nadd Al Shiba ✹

ABU DHABI HIGHWAY
AL QUOZ INDUSTRIAL AREA
Shaikh Maktoum's Palace

Dubai College ▲

THE ARABIAN GULF
Emirates Golf Club ✹
Jebel Ali Racecourse

▲ Jebel Ali Port

Municipality Boundary

To Abu Dhabi
To Al-Ain
To Hatta

DUBAI INTERNATIONAL AIRPORT

Burj Nahar Tower ❖

Al Ghurair Centre ✹
...ton Tower Hotel
...Continental Hotel

◇ Sheraton Hotel

Clock Tower Roundabout

Maktoum Bridge

Shaikha's Palace ✹
▲ Dubai Courts
▲ British Council
City Centre Mall ✹

Strand Roundabout

KHOR DUBAI

CREEKSIDE PARK

▲ Dubai English-Speaking School (DESS)

Nasr ...eisureland

DUBAI CREEK GOLF COURSE

Al Boom Tourist Village ✹
Wonderland ✹

Garhoud Bridge

✹ Wafi Mall

0 km         1

of Dubai was foreign, with Iranians the dominant minority.

**Rashid's vision**

Shaikh Rashid, when he succeeded his father in 1958, had the foresight to prepare his country to receive the benefits of oil wealth and even though oil was not exported from Dubai till 1969, seven years later than Abu Dhabi, Rashid ordered the dredging of the Dubai Creek in 1959, followed by the building of Port Rashid, extension of the airstrip and construction of the first bridge over the Creek, as well as the construction of the World Trade Centre which appeared at that time to be located out in the middle of nowhere. Many considered him mad and absurdly ambitious and optimistic for the future of his country, but his courage paid off. Much of the money for these projects came from Kuwait's Fund for Arab Economic Development.

When Shaikh Rashid died in 1993 his four sons ruled Dubai in a collegiate system. The eldest, Shaikh Maktoum, is the ruler, Prime Minister and Vice President of the UAE; the second son, Shaikh Hamdan is UAE Minister of Finance and Industry; the third son Shaikh Mohammed is the UAE Defence Minister and Dubai Crown Prince; and the youngest, Shaikh Ahmad, is commander of the Central Military region.

## The Dubai Creek (Al-Khor)

**Still dhow trading**

Dubai's only geographical feature is the Creek, the reason for its development as a successful trading port with Iran and India. Even today the destination of the hundreds of dhows that line the Deira side of the Creek remains Iran and India, only today instead of gold from India, the dhows arrive laden with caviar and carpets from Iran, and return laden with electronic goods and Levis. Since the 1970s the Indian government has clamped down on the smuggling, so the focus has switched to Iran. A small but steady trade has also been discovered of smuggling endangered animal species' products like ivory and leopard skin. Lacking fertile oases like Liwa and Al-Ain as refuge, Dubai has always looked to the sea for its livelihood. The inland oases of Khawaneej and Al-Awir, 20 kilometres from the coast, have only been created more recently through installation of pumps in water-wells, and though they are quite heavily wooded today, their dune setting and lack of palm plantations betray their modern origin.

The Deira side, where today the Hyatt Regency, the Inter-Continental and the Sheraton stand, has always been the commercial centre, where the majority of the souqs were located, while the fort and the ruler's palace stood on what was and still is considered the more residential side. It is on this side, known as Bur Dubai, where the phenomenal expansion of the residential areas has taken place, out through Jumeirah to Umm Suqeim, Chicago Beach and Jebel Ali.

Dubai's Creek was much the same as those of Sharjah, Ajman and Ras Al-Khaimah, except that it was bigger and extended much further inland. Some historical sources even suggest it once went as far inland as Al-Ain, 140 kilometres away. Today it is 12 kilometres long and on average 500m wide. In 1908 it became the port of call for the fortnightly steamers from the British India and the Bombay and Persia Navigation Companies, bringing additional custom and revenue. Traffic between the Deira and Dubai sides was by what were originally rowing boats called *abra* (Arabic across)

*'Abra' crossing point on the Dubai Creek*

and on Fridays passage across used to be free for Deira residents crossing to attend midday prayers in the big mosque beside the fort on the Dubai side. Transportation was not a problem at that time, as everyone lived within walking distance of each other and all heavy goods were moved by water. Today there are two bridges, Maktoum and Garhoud, and the Shindagha tunnel, but the abras still ply backwards and forwards between Deira and Bur Dubai from the landing stage by the Dubai old souq *(see map)* to the Deira side, except that now they are motorised, not oar-driven. When the Creek was dredged under the instructions of Shaikh Rashid in the late 1960s, the spoil was used in nearby low-lying areas to create new building land along the Creek shore which had

**Free for prayers**

**Clever dredging**

previously been flooded at high tide, and the sale of this new land greatly offset the dredging costs.

**Abra ride**

One of the musts for any visitor to Dubai is to rent one of these *abras* for an hour for a private tour of the Creek. The *abra* owner is always delighted since he makes a great deal more from that hour than he would stuck in the queue waiting for his boat's turn to fill up. At the time of writing the going rate for an hour was Dh50. The boats have their own shade awnings and you can take a simple picnic aboard to keep everyone happy. The standard hour gives enough time to get up as far as Dubai Creek Golf Course, and Garhoud Bridge is the furthest they will ever go.

**Opposite method**

Beyond Garhoud Bridge is the dhow construction yard at Al-Jadaf on the Dubai side, which still builds new boats, while old ones decay picturesquely on the bank. Teak for dhow building is imported from India, Pakistan and Burma, and the traditional method is used, where the outside is built with planks by eye and the frame inserted later, the opposite of the western method where the ribs are built first, then the exterior planking. Further on is the Gulf Dry Dock for ship repairs. On the Deira bank opposite, a public jetski area has grown up and on Fridays the Creek is alive with the buzzing of tens of these exciting toys whizzing round and round trying not to crash into each other.

**Wildlife sanctuary**

Such activities do not harmonise well with the plans to turn the end of the Creek into a Bird Wildlife Reserve. A special flamingo island was created at this end of the Creek, and artificial nest mounds constructed for them in an attempt to encourage the flamingos who were stopping over here on their migrations southwards, to stay and breed. These endeavours have not so far been successful and certainly the Dubai Watersports and Water Ski Club which is on the Dubai side just beside the island does not contribute greatly to the tranquillity of the Waterbird Sanctuary marked on the Dubai Municipality map. See the Birdwatching section later in this chapter.

Anti-pollution drives are in full swing and regular dredging takes place to bring out thousands of kilos of rubbish that ranges from cans and bottles to dead animals and refrigerators. There are two inspection vessels that work round the clock in shifts, in an attempt to prevent violations of waste disposal in the Creek. The water is monitored regularly and pollution levels are said to be within safe limits at present.

The Creekside elevations are having a facelift now on both sides of the Creek. On the Bur Dubai side the entire stretch from the renovated Bastakia district right along to the Grand Souq has had a smartening restoration of the old buildings that face the Creek, like the Al-Wakeel house, a project implemented by the Dubai Municipality Historic Buildings Section. On the Deira side the smart new office blocks like the 25-storey Twin Towers dominate the skyline as part of a programme to regenerate downtown Deira. Ironically the harsh climate takes its toll even on modern buildings like these, and their life expectancy is only around 20–30 years. The best place to view these elevations, old and new, is from the Creek itself, from an *abra*.

**Best view**

## HERITAGE SITES (OLD)
### Bur Dubai side

**Dubai Museum, Al-Fahidi Fort** *(2 hours)*
Open 8.30am–7.30pm daily, Fridays 1.30pm–7.30pm.
Tel: 531862.
No refreshments or cafe. Clean WC's. Uninspiring book/gift shop which is often shut in the afternoons. Typically for Dubai there is an entry fee, yet they still make an additional charge for the flimsy leaflet on the museum. (In Sharjah most museums are free and booklets are still handed out free.) As the Emirati lady cashier herself said, "In Dubai everything is money". Two other Emirati ladies sit behind the ticket office in case they are needed as guides, for which there is of course a fee.

The museum, established in the Al-Fahidi ruler's fort by order of Shaikh Rashid in 1971, is located in the busy market area of Bur Dubai near the head of the Creek which it once guarded, close to the Ruler's Office, the white building with new wind towers. Now even its view of the Creek is entirely obliterated by commercial buildings. Parking can be difficult at busy shopping times, so your best bet is to come between 1 and 4pm when most of the shops shut. The sandy coloured towers are instantly recognisable and a huge life-size dhow stands beside the fort in an open space, under which you later discover is the underground modern section of the museum. By 1987 the fort itself was found to be deteriorating as a result of subsidence and vibration from the surrounding area, and so a restoration project was undertaken, with the new under-

**Clever design** ground exhibition area very cleverly not compromising the old building through an ugly modern above-ground extension. The museum was reopened after renovation in 1995. It is a one-way system museum, so having entered through the old fort main gate flanked with cannon, you examine the old section of courtyard and rooms before moving down a spiral ramp to enter the modern underground air-conditioned section which presents Dubai through models and technology. The models, all life-size of a 1960s souq, a Bedouin tent, dhows, wrecks, pearl divers and fish, are extremely lifelike and indeed life-size, and have been very well thought out, so that you progress suddenly through the souq by stepping off a dhow onto the quayside and into the alleys of stalls, complete with heady smell of herbs and spices.

As you enter the main gateway of the fort, take a moment

**Splendid door** to examine the splendid teak door and the fine brass knockers. The old fort courtyard contains some fascinating examples of types of boats used for fishing, and a charming barasti hut with summer room to allow breezes through, and the snug winter room within. The kitchen was separate. Note too the huge wooden water tank used for drinking water on pearling ships. The far room on the right has a fine collection of weapons, including sharks-fin shields and chain mail suits. Weapons always held an important place, and all men traditionally carried a weapon. Though this later became decorative like the *khanjar* of Oman, it originated out of necessity in fairly lawless days where blood feuds and tribal conflicts were commonplace.

The other long room on the other side of the courtyard has local musical instruments from a harp to bagpipes made from goatskin and a shaker of goat's hooves. The upstairs section of the fort is out of bounds. As you leave the courtyard you pass a splendid European cannon dated 1785 which appears to be solid copper from its colour, though its label says it is bronze.

From here the spiral ramp leads down past stuffed sea birds and a flamingo to reach re-creations of the Creek as it originally was before oil was discovered. A display board here claims that the Creek originally went inland as far as Al-Ain, 140 kilometres away!

A brief film show then takes you through a visual kaleidoscope from the 1930s to the present day, giving its own highly simplified version of events, and from here you pop through into the reconstruction of the 1960s souq, startlingly real, with sound effects and smells. Beyond the souq the reconstruction runs to a Koranic School, and a traditional house with display explaining children's toys. The stuffed camel in the alleyway is especially fine, and can be patted and stroked.

**Realistic souq**

From here the theme progresses to desert, with camels, oasis and dates. The importance of water is explained and the corridor leads on into a wildlife display area with the desert by night and a Bedouin tent. Computer screens permit you to select snippets of film on various indigenous animals ranging from the Houbara bustard to the Rhinocerous beetle, which keeps children happy till they have exhausted the nine species. From here you move on to the Sun, Moon and astronomy section with stars and wind, all used by camel caravans to navigate as well as ships at sea. And you now step into the impressive marine gallery, designed so that you enter an underwater setting with boats above your head, displaying all the fish found in the local seas.

**Desert by night**

**Underwater setting**

The final section before the bookshop and exit ramp up, is archaeology, displaying finds from the Hatta tombs, the burials at Al-Qusais and the Mound of Serpents, as well as the Al- Jumeirah Islamic caravan city. The final room by the exit displays a varied collection of pots and jewellery from the sites found more recently.

Between the Fort/Museum and the Creek is the site for the new Grand Mosque, currently under construction. The mosque that was knocked down to create this space was from the 1960s but the original 1900 Grand Mosque also stood on this site, and the new one will be built on an enlarged plan in the style of the original.

The expansion of Dubai onto the Deira side of the Creek happened in 1841 when many of its inhabitants moved over there with the permission of the ruler of Sharjah, to escape a smallpox epidemic raging on the Dubai side. As the new

**Smallpox changes border**

settlement grew and flourished it pushed the dividing line between the Qawasim of Sharjah and the Bani Yas of Dubai which had originally been through the centre of the Creek, further northwards.

### Bastakia Quarter *(45 minutes)*

The Bastakia quarter on the Bur Dubai edge of the Creek is Dubai's only remaining district of old housing, complete with picturesque wind towers. Many were knocked down as recently as the 1980s, notably to make way for the Diwan Office itself on the Creekside, but the Historical Buildings **Conservation** Section has now designated the area for conservation, and is **area** currently restoring three old houses, one of which will be converted to a Tourist Centre. The houses here were all built after 1902 by a group of Iranian merchants. They had left their home town of Lingah on the Iranian coast after high customs dues were introduced there, threatening their livelihood, so they looked instinctively across to the trading haven of Dubai, where no taxes were levied at all. Their district was named Bastakia after the Bastakia region in southern Persia, where many of them originated, and they built it beside the Dubai souq and directly opposite the Deira souq which was the largest along the Gulf at that time with about 350 shops. Unlike most Persians who were Shi'a, these were mainly Sunni and of distant Arab origin anyway. The skills of these merchants played a large role in Dubai's ability to withstand the collapse of the pearling industry in the 1930s by enabling Dubai to develop an entrepôt trade with Persia and India throughout the 1940s and 1950s. Its cosmopolitan links gave it a head start in the 1960s when oil revenues began to flow in and the Iranian merchants were rewarded when the UAE Federation was set up in 1971 by being awarded UAE nationality.

**Persian wind** Until the beginning of the century, the wind tower *(barjeel)* **towers** had not been known, the local inhabitants living in barasti huts which allowed the breeze to pass through the walls. The Persians however introduced this architectural feature to Dubai and to all of the UAE, and soon even barasti huts were constructed with wind towers, as the one in the courtyard of the Dubai Museum demonstrates.

The foundations of the Bastakia houses were made of *Sarouj*, (a mixture of manure and red clay from Iran dried and baked in a kiln), and the houses themselves were made of coral stone cut from the banks of the Creek, limestone slabs and plaster for the decorative finish. There were a total of some 50 Bastakia houses, each designed round a courtyard for a large extended family. The principle of the wind tower is to collect wind from any direction and funnel it down the chimney to the room below, usually the majlis. In winter this could make the room draughty, so the base of the tower was generally sealed off with specially cut wooden sections till the heat arrived again.

One dedicated American dentist rented a dilapidated old wind tower house in Bastakia from its Arab landlord in 1990 and after wasting some weeks with two building companies, decided to take on the restoration project himself. He employed semi- skilled Indian and Sri Lankan labourers, carpenters, plumbers and electricians from the street and spent the next 18 months restoring the house to a habitable condition. The entire house was rewired and replumbed, balcony rebuilt, all the masonry and ceilings repaired using authentic traditional materials – an admirable labour of love. An English family and an Australian family also now live in restored houses here. The remainder, in a somewhat dilapidated state, are lived in mainly by Indians, with just a handful of Iranians left. Dubai Municipality aims to acquire all the houses eventually, as they come up for sale, so that it can implement a comprehensive tourism and housing scheme.

**Dedicated dentist**

**Labour of love**

There are now three new parking areas around the Bastakia quarter, making it easy to visit and have a stroll about the alleyways, watching the progress of restoration.

**Majlis Gallery** (*45 minutes*)
Open 9.30am–1.30pm, 4–7.30pm. Closed Fridays.
New car parks very close to the gallery.
Tel: 536233, fax: 535550.
The Majlis, a beautifully restored house, is set on the Al-Fahidi roundabout on the edge of the Bastakia Quarter. It houses a series of exhibitions, each usually lasting 10 days, and is run as a commercial gallery to promote art and artefacts of an international standard, but always welcomes anyone with an interest in the house itself. You can drop in for a guaranteed atmosphere of tranquility and calm. Before it opened to the public in 1989, it was the home for 10 years of an English

**Tranquil atmosphere**

family, the first westerners to make their home in the Bastakia area. The owner, a fourth generation Persian of the Amiri family, lived in it himself, moving out with his family to a more modern house in the late 1970s.

### Grand Souq, Bur Dubai *(45 minutes)*
### As-Souq Al-Kabeer

Over Dh30 million have been spent so far by Dubai Municipality Historic Buildings Section on the restoration of traditional buildings in the Bur Dubai and Deira souq areas. The paving and lighting of the souqs has been improved, with traditional style lanterns, and the stall frontages are being

**No more neon**     given a facelift. The ugly neon signs adorning many of the shops are being removed and replaced with traditional stone plaques giving a far more traditional feel. In the entire district surrounding the souqs the Municipality is altering specifications even for modern buildings, so that advertising and signs do not deflect from the traditional older structures.

Originally roofed with *areesh* (palm branches) the new wooden structures, though not traditional, were erected to create a longer lasting shade. Areesh had to be continually repaired and renewed after rains and high winds.

The main part of the souq, Dubai's oldest and most important, has a concentration of 8 wind tower shops, 4 on each side of the main alley, and this is where work has focused in the first phase of restoration. Care is taken to make the alterations in stages, so as not to disrupt the livelihood of the store owners. Most of these are Indian, though a handful are still local Arabs, whose families have always run shops in the market and whose sons wished to continue the tradition. Today the shops sell a hotchpotch of items like watches, jewellery, clothing, household and electrical goods.

### Wakeel House *(15 minutes)*

Designated as a Marine and Diving Museum, this house was recently restored. It was purpose built in 1934 as the office and

**British Agent's house**     residence of the agent *(Wakeel)* of the British India Steam Navigation Company. Its tower on the roof terrace was built as a lookout to watch ships arriving in the Creek. Fronting straight onto the water, you cannot walk in front of it, and the rear side overlooks the western entrance of the Bur Dubai

Grand Souq. The first floor was the agent's living quarters, while the ground floor housed his offices.

### Shindagha Tower *(5 minutes)*
Built in 1910 this is one of three huge watchtowers which defended the old town, the others being Burj Nahar and Al-Baraha, both on the Deira bank. The ruler used to employ black soldiers, mercenaries essentially, to protect the city from attacks by conflicting tribes. Dubai was especially keen to safeguard its trading activities and did not wish to have any interference in its lucrative business.

### Bin Suroor Mosque *(10 minutes)*
This little mosque, built in 1930 and now set by itself in Shindagha just off the tunnel approach road, was restored some years back and is now beginning to look shabby again.

**Tiny mosque**

Doubtless it will get a facelift when the Municipality builds the 30 or so traditional houses planned in Shindagha close to the Shaikh Saeed House. It is also the closest mosque to serve local visitors to the Diving and Heritage Villages. It is very small with one prayer room, and no separate place for women, making it difficult for women to visit.

**Shaikh Saeed House** *(1 to 1¹/₂ hours)*
Open 8.30am–1.30pm, 3.30–8.30pm daily,
Fridays 3.30–8.30pm. Tel: 535928.
Easy parking, clean WCs, Gift shop. No refreshments but can walk to Heritage Village cafés, 5 minutes away.

Shaikh Rashid took the decision in the late 1970s to restore the Shaikh Saeed House, the first action to restore a significant historic building in Dubai, thereby sowing the seed for interest in restoration projects at a time when a few old buildings still remained in existence. The original building dated back to 1896. The condition of the building was such that reconstruction was the only realistic solution to give it a longer life. Photos now in the house illustrate well the dilapidated state of the palace before restoration work began. It had been lived in continuously from 1888 till 1958 and was therefore maintained throughout that period. On Shaikh Saeed's death in 1958 however, his son Shaikh Rashid moved to the Za'abil Palace and the old Palace consequently soon fell into disrepair, since buildings of this sort deteriorate very quickly if not regularly maintained after the rainy season. The

**Lengthy reconstruction**

reconstruction project began in 1983 and continued till 1986. It only opened to the public in December 1996, because it was left to stand for 10 years while various departments tried to agree what purpose it should be put to. Such bureaucratic procedures used to take a long time, but it would appear that greater cohesion and cooperation have now been established to speed decisions up.

In this, and indeed in all buildings of that time, be they ruler's palace, wind tower houses or barasti huts, notice the width of a room is never more than 2.5–3 metres, a width found to be perfectly adequate when elaborate furniture was not required. It had in total 30 rooms, 20 verandahs, 3

**Six families together**

courtyards and ten washrooms, divided originally into six independent living quarters for different elements of the extended family.

Above: *The fruit and vegetable market, Deira side, Dubai*

Left: *Rare old back alley, Deira Grand Souq, Dubai*

Above: *Both foreigners and nationals alike shop at Sharjah's Fish Souq*

Right: *Crowds queue for entry at Dubai's Wonderland leisure park*

Above: *Bin Suroor Mosque in Shindaga, Bur Dubai*

Left: *The distinctive domes are a feature of Sharjah International Airport*

Left: *Sharjah's impeccably landscaped Culture Roundabout*

Above: *Stunning
tent-like architecture
at Dubai's Creek
Golf Club*

Right: *Rock pools at
Hadf*

The House today stands alone in its restored glory, the area all around having disappeared in the 1950s and 1960s. At that time however it had only one elevation fully visible, the side that faced the Creek and which formed part of a curtain of buildings fronting the water. All other sides of the house had only ever been seen from narrow alleyways around the other three sides. In an attempt to rectify this partially, the Historic Buildings Section of Dubai is starting work on a scheme to rebuild some 30 houses in the old style and setting out to recreate the atmosphere of old Dubai in this totally Arab quarter of Shindagha, where the Maktoums first settled when they broke off from Abu Dhabi. One of these houses will become a Museum for Traditional Architecture. The motive for such projects is avowedly threefold – first to give local people an awareness of their roots and heritage; second to encourage foreign tourists who expect to find historical buildings in places they visit; and thirdly to give resident expatriate workers an understanding and respect for the society in which they work. Dubai has as ever been quick to spot the commercial value of such restoration projects if it is, as stated, planning to have tourism revenues equal those of oil in years to come.

**Restored Arab quarter**

The Historic Buildings Section currently has 250 buildings registered, and has projects lined up till the year 2008. The hope is that such projects may lead to a questioning of current designs in housing and office building, and maybe one day some young local engineer may reject the power-guzzling imported air-conditioners and invent a wind tower with a solar cooling capability.

**Wind towers of the future?**

Today the house has been converted to serve as a Museum of Historical Photographs of old Dubai and the early rulers and their lifestyle, together with old archival documents, maps and coins. There is also a small exhibition room showing diving and the pearling industry. A few of the upstairs rooms can also be climbed up to via outside stairs and internal ones. Do not miss the little entrance to the tunnel staircase on the Creekside which leads up to the majlis room and outdoor gallery. The majlis room when unlocked, has delightful views when you open the shutters out onto the Creek, giving you a small glimpse of how pleasurable it must have been to sit here watching the dhows pass to and fro below. Today the place is also peaceful with an atmosphere of calm and reflection.

**Creek view**

**Majlis Umm Al-Sheif (Al-Ghoreifa)** *(30 minutes)*

Built around 1955 this majlis was where Shaikh Rashid used to spend his afternoons on the hot and humid summer days. At that time the surrounding landscape was simply palm groves and fishermen's huts, whereas now it stands incongruously in the built up residential district of Umm Suqeim, Jumeirah's extension. In an attempt to restore the original setting, palms have been planted with a network of falaj channels and a pool. In a corner of the palm garden a traditional café has been set up under a barasti roof with a rustic wind tower. There are also toilets at the Guard's entry hut, and the place is intended as a pleasant facility for local residents to come and enjoy the peaceful setting with the sound of running water.

**Rustic majlis**

### Jumeirah Archaeological Site

This extensive sixth century AD caravan site lies today in the heart of the developed residential district of Jumeirah, just inland from the Jumeirah Beach Park, and the intention is, that once digging is completed and the excavations protected, the site will be open to the public. First excavated by the American University of Beirut from 1969–70 and then by the Iraqis in 1975, Dubai's own local team of archaeologists are currently working on the site. Built a century before the coming of Islam, and contemporary with the Persian Sassanian culture, the series of stone walls that showed above ground were excavated to reveal a souq with a number of shops, a few stone-built houses and a large courtyard house thought to be the Governor's Palace, elegantly decorated with Persian-style sculpted plaster. One other large building was excavated which the archaeologists eventually concluded was a hunting lodge because of the little rooms with small arched openings round the edge. These were thought to be fox traps and would originally have had some device to flap a door down after the fox had been lured in by the bait. In all other respects the building is like the Governor's Palace with towers on the corners and semi-circular towers set at intervals along the sides. It too has the decorative plasterwork. The caravan station was used for two or three centuries in all, and is therefore unique in the UAE as the only site to span the pre-Islamic and Islamic period.

**Early caravan site**

## HERITAGE SITES (OLD)
### Deira Side of Creek
At the moment the chronic traffic congestion and lack of parking are a severe disincentive for visitors to Deira. The installation of car parking meters at Al-Ras opposite the Gold Souq has helped, and the construction of multi-storey car parks has begun. By the end of 1998 the Municipality plans to have made Deira into a pedestrian zone only, from the Inter Continental Hotel to the car park at Al-Ras. Special buses are planned to ferry people into the zone if they don't want to walk.

**Planned pedestrian-isation**

### Al-Ahmadiya School *(1¹/₂ hours for the whole complex)*
This school forms part of the restored complex of buildings consisting of four separate structures, all located in the heart of Al-Ras (meaning Head of the Creek) close to the Deira Grand Souq where the wealthy traders would have lived at the beginning of the century.

Opened in late 1997 as a Museum of Education, this old school building, Dubai's earliest proper school, is one of the most pleasing structures architecturally in Dubai. It conveys great harmony and the height and airiness of its rooms must have made it a pleasure to study here. The decorative elements are especially fine, with cusped arches on the ground floor verandahs and the doors to most of the class rooms having gypsum stucco inscriptions from the Koran. This delicate intricate work took a long time, which is why the building has taken four years to restore.

**Fine decoration**

Built in 1912 the name of the school comes from its patron Shaikh Ahmad bin Dalmouk, and Dubai's wealthiest and most distinguished sons (no daughters received education at that time) were taught here by leading teachers of the day in eight classrooms.

From the 1950s the building began to be neglected as new schools were built elsewhere. It was used by the Department of Islamic Affairs and Awkaf (Religious Endowments) for a few years but in the 1960s they too moved out to a more spacious modern building.

Beside Al-Ahmadiya on the north (street) side is a building originally earmarked as the Museum of Traditional Architecture, built in 1880, now destined to be Deira's Tourist

**Tourist Centre**

Centre while behind Al-Ahmadiya, further into the heart of Deira is a group of small old huts, undergoing restoration for some future as yet unresolved purpose, maybe as a series of souvenir shops or tourist café.

## Heritage House

Fronting onto the street and joined onto the Al-Ahmadiya school stands the impressive private house of a wealthy merchant, now known as Heritage House. It is planned to be decorated in a traditional style with old furnishings and will then be open to the public. Restoration took 18 months and was begun in 1994, costing Dh1 million. An aesthetically pleasing structure built in 1890, it is very spacious inside with high ceilings. Especially attractive is the upstairs summer majlis designed to catch the breezes from the Creek. At the time it was built the Creek beachfront was just in front of it with no obstructions. The decorative crenellations along the top of the walls are very striking.

**Changing waterfront**

## Bin Dalmouk Mosque

Part of the Al-Ahmadiya and Heritage House complex, this charming little mosque built in 1930 belonged to the wealthy Lootah family. It was totally demolished before its architecture could be recorded so it has had to be rebuilt from old photos. Traditional building materials were used throughout and the main pillared prayer hall is now air-conditioned, making it a blissfully cool haven on hot summer days. The mosque is in use, but can be entered after taking off shoes.

**Cool retreat**

## Grand Souq Deira 1850, Bandar Taalib Souq 1920 *(1 hour)*

Since restoration work began in 1994 vehicular access to the souq has been prohibited, making it a far pleasanter place to stroll. The entire project has been scheduled for completion in 1998 with a fund of Dh6 million.

Some of the shops in the Iranian section of the souq have traditional wind towers and this part is known as Bandar Taalib Souq. Teak wood shutters are being added to the stalls to help preserve the original atmosphere. The paving and lighting has been carefully re-done in a traditional style. The ugly and inappropriately garish shop signs will gradually be replaced by more tasteful carved plasterwork, reconstructed

**Traditional shutters and paving**

with the help of old photos. This souq was Dubai's oldest and busiest, the point at which the dhows from Iran and India would unload their goods. Today the shops here are run by Indians and sell a variety of wares, from cloths to spices and household items.

**Old Municipality Building, 1950** *(10 minutes)*
Set on the Deira Creekfront just a short way before (east of) Deira Grand Souq, this corner building with its green painted overhanging first floor balcony and roof, is only interesting by way of contrast to the huge red marble building further east along Deira Creekside which serves today as Dubai Municipality. Today the corner shop is called Latifi Stores.

**Old/new contrast**

*Burj Nahar and its garden, Deira*

**Burj Nahar** *(10 minutes)*
Built around 1870 the Nahar tower was one in a line of defences to the east and north of the city, along with Al-Baraha Tower built in 1910. It still stands incongruously by itself in Deira's business district, surrounded by a small garden.

**Naif Fort/Tower, 1938** *(15 minutes)*

The Naif Fort was one of the city's oldest defences, serving for many years as a police station. Since 1995 it has been extensively restored to resemble the original fort, though the only original structure remaining is the tower itself. The new police station has a Police Museum in the ground floor open to the public, alongside all the normal police offices like traffic and CID divisions.

**Working police station**

**Al-Qusais Archaeological Site** *(Not open)*

This suburb of Dubai just north of Dubai International Airport off the Sharjah highway is Dubai's most important site in archaeological terms because of the rich finds in the graves there, though nothing remains to be seen that would interest the layman today. The site is officially closed, lying in the modern cemetery of Al-Qusais. The three tombs found here were dated between 2,500 and 1,500BC. The nearby Mound of Serpents which yielded such rich finds has now disappeared or at any rate cannot be found because the excavators of the 1970s left inadequate records. The whole area has been extensively built over with the growth of the city and the chances of being able to trace the original site are slim. The mound acquired its name from the many models of bronze snakes unearthed here which, together with hundreds of bronze arrowheads, tiny bronze daggers, vases and bowls with snakes moulded on, suggested it was some kind of ritual site with offerings, the snake having long been associated with immortality in ancient legend, because of its ability to shed its skin and emerge as new. The snakes and all the grave finds are on display in Dubai Museum.

**Missing Mound**

## HERITAGE SITES (NEW)

These are all on the Dubai side of the Creek, and have been built as attractive places for locals and foreigners alike to go to eat and shop in a traditional setting. The Emirates are in the unfortunate, or depending on your viewpoint, fortunate position of having to recreate history and traditional culture for the benefit not specifically of tourists but for their own youth, for the under 25s, who have only known life since oil wealth. This necessity to illustrate life as it was lived pre-1960

**Heritage creation**

has given the Emirates a wonderful opportunity, a sort of *carte blanche*, to write history from an entirely controlled standpoint.

### Diving and Heritage Villages, Shindagha

Open 4.30–10.30pm. Easy parking.

Located at the head of the Creek on the Dubai side, between the Shindagha Tunnel and Shaikh Saeed House, this pair of newly-built traditional style villages set side by side were opened in time for the Shopping Festival of 1997. They are closed in daytime, opening from about 4.30pm in winter and 5.30pm in summer, staying open till 10 or 11pm according to the season. Extensive parking has been provided, accessible as you approach from Falcon roundabout towards Shindagha Tunnel, filtering off to the right before the tunnel.

The whole area along the Creekside here has been landscaped and paved, equipped with benches, waste-bins and public toilets. This makes it an attractive promenade that now links up to the entrance to the Grand Souq, one kilometre away. As in all such villages, food figures large, with many breads prepared by local women as you watch, as well as a big seafood restaurant and a traditional café. There is also a playground area where children can learn to play the games of earlier times.

**Abundance of food**

The Diving Village will have an aquarium and all marine equipment on display that was used for pearl diving in the pre-oil days, with models of different types of fishing boats. There is a diving souq selling fishing tools and instruments. During the Shopping Festival, fresh oysters are collected daily and sold for Dh5 to be opened before your eyes. If you are lucky you could find a pearl worth Dh60,000. Demonstrations are held on how to rig a dhow.

**Oyster lottery**

The Heritage Village also has a restaurant for 200 people and a souq with over 20 shops selling traditional handicrafts. At the time of writing many of these were clearly made in India, but there are moves afoot to try to introduce more Islamic-style souvenirs. There is also a camel and a donkey for children to ride. The Folklore Yard in between the two villages will be used for folk dance groups and musicians to give open air performances.

### Mamzar Park Traditional Café

Set in the centre of Mamzar Park, this recently completed traditional café is designed to show today's youth how traditional meals were served in a simple setting. The central courtyard café and gateway are built of coral-stone from the shoreline, and the remainder of the structure is all of barasti palm fronds.

**Homely setting**

The seating area is pleasantly divided into barasti open tables designed to seat 6 and the light fittings have been crafted in the shape of antique kerosene lamps which were used in the 1950s before electricity. One section is reserved for families and mats are laid out for overflow seating or for those who simply prefer to sit on the floor. The project took a mere three months to complete.

### Creekside Park

Within the park a group of buildings has been constructed in the old style to illustrate a typical mountain house, with its falaj or irrigation channels watering the date palms around it.

**Mountain house**

The house is built from traditional mountain materials of mud and stones, not the coral stone and gypsum plaster used on the coast. There are three rooms round an open courtyard, and a small kitchen. The exterior has no decorative elements and is very simple. Part of the roof construction has been left open to demonstrate the construction technique.

### Al-Boom Tourist Village

Now located in a new site donated by the government beside Garhoud Bridge on the Dubai side of the Creek, next door to Wonderland Water Park, Al-Boom is an ambitious project all based on dhows and the Creek. The 30 year-old hand-made dhow restaurant previously moored outside the British embassy and called Al-Boom, is now called Al-Mumtaz but continues to operate as a floating restaurant.

**Ambitious plans**

A 15-storey hotel will be built here partly overhanging Creek waters. It will resemble two racing dhows in full sail and will have 150 rooms and a top floor royal suite. There will be a café partly submerged in the Creek, with shops and swimming pools and a marina. There are ball rooms, conference and exhibition halls and 6 cruising dhows of various capacities from 150 down to 10 people. There is also a

---

**MORE ARAB PROVERBS**

Trust in God but tie your Camel.

You cannot carry two watermelons in one hand.

It is better to endure the wind of a camel than the prayers of a fish.

He wears his secret in a sling (for all to see).

The man who cheats you once will cheat you 100 times.

When the child falls silent mischief follows.

Dine with a Jew but seek shelter from a Christian.

When a merchant criticises the merchandise it is because he wants to buy it.

Too soft and you will be squeezed; too hard and you will be broken.

Better to ride a dung beetle than to tread on soft carpets.

The more devils that disappear the easier it is for the angels.

Craftsmanship spouts gold.

Nobody steals a minaret unless they know where to hide it.

When danger approaches sing to it.

The thing dearest to the heart of man is that which is forbidden him.

Who does not think his fleas are gazelles?

The well is deep the rope is short.

Fight for honour, for dishonour is easily won.

He who takes a donkey up a minaret must bring it down again.

---

plan to get another boat for fishing so that visitors can fish and eat their own catch. On Fridays there will be a fishing competition with prizes. Quite how this plan tallies with the large notices beside Garhoud Bridge saying "No Fishing" remains to be seen. There are also plans for pony rides and horse-riding, with children's playgrounds.

## City Mosques

Mosques are the focal point of every Muslim community and in Dubai there is a law that no one should need to walk more than half a kilometre to reach one. Their density is in fact higher than that in many Arab countries, and there appears to be a small mosque on most street corners. Even petrol stations have their own small one for employees, as do police stations, and each ruler's palace or wealthier house has his own private one.

In Dubai's early days the Grand Mosque was the centre of the town's cultural and spiritual life. It was situated between the Al-Fahidi Fort and the Bur Dubai Souq and this today is the same site chosen for the new Grand Mosque being built in an enlarged version of the original. All the earliest schools were part of the mosque, known as Kuttabs, where children **Rote learning** from the age of six would learn the Koran by heart and then practice writing it. Their schooling was considered complete once they had completed this, a task which took two years or five years depending on the memory the child was blessed with. Such mosques were generally built by wealthy individuals rather than by the ruler or by the community.

Mohammed Al-Fahim recalled "The school started early, about 6.00am, and lasted until noon with an hour-long breakfast break between eight and nine... Twenty-five or thirty of us sat silently reading, each struggling over a different page of the Koran... There was no question of progressing to a new page until we had completely mastered the one which preceded it."

**No hierarchy** Islam has no ecclesiastical hierarchy – one of its most attractive features – and the many mosques are not linked by any supervisory body. The custom was for leading families to build local mosques for their own use and for that of the neighbourhood. Some property *(waqf)* was generally attached to it to bring in income to pay before its maintenance. In towns this is usually a row of shops rented out to local merchants. The rent is then used to pay the salary of the *muezzin* (prayer leader) and for the cleaning and maintenance of the mosque.

In poor rural areas the mosque is often built of the same materials as the village houses, the only outward distinguishing feature being the *qibla* or prayer niche which indicates the direction of prayer towards Mecca. In such communities no *imam* was employed to lead prayers or conduct the Friday sermon. The eldest, best-read or most respected person in the village would simply do it.

As in most religions, the women are probably the most

devout, observing the correct prayer times and praying for longer – but they rarely visit the mosque, preferring instead the privacy of the home. One source said that the Friday Mosque in Dubai had a women's gallery in the 1950s. If men do not find themselves near a mosque at prayer time, they simply spread out a prayer mat or their headcloth on the ground and perform at the roadside.

Burial, a matter for some ceremony and pomp in Christianity, is an extremely simple and quick affair in Islam. The deceased must be buried before sunset on the day he died and the body wrapped only in a white cloth is carried by the male mourners. A brief prayer is spoken by the most respected man in the group, the body is buried and the spot marked only with a headstone and footstone. Death is accepted with remarkable composure as the will of God.

**Simple burial**

The elaborate Jumeirah Mosque is Dubai's most admired mosque from the outside. Here, the curious hotchpotch of proportions that results from Indian architects borrowing designs from Egypt, Syria, Jordan and Turkey, happens to have resulted in a pleasing final effect. It stands on the Beach Road close to the Jumeirah Beach Road Spinneys and MMI. Non-Muslims do not generally enter mosques here unless invited.

**Pleasing architecture**

### The Gold Souq *(Closed Fridays)*
Set in the back-alleys of Deira, at least the Gold Souq is now easier to visit since the introduction of the metered car park opposite its entrance. Evenings are the busiest and the souq stays open till around 10pm or later depending on season and trade.

This is one of the largest retail gold markets in the world, with hundreds of small stalls selling gold from all over the world, from ingots to finely worked jewellery, as well as precious stones and pearls. The alleyways appear endless and you may find it difficult to retain your sense of direction.

Dubai promotes itself as the City of Gold and in 1997 became the world's largest gold distribution centre having overtaken Singapore. The UAE and Saudi Arabia have the world's highest per capita annual consumption of gold, at 15 grams. The country's total annual demand, including re-exports, exceeded 350 tonnes in 1996. Dubai's gold is imported

**Highest gold consumption**

from 16 countries, led by Switzerland, then the UK, then South Africa. Dubai's main export markets, the bulk of which is for gold, are Japan, India, South Korea, Taiwan, Switzerland, UK, US, Oman, Thailand and Germany. Dubai gold prices are on average 18% cheaper than Hong Kong and 40–50% lower than in most European countries.

**Cheaper prices**

### City Parks and Amusement Parks

Dubai has recently announced, in addition to its existing parks, a new programme of Greenification, especially along the main streets, conspicuous till now by their lack of plantlife especially compared to Abu Dhabi. It is hoped that these will help keep pollution at bay as the number of cars on the road increases, since the trees absorb the carbon dioxide of the cars' exhausts and release free oxygen instead.

### Al-Mamzar Beach Park

Open 8am–9.30pm Saturday–Wednesday. Thursday, Friday and holidays 8am–10.30pm.

At 99 hectares easily Dubai's largest beach park, Al-Mamzar has the advantage of being on a promontory and surrounded on three sides by the sea. Its eastern side is flanked by its own Creek Khor Al-Mamzar which forms the border with Sharjah. In the centre is the Traditional Café built largely of barasti and there are a further 12 fast food and drink kiosks scattered throughout the Park. This is the only Dubai park to have swimming pools (3 in all) with water slides, showers and changing rooms, and for the beach there are chalets for rent by the day with showers and changing rooms at regular intervals on the shoreline. There is a fine wooden viewing tower in the centre of the park and an interesting children's playground. There is parking for 1200 cars outside and 460 inside for those using the pools and the chalets. Barbecueing is allowed in special areas throughout the park. The park cost Dh 100 million to establish. No football is allowed on the grass, but bicycles and pets are not specifically excluded.

**Traditional café**

**Pools as well as beaches**

### Jumeirah Beach Park

Open 8am–9pm daily. Mondays ladies and children only. No pets, bicycles, football or barbecueing on the grass. The park is extensively used by Russian visitors to Dubai who are shipped in by the bus load. Notices have been erected in the park in

Russian giving the park rules. It is a very attractively landscaped park, with wooden steps down onto the beach which is well equipped with showers but no changing rooms. There is a children's playground and a designated picnic and barbecue area.

**Barbecueing allowed**

### Mushrif Park

Open 8am–9.30pm Saturday–Wednesday. Thursday, Friday and holidays 9am–10.30pm. No cycling, pets or football. Entry fee Dh10 with car.

Set 15 kilometres outside Dubai City centre on the Khawaneej road and beyond the Airport, Mushrif Park was opened in 1975 as a drive-in "semi-park". Even before its official creation, this area was noted for its *ghaf* and goliflora trees and the greenery used to draw local families here at the weekend for rest and recreation. The particular character of this 125 hectare park is of a less manicured environment, with wilder forest vegetation especially towards the perimeter. Its other unique feature is the World Village in which miniature houses from around the world have been built ranging from an English Tudor cottage to a Chinese pagoda. There are designated barbecueing and picnic areas, a small fun fair area, a train that does tours of the park (it does not run between midday and 4pm), a swimming pool, a children's playground, and area for camel and pony rides. Scattered throughout the park are the usual kiosks selling fast food and soft drinks, and a central restaurant.

**Fun World Village**

Birdwatching is especially good round the perimeter areas. There are six separate parking areas inside the park and you can study the map at the entrance to work out which to plump for, or just do a huge circuit to decide.

**Good birdwatching**

### Safa Park

Entry fee. No bicycles, no pets. Opens 6.30am–9.30pm Saturday–Wednesday. Thursday, Friday, and holidays 7.30am–10.30pm. Tuesday ladies only.

Probably the most popular park with resident western expatriates, this 64 hectare park is one of Dubai's oldest, established in 1975. Set in Jumeirah, the park spans the gap between Al-Wasl road and the Dubai-Abu Dhabi Shaikh Zayed Highway. There are three entrances and cars must be left outside in the designated parking areas. The usual rules of no football or barbecueing on the grass apply. There is a big wheel, a dodgem area and a roundabout together with an indoor air-conditioned gaming hall. Double or quadruple bicycles can be hired which fit adults, but children below 10 will have trouble reaching the pedals. There are children's playgrounds scattered everywhere and in the centre is a landscaped hill and lake area with pedal boats for hire. Grouped together are three model gardens, Dubaian, European and Oriental, and there is also a small maze in a separate area. Unlike other parks Safa Park has a tennis court, volleyball, basketball and football pitch, as well as jogging and fitness circuits. Dogwalking and jogging round the outside perimeter of the park is a popular expatriate activity, early morning and evening.

**Playgrounds galore**

### Creekside Park
Open 8am–9.30pm Saturday–Wednesday. Thursday, Friday and holidays 8am–10.30pm.

Though in a fine Creekside setting, no swimming is permitted in the Creek water from this Park. The usual rules apply of no pets, no bicycles and no football or barbecues on the grass. It stretches for 2.6 kilometres between Maktoum and Garhoud bridges on the Bur Dubai side. There is parking for 900 cars, and besides the usual restaurants and kiosk facilities there is even an 18-hole mini-golf course, children's playground and a park train to do the circuit. These trains tend not to run between 12 and 4 pm. Like all parks there are public toilets and cool water dispensers at intervals throughout. The cost of this park, the Municipality tells us, was Dh109 million.

**Mini-golf**

### Al-Nasr Leisureland
Open 9am–10.30pm daily

Dubai's oldest leisure park, Al-Nasr seems a bit outdated now, but is still popular for its ice skating rink, bowling alley and amusement park. It also offers a fitness centre, swimming, tennis and a sauna, and this part operates like a club with annual membership. Nearby is the Indian Sports Club and Indian High School and the Club is largely frequented by Indian clientèle. It is located in an area given over to schools, churches and hospitals between Creekside Park and the Karama district.

## Wonderland

Friday families only. Wednesday night women only.

This 33 acre fun park is set between the Garhoud Bridge and the Wafi Mall and opened in 1997. Costing Dh120 million to build, it currently offers 30 rides including roller-coasters, go-carts, water slides and swimming pools for adults and children. The water park section is called Splashland and has a relatively high one-off entry fee. In winter the water is not heated and gets cold. The businessman behind the scheme, Ali Albwardy, has entered many ventures successfully before and in fact runs Dubai's luxurious Polo Club as a hobby. He plans to expand Wonderland, American-style, to be a three-day park with a hotel, by adding more rides. Many of the managers were poached from the UK's Alton Towers. There are two restaurants, one fast food, one more sophisticated.

**Water rides**

## Dubai Zoo

Open daily except Tuesday, 10am–6pm. Entry fee.

The controversial Dubai Zoo began life 30 years ago as the private collection of Hans Bulart, an animal lover who had come to Dubai in 1962 to make underwater films. On the roof of the buildings where he lived in Al-Nasr Square he began collecting animals from all sorts of places, some given by local people. His cow was given by Shaikh Rashid, and when the collection reached the point of bursting from the rooftops, Shaikh Rashid granted 5 acres of land in Jumeirah which is the site of today's zoo. The space was generous for a private collection, but once it evolved into a full-blown zoo with creatures like giraffes, lions and tigers at the insistence of his patrons, the space was far too cramped and Hans Bulart eventually left in 1969 somewhat disillusioned. His father Otto, who went on to build the Al-Ain Zoo, looked after the Dubai Zoo till 1971 when Dubai Municipality appropriated it. It was managed by various people till the current manager Dr Reza Khan came in 1989 from Al-Ain Zoo. Dr Khan built the aviaries which have been very successful, and the African Spoonbill has bred here even though it rarely breeds in captivity. He has also succeeded in breeding Socotra cormorant, making him the first successful breeder in the world of these, and has donated pairs to Kuwait and Riyadh zoos. The zoo actively participates in animal exchange

**Bursting collection**

**Successful breeding**

programmes for breeding and is the only one in the Arab world so far to have successfully bred chimps, Nile crocodile and African turtles. The zoo has also bred Arabian wolves which are on the verge of extinction in Arabia because of urban sprawl. It has been hunted like the leopard by farmers who see it as a threat to their cattle and poultry.

There are now 1, 400 animals in the five acre space granted for the private collection. Many of these animals were not solicited but sent there for housing by the authorities after having been confiscated at the airport from irresponsible animal dealers. To that extent the zoo has become a sort of haven for illicitly smuggled animals, or even animals just mysteriously happened upon. One man recently brought in a Cobra complete with fangs in a biscuit tin.

**Expansion plans**

A new zoo is now in the planning stage that will be set outside the city behind Mushrif Park in a 440 hectare site (three times the size of Safa Park), a 5 kilometre long expanse where authentic habitats will, as far as possible, be simulated. Projected completion date is 2001, so till then the over-crowding will continue. The problems are exacerbated by the many local visitors to the zoo who clearly have no understanding of the animals or their needs. They throw stones at the animals to make them move, taunt them, feed them inappropriate food (which has resulted in the death of some animals, like the emu who was found on cutting open to

**Baby's dummy**

have a baby's dummy blocking its gut), and dangle their children over the fences to get better photos. Slowly through educational programmes like Adopt an Animal, visitors may come to grasp and even participate in the well-being of the animals. Modern zoos exist to save rare and endangered species and to educate people about animals and the new Dubai Zoo may hopefully get a chance to tackle this issue.

### Shopping Malls

Dubai is like a shrine to shopping. Shopping is probably the national pastime, followed by sport. Dubai used to be the great centre for pirate cassettes, videos and software, but these have all been severely clamped down on. However in 1996 video piracy was still at 40% and software piracy at 87%.

**Long opening hours**

The biggest and glitziest of the malls are usually open from 10am to 10pm daily and in the evenings become crowded with locals, who love to sit in the cafés or just mill about.

## SHOPPING FESTIVAL

Inaugurated in 1996, Dubai has found its month-long Shopping Festival to be so lucrative that it has now become a spring fixture, along with many other events geared to coincide with its timing, like the Dubai World Cup Horse Race. The 1998 dates for the festival are 19 March–18 April. These dates have been carefully chosen to coincide with Eid Al-Adha, Easter, Iranian Nawrouz and school holidays in GCC countries. The build-up to the annual festival is on an impressive scale. All projects to do with retailing or encouraging people to spend money pull out the stops to ensure their completion coincides with the start of the Shopping Festival. Hence Dubai's Heritage Village on the Creek was completed from scratch in a remarkable six months to make sure it was ready in time for the festival, as was Umm Suqeim's new Spinneys Centre. All the major shopping outlets reduce prices (through resident sceptics say that prices are inflated artificially before the festival so that they can appear to be reduced when it begins). The malls like City Centre and Lamcys offer spectacular prizes to be won in lottery-style draws which can be entered by anyone spending over a certain amount usually Dh 100. The prize draws take place daily around 9 pm, the time when the hopefuls congregate in droves. Fireworks and laser shows over the Creek take place for all to see each evening and each day the Gulf News paper has a special supplement detailing the special events of the day, like bungee-jumping at the Creek or the International Gold Conference.

Terrific publicity is bought for the event, with Dubai for example flying out British TV teams on full expenses to cover the event. Hotels record full capacity and some offer 40% discounts.

The Carpet Oasis set in a specially constructed tent had 93 stalls in 1997 displaying over 100,000 carpets with 20–25% discounts. Many of the special features designed for the Festival, like the Rigga Street pavement cafés and pedestrian zone, become permanent fixtures afterwards. The numbers of visitors arriving for the Festival, mainly from the sub-continent and the rest of the Arab world, exceeds the total UAE population. Neighbouring Emirates of Abu Dhabi and Sharjah are said to feel the pinch during the festival, as Dubai creams off all the business for itself, with little or no spillover for them.

## City Centre

Recently expanded onto a third level the Deira City Centre is the largest mall in the Gulf region. It opened in late 1995 and boasts the only French food store in the Emirates, Continent, renowned for its cheap fresh produce. Unlike other large foodstores, it sells no pork, a sign that it is very much pitching

**IKEA and Woolworths**

itself at the local Arab market. The mall also has the hugely successful IKEA, Woolworths and Magic Planet.

### Al-Bustan

Opened in 1997 with 100 retail outlets close to the Airport and the largest children's indoor playground in the Middle East called Fantasy Kingdom.

### Bur Jaman

Major pink landmark of Bur Dubai with little green hats on. Three floors of shops and outlets of every type linked by a maze of escalators and glass lifts in the centre. Underground car park.

### Lamcy Plaza

**Pink giant**

This giant pink palace on the edge of Karama dominates the left side of the Shaikh Zayed Highway as it turns to approach Garhoud Bridge. Costing Dh200 million it opened in 1997 and offers 100 plus stores, including a giant food court. It boasts one of the biggest music stores in the Middle East and the biggest book store in the UAE, and has outlets for jewellery, toys, sportswear, fashion collections, cosmetics, perfume and electronics. It also has a cinema complex and a café.

### Camel and Horse Race Tracks

**Big business**

The camel races at Nad Al-Shiba are quite a spectacle, held in the winter racing months from October to March on Thursday afternoons and Friday mornings. Camel racing is serious business and the price of a racing camel starts at around £40,000 and a champion thoroughbred recently fetched £1.5 million. The average length of the race is eight miles and the winner generally gets a prestige car or 4WD. Owners follow the race alongside the track yelling encouragement from their 4WDs. The National Day Races and the races on the two Muslim eids are the most important of the year.

Horse-riding, much patronised by the ruling Shaikhs, is fast becoming the most lucrative and exciting spectator sport in Dubai. Renowned as it is in Arabic literature the horse was in fact a late importation into the Arabian Peninsula. It was not known to the early Semites, but having been domesticated by nomadic Indo-European herdsmen east of the Caspian Sea in

---

### DUBAI WORLD CUP

The World Championship horse race over one and a quarter miles on sand, the race immediately caught the world's attention by offering US$4 million in prize money with no tax, plus excellent facilities for the horses and their entourage. The veterinary clinic here, run by an American and set up by Shaikh Mohammed, is one of the most sophisticated in the world. The inaugural race was watched in 197 different countries and read about in leading international papers. The facilities at Nad Al-Shiba are being continually improved and so is the prize-money for the race-goers. At the 97 World Cup, the public were invited to select all six winners, to enable them to win one kilogram of gold, by filling in their forecast sheets.

The whole event is Shaikh Mohammed's personal creation and he capped it all in 1997 when his own horse Singspiel won it, thereby saving himself a great deal of prize money. He also flies in celebrities of his choice to provide additional glamour to the occasion. Last year's choices were Rod Stewart and Andrew Lloyd-Webber. The total cost of staging the event is reckoned to be around 15 million dollars.

---

early antiquity, it was imported by the Hittites of Turkey and thence into Syria. From Syria it was introduced onto the Arabian Peninsula sometime shortly before Christ, and once there it had its best chance to keep its blood pure and free from admixture. (The ancient horse fossils found in Abu Dhabi belonged to a quite different, now extinct animal called Hipparion, a small pony with three toes on each foot.) The Arabian thoroughbred is renowned for its physical beauty, endurance, intelligence and touching devotion to its master. Unsuited to the desert, the horse is an animal of luxury whose feeding and care is a difficult matter for the desert dweller. Its possession assumes wealth, and its chief value was in providing the necessary speed for a successful Bedouin raid. It was also used in hunting and sporting tournaments, and today Shaikh Mohammed continues the tradition of endurance races up to 120 kilometres which get completed in under eight hours. His own teenage son Rashid recently set a record in such races.

**Pure blood**

**Record for Rashid**

The camel by contrast is a creature of necessity, without which man would not have survived in the desert. He drinks its milk instead of water (which he saves for the cattle), eats its meat, wears its skin, makes tents from its hair, uses its dung as fuel and its urine as medicine and hair tonic. The Bedouin is in effect a parasite of the camel. The Bride's dowry, the blood price, gambling profits, wealth of a Shaikh – all were calculated in terms of camels. It is the Bedouin's constant

**A thousand names**

companion, his alter ego. Arabic is said to have a thousand names for the camel, such is its importance. It can go five days without water in summer, 25 days in winter. The Arabian Peninsula remains the chief camel breeding centre of the world.

In addition to the race meetings at the Jebel Ali and Nad Al-Shiba racecourses, polo is also taken seriously in Dubai with two polo clubs out in the Nad Al-Shiba area.

### Golf Courses

As with so many other sports Dubai has here too carved out a niche for itself as the premier golf destination of the Gulf and Middle East, hosting the Dubai Desert Classic since the early 1990s, at the magnificent Emirates Golf Club at Jebel Ali (Tel:

**Expensive nurturing**

480222). The course is maintained at terrific cost with an immensely complex automatic watering system. It is mown three times a week and the greens daily, and fed every three days with a blend of fertilisers. Before the days of grass courses in the Middle East, golfers had to walk round carrying a small patch of astroturf to put down on the sand fairways for each stroke. In addition to the Emirates Golf Club there are now two further grass golf courses in Dubai, one at Dubai Creek (Tel: 821000) and the other at Nad Al-Shiba's Dubai Golf and Racing Club (Tel: 363666). The latter is a 9-hole grass course set behind the World Trade Centre in amongst the Horse Racing Course Grandstand and is floodlit till 11pm.

### Birdwatching

Within the Dubai area, the prime birdwatching spot is the lush greenery of the Emirates Golf Course, best visited in the early

**Plethora of birdlife**

morning. The seasoned eye here can spot up to 200 species, including wheatears, bulbuls, shrikes, doves and hoopoes. A flamingo was recently killed by a flying golf ball! Safa Park is also rich in birdlife, especially round the sewage treatment plant area. Mushrif Park with its wilder vegetation is good for birdwatching round the perimeter, and the other wilder area is the Za'abeel fishponds behind Shaikh Mohammed's Palace, where you can spot heron and egret. At the most inland point of the Creek there is also the Waterbird Sanctuary which is noted for the flamingo population above all, though it also supports 30% of all wader birds in the UAE and is an important fuelling stop for migrating birds. The flamingo come from the lakes in northeastern Iran to Dubai to overwinter and are supposed to breed in May. The Flamingo Island was built here 10 years ago to encourage this, but so far breeding has not taken place successfully. One year the island was invaded by wild dogs, then there is disruption from low-flying aircraft and 4WD rallies around the Creek. Bulldozers have also been known to turn up unexpectedly, carrying out some project for the Municipality about which the other arms of government seem to know nothing. Shaikh Mohammed has lent his support to the idea of establishing a breeding colony of flamingos at the Khor. The UAE authority on birds, Colin Richardson (tel/fax: 313378) runs excellent birdwatching tours in and around Dubai for enthusiasts, which can be for half day or full day, and which even go as far afield as Ras Al-Khaimah and Al-Ain.

**Fussy flamingoes**

*(See also section on Birds and Wildlife.)*

---

### CHICAGO BEACH HOTEL RESORT

High profile in every sense, this phenomenally ambitious project is the personal brainchild of Shaikh Mohammed, designed to enhance the status of Dubai as a top class destination. The 600-room Jumeirah Beach Hotel in the shape of a wave opened late 1997 with the exclusive tower and aquapark scheduled to open end 1998. The sporting centre will be the most advanced in the region, with even a grass soccer pitch. The stated intention is to attract international sports stars and teams to come to Dubai as part of their winter training schedule, which would also encourage local sporting talent. The tower at 321 metres will be the world's tallest hotel, standing on a huge artificial concrete island. The plan is that this tower, dwarfing the World Trade Centre, will become the symbol of Dubai, like the Eiffel Tower is to Paris. The 7-star Tower Hotel will have 200 luxurious suites aimed primarily at wealthy GCC nationals.

### Beach Clubs and Sports Clubs

There are some public beaches in Dubai, but on Fridays and holidays they are very heavily frequented and most western expatriates prefer to join Beach Clubs where they are guaranteed privacy and congenial surroundings as well as the convenience of showers and a bar. Most have high joining fees and then an annual membership fee which varies according to the plushness of the facilities. Full listings and fee details are given in the excellent Dubai Explorer Guide, and most people do a circuit of them all, collecting brochures and carrying out an inspection before committing themselves.

**Range of facilities**

### Nightclubs

Dubai is positively bursting with nightlife, boasting at least 12 western-style nightclubs and an equal number of Arab nightclubs, with bellydancers and ethnic colour. All tend to open around 9–10pm and stay open till 3am. Single women often get served free drinks in the western style ones, to encourage single men to come in and spend their money. They are mostly located in hotels or other leisure complexes, like the Cyclone which is on the Al-Nasr Leisureland compound.

### Cinemas

There are an ever-increasing number of English-language cinema complexes in Dubai, usually part of a hotel complex like the Galleria at the Hyatt Regency or the Almassa at the Metroplex, or part of a shopping mall like the new Lamcy Plaza complex, or part of a leisure complex like the Al-Nasr at the Leisureland complex. There tend to be matinée and evening showings, and prices are reasonable.

**Reasonable prices**

### Hotels and Restaurants

Huge numbers of both, always being added to and improved. A few are picked out in the Practical Information given at the end of the Dubai chapter, but for a complete listing consult the Dubai Explorer Guide whose details are given in the Further Reading at the back of the book.

## ORIENTATION WALKS AND DRIVE
*(see Dubai map to aid with navigation)*

### Orientation Walk round Old Dubai *(Allow 2 hours)*
The buildings visited in this walk are described in detail in the earlier text, and can be looked up in the index.

Drive to the easy parking at the Diving and Heritage villages by forking off to the right just before the Shindagha tunnel, having approached from Falcon (alias Budgie) roundabout. This walk is best done after 4.30–5 pm when the stalls in the heritage villages will be open. The total distance is 2 kilometres one way, easy walking along wide pavements bordering the Creekside, away from traffic. The easiest option is then to take a taxi back to the Heritage Village carpark, where you can eat in one of the restaurants attractively illiminated beside the Creek water's edge.

**Creekside Walk**

After visiting the stalls of the heritage villages, head for the Creek-side promenade and walk towards the Shaikh Saeed House. Continue round to the *abra* crossing points where, if you are feeling energetic and want to link this walk to the Deira orientation walk, you can cross over and then catch your taxi back from there.

From the Bur Dubai *abra* crossing point, a little square brings you to the entrance of the Dubai Old Souq, with its modern carved wood entrance in traditional style. The stalls here are mainly selling textiles, with a couple of gold jewellers and clothing and shoe shops. 90% of the traders are Indian. You will pass the Wakeel House and then emerge from the souq in front of the impressive *Diwan* (government office) building behind high railings. This joins on to the Bastakia quarter and you can finish by exploring the alleyways between the wind tower houses, to end up at the Majlis Gallery, from where you can take a taxi back, or simply retrace your steps.

**Bastakia alleyways**

### Orientation Walk round Old Deira *(Allow 2¹/₂ to 3 hours)*
The places covered in this walk are all described earlier in this chapter on Dubai. Consult the index for the relevant page numbers.

Drive to the metered car park opposite the Gold Souq. The best approach is from the Hyatt Regency traffic lights or else along the Deira corniche road past the Sheraton, Inter-Continental and dhow wharfage. The total distance is about 2km in a loop back to the starting point. If you are not interested in buying anything but only looking at the buildings and architecture from the outside, you can do this walk at any time. Choose after 5pm if you want to be sure shops and stalls will be open.

**Evenings for shopping**

Enter the Gold Souq and explore at leisure. Continue out the far side to the Deira Covered Souq where merchandise is grouped by type in typical Middle Eastern fashion, so you get a streetful of shops selling pots and pans, then a streetful selling textiles, and so on. Loop back through the Deira Grand Souq with Bandar Taalib windtowers to enter the Deira Old Souq, sometimes known as the Spice Souq. From here you can navigate the short distance to the Ahmadiya School complex of four old buildings, where a café may hopefully have opened to refresh you after your exertions.

**Orientation Drive around Dubai** *(Allow 1½ hours)*
The timing assumes you are driving slowly, with occasional hovering.
Starting point Safa Park, by the Choithrams and Union Co-op supermarkets.
Turn off Al-Wasl Road by the Safa Park Big Wheel and head for the sea, passing the Turkish Bakery on your left, till you

**Beach road**

reach the Jumeirah Beach Road.
Turn right along the Beach Road, passing the Jumeirah Beach Park and the Hilton Beach Club on your left, then Dubai zoo, Magrudy's Shopping Mall, the Beach Road Spinneys and the Jumeirah Mosque on your right.
Continue past the Dry Dock at Port Rashid to Falcon (Budgie) roundabout.
Head for the Shindagha Tunnel, passing the Shaikh Saeed House and Diving and Heritage Villages to your right before you enter the tunnel.
Emerge on the Deira side and turn left at the Hyatt/Galleria traffic lights, through the Hyatt carpark and onto the corniche, where you turn right.

**Big lap**

Double back on yourself at the first crossing point in the dual carriageway, and head back into the Fish and Vegetable market (closed Fridays). Stop to explore if you feel robust.

Follow signs to Al-Ras, turning left on leaving the Fish Souq, and follow the road round to lead onto the Deira side of the Creek corniche.

Pass the carpark in front of the Gold Souq.

Follow the corniche curve to where the dhows are moored and on your left is the Old Deira restored Grand Souq with wind towers. **Dhows**

Pass the Sheraton Hotel on your right and follow signs to cross Maktoum Bridge.

Bear right at the roundabout and follow signs to Al-Souq to follow the corniche on the Bur Dubai side.

Pass the British Embassy compound on your left and continue to the roundabout on the edge of the Bastakia quarter.

Pass the Majlis Gallery, then keep right whenever there is a choice, passing through the busy new souq area. Pass the square with British Bank, then enter the square with the Dubai Museum/Al-Fahidi Fort. **Museum/Fort**

Pass the Shindagha Tower on your right and the Plaza Cinema on your left.

After the traffic lights, pass the Shindagha Market on your right, then rejoin the Falcon (Budgie) roundabout, to retrace your way back to Jumeirah.

### Jebel Ali

This is the world's largest man-made port and the UAE's biggest free zone. The incentives are exemption from corporate tax for 15 years, no personal income tax, no currency restrictions, 100% repatriation of capital and profits, superb communications, easy labour recruitment, and no import or export duties. **Incentives**

Whereas in the UAE as a whole companies must be at least 51% owned by nationals, in the Jebel Ali Free Zone 100% foreign companies can be registered. Big names here include BP, Sony, Kodak, IBM and Acer computers.

Shaikh Rashid conceived the idea of the Free Zone in 1976 whilst out on a camping trip in the Jebel Ali area, and the story goes that he struck his walking stick into a dune and announced that the $1,000 million industrial port would be constructed on that spot. **Rashid's stick**

By 2012 Dubai International Airport plans to have moved close to the Jebel Ali Free Zone, to cope with an estimated city population of over two million.

## EXCURSIONS FROM DUBAI

*Half Day*
### Qarn Nazwa Dunes
Leaving Dubai on the Hatta road which forks away from the Al-Ain road at the Nad Al-Shiba/Country Club roundabout, you pass through dirty industrial outskirts of Dubai City, where the road skirts the edge of the most inland point of Dubai Creek to the left. Follow signs to Hatta or Lahbab at the roundabouts.

After 15 kilometres beyond the Lahbab roundabout (just over half an hour's drive from Dubai) the dunes start to become red. There is a dramatic rocky outcrop by a petrol station on the left, with a further outcrop to the right. Shortly after, there is a break in the fence where the Nazwa dune rises up on your left, favoured by 4WD enthusiasts as the closest place to the city where you can test your desert driving skills. On Fridays it gets positively crowded, and is a good spectator sport. If you are a newcomer to the desert, you can go on foot to watch the enthusiasts perform. In the distance to the left (north) is Jebel Nazwa, a large limestone outcrop with the village of Tawi Nazwa at its foot.

**4WD favourite**

---

### DESERT DRIVING

Driving in soft sand the cardinal rules are:

1   stick to a steady speed in second or third gear.

2   try not to change gear unless imperative.

3   turn the steering wheel gently from side to side as you drive, to help stay on the crest of the sand.

4   carry four pieces of carpet, one for each wheel in case you get stuck. The best way is to keep carpet anyway in the footwell of each seat.

5   deflate tyres if you get stuck to 20 psi or a little lower to improve your grip.

6   travel with another vehicle, unless you are very experienced and know the route well.

7   always carry a tow rope and a shovel.

Desert Driving courses are run regularly at weekends, some even specialising in women only. Look out for adverts in the press.

---

**Ajman Fort / Museum** *(see Ajman section)*

**Sharjah Museums**, half day each *(see Sharjah section)*

**Sharjah Old Restored Souqs** *(see Sharjah section)*

**Jebel Buheis,** scenery and archaeology *(see Sharjah section)*

**Jebel Maleihah,** scenery and archaeology *(see Sharjah section)*

**Al-Hadf / Sanaadil Gorge,** wadi scenery *(this can be easily extended to a full day).* 4WD preferable but not essential.

About the easiest and quickest of any excursion to the mountains, this trip serves as an excellent introduction to gentle off-road driving with striking scenery, the gorge and rock pools. There is no need to be more than one vehicle. The trip can be as short as three hours, one hour for the drive itself from Dubai each way, and one hour for walking in the gorge. Alternatively it can be extended to a gentle whole day by taking a picnic and exploring the wadi beyond, which has a few ruins and more rock pools. You are not likely to encounter anyone beyond a few Beluch and Pakistanis tending the cultivated date gardens in the villages. Al-Hadf and Sanaadil both lie in Omani territory, in the bulge that can be entered from the UAE without a visa, before popping out of Omani territory again and re-entering the UAE shortly before the Hatta enclave.

Having entered Omani territory where the signpost announces 'Welcome', and arrived at the first mountains shortly after the Madam roundabout, the signpost off to Hadf 6 kilometres is marked to the right, just a few kilometres later. (The earlier signpost off to the right is marked Mahdah, a well-graded wide track which leads all the way to Al-Ain via Wadi Sumaini and Al-Juwayf, an easy one and a half hour drive till you reach tarmac at Mahdah, 30 kilometres before Buraimi/Al-Ain. This track too makes an interesting simple outing and has several forks off into outlying valleys which make worthwhile exploring.) The impressive mountain with greenish deposits to the left immediately opposite the turn off to Mahdah is called Jebel Rawdah, a good hunting place for fossils.

**Excellent introduction**

**Oman without visas**

Having turned off to Hadf, follow the track as it bends round to the left to meet a T junction after some 3-4 kilometres, with a wide graded track in front of the small village of Sanaadil. Turn right, towards the mountains, skirting the villages and within a kilometre you come to a date palm grove

**Deep gorge** on your right, with the beginnings of the gorge down below to your left. In a saloon car you can stop at any point here. In 4WD, drive on a further kilometre to where the bumpy track flattens out beside a wadi bed, and park the car. From here you can walk back on your tracks into the wadi bed itself, passing rock pools as the gorge narrows and deepens. Where it gets too narrow to continue, clamber up and follow the gorge from the top. At certain times of year the gorge culminates in a large lake-size pool where you can swim easily.

### Full Day Excursions
Dubai is the most centrally located of the emirates, with the best road connections, and therefore if you are prepared to make early starts and do not mind  drives of 2–3 hours each way, most of the places described in this book can be reached from Dubai in a day trip.

### Hatta
Hatta is Dubai's mountain enclave, surrounded on three sides

**Mountain enclave** by Omani territory. Only one hour's drive from Dubai, it is totally accessible even for a day trip, though many prefer to stay at least one night in the splendid Hatta Fort Hotel, arguably the most attractive place to stay in the UAE. From Abu Dhabi it is two and a half hour's drive. Follow the Hatta signs from the Nad Al-Shiba roundabout (98 kilometres to Hatta from here), then follow Al-Awir, then Lahbab till you reach the Madam roundabout just before the mountains. Shortly after Madam, a sign with the Omani crossed daggers announces you are entering Omani territory and you are urged to put on your seat-belts, law in Oman. The Omani Police headquarters on the left is the low brown fort-like building just before the mountains.

The mountains of the Hajar range all around Hatta are especially striking, jagged and volcanic with shades  of red, purple and even green sometimes where the copper is prevalent. In the mountainous approach to Hatta you enter an area of wealthy modern houses in a range of extraordinary designs from Swiss chalets to impregnable forts, all weekend places for wealthy Dubaians. The first roundabout you reach is the Hatta Fort roundabout, the hotel lying off to the left. From here it is 11 kilometres onwards to the Omani border post. The hotel makes the most of its setting, with even a mountain or two in its grounds. The barrenness of the rock makes an interesting contrast with the lush green lawns and semi-tropical foliage that greet you as you turn off the Hatta roundabout to enter the hotel's grounds. Built 16 years ago, the 54 rooms are designed almost like stone-built Swiss chalets. The range of sports is impressive, with a 9 hole fun golf course, mini-golf, tennis, archery and shooting under supervision. There are three jogging tracks round the grounds from a 1.8 kilometre cross-country circuit to a 5 kilometre mountain run, depending on fitness. The food is excellent, in both the restaurant where live singers entertain or at the open-air Gazebo restaurant for breakfast and lunch, with an attractive setting overlooking the pool. A 200 person conference room has recently been added. The hotel has its own aviary and even issues a specially printed leaflet in each room to help visitors identify the 50 or so species of bird to be seen in the grounds. Special Safaris are offered, expensive, but ideal for those without a car, ranging from three hours at the Hatta Pools, to a full day in the wadis and dunes.

**Splendid hotel**

**Safaris on offer**

## Hatta Heritage Village

This recently completed project has been to restore and preserve an entire area, including landscaping of the spaces between buildings. Opened in 1996 the village is set between the two hills crowned by watchtowers in the centre of new Hatta town, and recreates the old village which had fallen into disuse. The original settlement here is thought to date back to the sixteenth century. Apart from the buildings themselves, probably the most charming aspect of the place is the restored falaj system with a fine strong flow of water and several areas where access to it has been made easy by steps. A particularly attractive spot is under some shady trees below the Hatta mosque, the distinctive building with a short spire like an oast-house cone, raised up on a mound. The original mosque has been dated to 1850. From here the falaj flows off through the

**Charming settlement**

date palm gardens, a popular spot for picnicking locals on Fridays. Indian families are especially fond of shampooing themselves under one of the high gushing currents.

In the centre of the village stands the 1800 fort, a strong simple structure round a courtyard. There are then some 30 houses of various sizes and types, all true to the original pattern, with only their roofs needing reconstruction. Several are built right into the hillside, and are made of barasti, while others belonging to wealthier houses are built of mountain stones and mud. At the time of writing the houses were not in use, but the plan is to turn them into shops, restaurants, **Craft** displays of traditional lifestyles and traditional craft **workshops** workshops. House number 15 is even earmarked to highlight traditional UAE poetry, dance and song. The path winds up through the houses to approach the watchtower dated to 1850, from which you have an excellent view of the surroundings, including the cemetery to your left.

### Hatta Tombs

There are a total of 60–70 fenced tombs, mainly of the Umm Al-Nar style, scattered over 5 kilometres. They are small to **Not yet** medium, 8–10 metres in diameter, dated 2,000BC. None has **excavated** yet been dug, but they have been fenced for protection. They lie east and south of the village just above the wadi line.

Follow the brown Heritage Village sign forking left to reach these tombs, and skirt round the hill, past the Heritage Village to reach a T-junction with a white mosque after 0.7 kilometres. Turn left here and follow the tarmac road for 0.9 kilometres till you come to a junction with a tarmac road forking right at right angles. Straight on becomes a dead end. Follow the right fork with its many speed humps for 3.4 kilometres and then take the track to the left that leads between two farms. Follow the track for 0.8 kilometres till you come to a fork. Left continues on the same height and right leads down into a rocky wadi and up the other side. On that other side you will see a green wire fenced tomb near a simple shack-like farm, which houses probably the most impressive Umm Al-Nar style circular tomb divided into chambers. The tomb measures about eight metres across. Two more fenced tombs can be seen close by, in a worse condition. Staying on the left track for 0.4 kilometres you reach a point where you see other fenced tombs on the hillside opposite. They cannot be reached by vehicle, and you should allow at least an hour for a thorough exploration on foot. The whole area is relatively unpopulated and picnicking would be possible for those prepared to carry it a little way onto the hillside.

**Walking is best**

### Hatta Pools *(4WD preferable)*

The track from the tombs just described returns to join the tarmac road that leads on to the famous Hatta Pools. From here you turn left and it is a further 6 kilometres to the point where the tarmac ends and the well-graded wide track forks right (south) into the mountains. The track is like a roller-coaster up and down in an endless series of hills. There is a turn-off to Al-Tuwayah, then to Al-Karbi Al-Gharbiya, then to Al-Bon, before the track opens out into Wadi Qahfi.

**Roller-coaster**

After a long steep descent, look out for the first small track to the left at exactly 6 kilometres from the end of the tarmac. This track descends into the wadi and down to a rough parking area above the pools. There is very little vegetation and therefore shade in the area of the pools, so it is best to keep your exploring and walking to either end of the day. On Fridays the sheer volume of vehicles, 4WD, pick-up trucks and saloon cars is depressing, many of them complete with blaring transistor radios and of course attendant litter. The crowds can been avoided by choosing any other day, or by waiting till late on Friday when most people are making their way home.

**Busy Fridays**

The main track through Wadi Qahfi crosses over the wadi itself some 2–3 kilometres after the left fork to the pools, and many saloon cars get stuck in the water here. They usually make it in the end, pushed out by spectators or towed out by helpful passers-by. The track, once the wadi is crossed, continues on towards Subakh and Rayy, with more pools and waterfalls. As usual the best way to appreciate the landscape is on foot, and the best approach is from the wadi water crossing point. Once down in the wadi bed, turn left (north) to slightly double back on yourself and park after about 500 metres. From here you have a very interesting walk, following the course of the wadi, along towards the point where it enters the gorge-like rocks. You walk high along the top for this stretch, peering down periodically into the gulleys to watch the waterfalls from above, till after about 30 minutes, you

**Wadi walk**

reach the pools and waterfalls proper, below the parking area first described, reachable by the earlier left hand fork.

**Ad-Dour, Tell Abraq**, archaeology and scenery *(see Umm Al-Quwain section)*

**Al-Ain** *(see Al-Ain section itineraries, Abu Dhabi)*

**Umm Al-Quwain Fort / Museum, Aquarium** *(see Umm Al-Quwain section)*

**Ras Al-Khaimah Fort / Museum**

**Sheba's Palace and Shimmel** *(see Ras Al-Khaimah section)*

**Fujairah Fort and Museum** *(see Fujairah section)*

**Bithnah Fort and Wadi Hayl** *(see Fujairah section)*

---

### EMIRATES AIRLINES

The national carrier, operating out of Dubai, set itself up under Shaikh Ahmad, youngest of the four Dubai ruling brothers. It has received many international awards and has won the Best Airline award now for four years running, an astonishing achievement for an airline that started in 1985 with two aircraft and its crew on lease from Pakistan International Airways. It keeps ahead of the competition by offering facilities like personal videos even in economy class and by offering excellent quality food. It flies to London three times a day, thereby offering an unrivalled choice of timings and the choice of Gatwick or Heathrow. For Club Class passengers it also offers a chauffeur driven limousine service to the airport from your home or office, plus an offer whereby each club class return purchased from London entitles you to a free economy class return ticket for use by yourself or a member of your family. It was the first airline in the world to offer in-flight fax facilities for passengers, and satellite telephone communications. It now has over 35 destinations worldwide and has an ever expanding fleet of aircraft. Its tourism branch, Emirates Holidays, offers holidays in 23 locations worldwide.

---

## DUBAI PRACTICAL INFORMATION

### Airport
Tel: 04-2066666 to check flight arrivals.
Recently opened a second terminal and the eight million passengers handled in 1996 are projected to rise to 17 million by 2000. It is currently the second busiest airport in the Middle East after Cairo. Duty Free sales in 1996 were $180 million, ranking with Singapore and Amsterdam as one of the top three in the world – gold and jewellery are the most popular items, followed by electronics, alcohol, cigarettes and perfume.

Only government taxis are permitted to collect passengers from the airport. Rates are metered and fares to the city centre, about 4 kilometres away, are Dh20–30 at the time of writing. There is also a luxury limousine taxi service from the airport, costing Dh50–60, with vehicles such as Cadillacs. There is no departure tax.

### Tourist Offices
The plan is to open a Tourist Centre in a restored house in Bastakia in Bur Dubai, and by the Heritage House in Deira, and one on the Abu Dhabi Highway at the border with Abu Dhabi.

### Embassies/Consulates
British Embassy Tel: 04-521070  Open 7.30am–2.30pm daily. Shut Friday and Saturday.
USA Consulate Tel: 04-371115. Same hours.

### Post
There are not enough proper addresses and streets to make delivery feasible so a P O Box system operates. Stamps can be bought at the bigger hotels as well as at the post offices which are generally open mornings only.

### Telephone
There are many phone boxes along the streets, most of which require phone cards. On Fridays there are queues because of all the Indians phoning home.

There is an excellent Directory Enquiry service on 180.

Mobile phones are very widely used, as are pagers.

### Bookshops

Magrudy's on the Beach Road, Lamcy Plaza bookshop, Books Plus in the new Spinneys Centre at Umm Suqeim, and the big supermarkets like Spinneys, Choithrams, Park 'n Shop and Continent.

### Driving

Accidents are commonplace in Dubai and resident expatriates expect two or three prangs a year. The excellent road network with three and four lane highways in each direction encourages excessive speeds, and since it is widely known that the speed limits can be exceeded by 20kph before the automatic cameras bother to click you, most simply break it, especially as the nationals reliably say that if you are driving fast enough the camera cannot get a clear shot of your registration plate anyway. Lane switching on the wide highways and poor roundabout discipline are the major causes of accidents. The system of flyovers and underpasses also takes a little getting used to for a newcomer.

**Speed traps**

### Taxis

These are metered and regulated. Ring 313131 to call a taxi. Teenage girls are not recommended to use taxis alone at night. By the end of 1999 all private taxis here will have been phased out, and only Dubai Transport Corporation taxis, metered and regulated, will exist.

### Emirates Airlines

Tel: 04-215544 reservations.

Always getting international awards for providing high quality services, even in economy class. They have a separate terminal at Dubai Airport which makes the checking-in process much smoother.

Arabian Adventures is part of Emirates Airlines and have had steady growth each year. In association with Budget Rent a Car they offer Self-Drive Holidays (Tel: 971 4-3034444, fax: 314696)

**Creek Cruises**
Traditional dhows with seating for up to 125 are available for private charter, weddings, birthdays etc.
Al-Boom Tourist Village Tel: 341000
Malika Al-Khor Tel: 721100/721937.

**Restaurants**
So profuse and omnipresent in every street that no attempt will be made to catalogue them. Suffice it to say that in Restaurant Guides to the UAE put out monthly by publications like Aquarius, What's On and Connector, Abu Dhabi listings take up two pages, Sharjah, Fujairah, Ajman, Umm Al-Quwain and Ras Al-Khaimah take one page between them, and Dubai takes eight pages. It likewise has at least 12 nightclubs, compared to Abu Dhabi's three and none in the rest of the Emirates. The range as listed in such publications, is African, American, Arabic, Chinese, Filipino, French, German, Greek, Indian, Irish, Italian, Jamaican, Japanese, Korean, Lebanese, Mediterranean, Mexican, Mongolian, North-west Frontier, Pakistani, Persian, Polynesian, Pub Grub/Bars, Russian, Scottish, Seafood, Sri Lankan, Steak Houses, Swiss, Thai, Vegetarian, Vietnamese, Fast Food/Take Away. The cheapest places to eat are generally thought to be the unlicensed Indian restaurants in areas like Satwa. Otherwise most are fairly pricey and the hotel restaurants are difficult to eat cheaply in unless you confine yourself to a wholesome starter.

Here are some sample ones. Prices are per person for a 3-course meal without drinks.

*Cheap (under Dh50)*
Ravi's in Satwa for Pakistani food in simple surroundings. Open 5am–midnight. Tel: 315353.

*Moderate (Dh50–100)*
Da Vinci's at the Airport Hotel, Deira for good Italian food. Open 12am–12pm. Tel: 823464.

*Expensive (Dh100–150)*
Lou Lou'a in the Sheraton Hotel, Deira for excellent French cuisine. Open 12.30pm–2.45pm, 7.30–11.30pm. Tel: 2071717.

**Hotels**

The UAE has 304 hotels at the time of writing, offering 21,000 rooms, and Dubai has well over half of these. More are opening all the time, yet occupancy in summer 1997 was lower than ever before, a fact blamed on the drop in visitors from Russia and the CIS countries. In summer 1996 hotel room occupancy was 70–80%, but in summer 1997 it dropped to 30–40%, causing hotels to slash summer rates incredibly low. This may be the signal that Dubai has for the time being reached saturation point, yet more luxury hotels are being built each year, notably the Al-Bustan beyond the Airport and Chicago Beach at Umm Suqeim.

Here is a sample. Prices are for a double room.

*Cheap (under Dh300)*
Copper Chimney Hotel, Bur Dubai, within walking distance of the Al-Fahidi Fort and Creek. No bar, no restaurant.
Tel: 524005, fax: 513181.

*Moderate (Dh300–500)*
Carlton Tower Hotel on the Deira corniche.
Tel: 227111, fax: 228249.

*Expensive (Dh 500–800)*
Hyatt Regency Hotel, overlooking the sea on the Deira side, with the luxurious Galleria appartments where new arrivals are often put up whilst seeking villas. Shops, ice rink and cinema complex attached. Tel: 731234, fax: 713868.

**Walking**

The best walking areas from among the places described in the Dubai section are:

the hinterland of Jebel Ali, good undulating scrub desert;

the dunes around Qarn Nazwa and Tawi Nazwa;

mountains behind Hatta where the tombs are scattered;

Hadf and Sanaadil Gorge, all the valleys and hills beyond make good hiking;

# Sharjah

Area: 2,600 square kilometres
Population: 380,000

*Itineraries*

## Overview

**Cultural giant**

Sharjah stands out among the Emirates as the cultural giant. Hardly a month goes by without the Sharjah authorities announcing yet another restoration project for an old building or the opening of yet another museum. This bias stems of course from the ruler himself, the culturally enlightened Dr Shaikh Sultan bin Mohammed Al Qasimi, a man of rare sensitivities and the only ruler of the Emirates to hold a PhD from a British University. His first degree was in Agriculture. His wife too must take much credit for initiating many facilities for women, such as the Sharjah Women's Club in pride of place beside the Ruler's Palace. The first girl's school was opened here, and in the late 1960s Sharjah was still the only emirate to have a girl's secondary school. Education remains a major preoccupation for Sharjah, and even its TV station produces many of its own programmes with an educational or cultural content. Its Cultural Centre stages many educational programmes for school children.

**Prosperous past**

In the pre-oil days Sharjah was the most prosperous and dominant of the emirates, a bustling trading port with its Creek the headquarters of the great Qawasim seafaring tribe, while Abu Dhabi was a simple fishing village and Dubai a modest trading town on its Creek. Inland too, it had the fertile agricultural area around Dhaid where much fruit and vegetable produce could be grown to supply Sharjah town.

**RAF base**

Earlier this century Sharjah was the headquarters of the British sponsored Trucial Oman Scouts, an RAF base, and a residence for the British political agent and therefore had more of a British presence than any other emirate. The reason for this was that the ruler in the 1930s had offered the British the right to build a landing strip and airport, the UAE's first, whereas the rulers of Abu Dhabi, Dubai and Ras Al-Khaimah had all refused. This brought Sharjah valuable extra income at a time when the pearling industry had virtually ceased because of the advent of Japanese cultured pearls.

Oil was discovered here in commercial quantities in the 1970s and Sharjah produces some 60,000 barrels a day. Funds ran very low in the early 1980s but then improved when condensate and gas fields were discovered and started production in the late 1980s and 1990s.

The third largest emirate with an area of 2,600 kilometres,

the 1992 population was 330,000. Its three enclaves of Dibba, Khor Fakkan and Kalba are treated separately in the Fujairah section for geographical and touring convenience. It also owns the two islands of Abu Musa and Sir Abu Nuair.

In 1985 the Sharjah government banned the sale of alcohol in public places, so all hotels and restaurants are "dry". This has of course had a damaging effect on Sharjah's tourism trade and encourages many residents and visitors to go to Dubai for eating out rather than staying in Sharjah. Non-Muslims are generally allowed to have their own alcohol, as long as they drink it in their room and not in public. Far from being a bigoted extremist however, Shaikh Sultan has even donated land in Sharjah for separate Christian faiths to build their churches, including the Church of England and the Armenian church.

**Dry hotels and restaurants**

### Approach and Orientation
The approach from Dubai to Sharjah is hardly prepossessing. You appear simply to be moving from one set of modern buildings and faceless skyscrapers into another virtually identical set after a short gap of desert scrub land, except that the buildings appear less affluent and the streets narrower. There is now a sort of bypass for those who simply want to head through as fast as possible, marked Ras Al-Khaimah and Sharjah Airport. This new road sweeps inland and takes you through Sharjah's apparently endless industrial hinterland, before emerging at Culture Roundabout on the far side. Sharjah is in fact the most industrialised of any of the Emirates, with over 500 small to medium sized industrial companies, attracted here by incentives from the authorities to encourage business. Sharjah Airport, in support of these industries, is a very busy cargo centre. For expatriates too, the Sharjah rents are considerably cheaper than neighbouring Dubai, so many brave the busy commute and live in Sharjah, whilst working in Dubai. Though cheaper, Sharjah housing is also reckoned to be less well finished than Dubai equivalents, with more problematic plumbing and wiring.

**Cheaper housing**

As well as the endless industrial areas, the residential and shopping areas of Sharjah too are extremely spread out and difficult to reorient yourself in. The beach and lagoon areas that currently separate Dubai's Mamzar Park and Sharjah's Al-

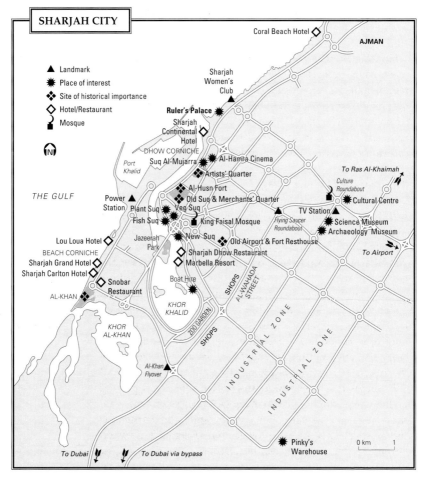

**SHARJAH CITY**

▲ Landmark
✹ Place of interest
❖ Site of historical importance
◇ Hotel/Restaurant
▮ Mosque

Ⓝ

Coral Beach Hotel ◇

AJMAN

Sharjah Women's Club

**Ruler's Palace** ✹

Sharjah Continental Hotel ◇

DHOW CORNICHE

Port Khalid

Suq Al-Mujarra ✹

✹ Al-Hamra Cinema

❖ Artists' Quarter

To Ras Al-Khaimah

Culture Roundabout

THE GULF

Power Station ▲

❖ Al-Husn Fort

❖ Old Suq & Merchants' Quarter

▮ Cultural Centre

Plant Suq ✹   Veg Suq ✹

Fish Suq ✹

▮ King Faisal Mosque

TV Station ▲

Flying Saucer Roundabout

✹ Science Museum

Archaeology Museum

Lou Loua Hotel ◇

Jazeerah Park

✹ New Suq

❖ Old Airport & Fort Resthouse

To Airport

BEACH CORNICHE

Sharjah Grand Hotel ◇

Sharjah Carlton Hotel ◇

◇ Sharjah Dhow Restaurant

◇ Marbella Resort

Boat Hire

◇ Snobar Restaurant

AL-KHAN ❖

KHOR KHALID

ZOO GARDEN

SHOPS

SHOPS

AL-WAHADA STREET

INDUSTRIAL ZONE

INDUSTRIAL ZONE

INDUSTRIAL ZONE

KHOR AL-KHAN

Al-Khan Flyover ▲

✹ Pinky's Warehouse

0 km      1

To Dubai ↓   ↓ To Dubai via bypass

Khan fishing villages are all scheduled for development with gardens and cultural buildings and some reclamation of the tidal flats. Work has already begun, so that eventually, there will barely be a gap between the urban sprawl of the two emirates.

The safest way for a newcomer to explore is to turn off the Dubai-Sharjah highway at the Al-Khan flyover (the first flyover) and then follow the signs to Al-Khan towards the sea, passing on your left the Sharjah Expo Centre and the new Book Mall. At the next major junction 2 kilometres later, turn right and the road will lead you over Khor Khaled, Sharjah's lagoon, across the amusement park island of Jazeerah and over the bridge again for views towards the fine blue Al-Souq Al-Markazi, Sharjah's central market. At the next rather complicated junction you want to turn left, again towards the coast, which you achieve by staying to the right to exit onto a roundabout. Having achieved that, you now simply stay on this road as it passes the Sharjah plant nursery stalls and harbour and turns right to follow the line of the corniche. This is the area where most places of interest to visitors lie, so the description given follows this order of approach.

**Complex of roads**

## Al-Khan – Old Fishing Village *(30 minutes)*

Once you have exited the main Dubai-Sharjah highway at the first flyover and are heading for the coast following the signs to Al-Khan, you continue for some three kilometres till you reach the coast at a roundabout. To the left here, beside an old watchtower and huge red and white electricity pylon, are dirt tracks that take you into Al-Khan, the traditional old fishing village that occupies this isolated promontory, guarding the entrance to its own Creek, Khor Al-Khan. Unique among all the Emirates, this village is like a community in a time warp, their lives continuing, apart from the welcome additions of electricity, air-conditioning and TV, much as they did before the oil-era. The villagers appear to be a mix of local Arab and Sub-continentals, going to the mosque together and playing on the village football pitch together. Among their houses are the remains of older houses, one large courtyarded house near the mosque, another watchtower and several other ruined houses especially as you near the tip of the promontory. Closer examination reveals they are made mainly, not of mud brick, but of coral rock cut from the shoreline. By itself on the very tip of the promontory, stands a small ruined mosque, abandoned in favour of its larger newer one in the village centre. These old houses in Al-Khan are all scheduled for renovation and conservation on the ruler's instructions, in recognition of the fact that they represent a unique example of the lifestyle of a Creek settlement in the pre-oil days. On the southern edge of the promontory, in the Creek and hence well sheltered from the rough seas, a few fishing dhows are still built using teak wood imported from India as it always was in the old days.

**Time warp village**

**Renovation planned**

### Beach Corniche

Returning to the roundabout you now continue straight to follow the corniche, lined here with Sharjah's beach hotels, from the Carlton to the Lou Lou'a *(see practical information for details)*. In between are areas of public beach. The lack of alcohol has affected these hotels, which have had to build a clientèle based on Arab and CIS custom leading to them acquiring a largely deserved reputation for Russian prostitution.

### Port Khaled

Beyond the next roundabout the landscape abruptly changes from grand beach hotels to industrial port, with the Sharjah Ports Authority and Port Khaled, a man-made deep water harbour at the entrance to Sharjah's Creek, where container **Ports –** ships can berth. Sharjah is the only emirate to have a port on **east and west** the East Coast (Khor Fakkan) as well as on this coast, and the two ports strongly support each other. It does not have the facilities to compete directly with Dubai, but has found a niche for itself in trade with East Africa.

### Sharjah's Creek

Called Khor Khaled, you now head for the roundabout which leads over the Creek lagoon, crossing halfway over Jazeerah Island (Arabic, island), on which stands Sharjah's largest park and fun-fair, Al-Jazeerah Park, with its big wheel, water rides and little train.

**Changing** Changing currents leading to shifting sand banks have long **currents** been a hazard to these creeks, and Sharjah's suffered from severe silting in the mid-20th century, worse affected than that of Dubai, so that by the 1950s dhows that used to call in at Sharjah went instead to Dubai. With money from oil revenues, they tried to make a new entrance through to the Creek from near the power station, but this only made matters worse, so in 1975 the original entrance, by the Sharjah Continental Hotel, was dredged and the other entrance filled in again. Occasional dredging is done to keep it clear, so that today the Creek is once again bustling with dhows and ships and all along the Dhow corniche these colourful wooden boats add life and character to the modern city. A canal is planned to link Khor Khaled with Khor Al-Khan to improve water flow through both. Black 4-columned oil rigs are frequently to be seen moored in the Creek for repair, a good chance to see these monsters which are usually far out at sea.

Sharjah was the first of the Emirates to commission a town plan. Devised by Halcrow's in 1963, this plan provided for green areas like the Jazeerah Park on the island and the gardens that run all round the edge of the Creek itself, together with the dramatic 100 metre high fountain, third highest in the world, after Lake Geneva and the recent one in Jeddah, Saudi Arabia. These Creek gardens with their shady trees and little zoo in the south-west corner are where most local families congregate in the late afternoon and evening for strolls or picnics.

**Strolling areas**

## OLD MONUMENTS

With the advent of oil money, the towns all along this coastline of the emirates knocked down their old houses that used to line the Creekside and replaced them with concrete high-rise and plate glass structures. By the 1980s little remained of the traditional architecture that had been the essential character of these settlements. Sharjah was the first to realise the importance of preserving what remained, and mercifully, more remained here than in any other emirate. Despite the dilapidated condition of much of it, it was nevertheless salvageable for restoration. Thus in the early 1980s work began and still continues on carefully renovating some areas of the old Souq and some fine old merchants' houses, projects for which Sharjah deserves warm congratulations. No other emirate has such a finely restored area of authentic buildings. Entry to all is free.

**Striving for conservation**

### Naboodah House/Bayt Al-Naboodah (Heritage Museum)
*(45 minutes)*
Open 9am–1pm, 5–8pm, Fridays 4.30–8.30pm only.
Shut Mondays. Wednesdays women only.
This two-storey house made from coral stone belonging to the wealthy merchant Al-Naboodah family was the first to be restored, and now doubles as Sharjah's Heritage Museum. The unassuming entrance does not prepare you for the extremely smartly presented interior, in which every last detail has been carefully executed. The Naboodahs were among Sharjah's

*Naboodah House, the restored home of a wealthy merchant family*

wealthiest merchants, of Iranian origin, and the splendour and relative luxury of this late nineteenth century house exceeds that of most of the rulers' palaces at that time. The house is well equipped with WCs upstairs and downstairs, and a water dispenser and gift shop. The delicately fluted columns of the courtyard are made of wood brought from India by Obeid Al-Naboodah, the cloth merchant. Each of the 20 or so rooms has been carefully recreated with relevant furnishings. Of special interest is the children's room, where the original children's toys can be seen, ingeniously made dolls' houses, model cars and boats. Behind the kitchen, steps lead up to the original toilet next to the well. Water was fed up here from the well and the excrement was collected in a tank below, concealed by the little wooden doors at ground level. This was periodically emptied just like a modern septic tank. Much of the upstairs is reserved for offices, but from the open walkway round and the shaded verandahs, good views over the surrounding area can be had towards the round wind tower of the Midfa House.

**Early toys**

### Souq Al-Arsah *(1 hour)*
The courtyard in which the Naboodah House stands has been imaginatively supplied with children's swings and see-saws made in traditional style from wood and rope, and to the left of it, the passage leads into a wonderful maze of alleyways which is called the Souq Al-Arsah. Al-Arsah means Open Space, and it was here that camels of travelling merchants stopped and where bartering took place.

Roofed with barasti in the traditional way, the stone-built stalls with their wooden shutters are a delight compared to the synthetic versions to be found in the Heritage Villages of the other emirates. Sharjah has no need of such artificial creations, for it has been able to save the real thing. The series of stalls, some 100 in all, are run partly by local Arabs and partly by Indians (locals are especially encouraged by preferential deals), and are the perfect place for souvenir shopping, with antiques, traditional jewellery, bric à brac, and other stalls ranging from musical instruments to model dhows and date stalls, all set in the clean and shaded lanes. The shops are never crowded, and whilst the stallholders may wish for more visitors, the shoppers are generally glad to have it to themselves. There are also benches in the attractive central area to rest weary shoppers' feet, while sipping refreshments from the Coffee Shop. There are four gates to the souq which are kept closed at night. One 60-plus grandfather who runs an antique shop, Gulf Antiques, can still recall how he used to come to the market place here as a child to see pearl divers and foreign ships. The antiques business is taking off, he says, even among nationals. Omani chests used to cost a mere Dh300. Now they cost anything from Dh3000–Dh10,000, depending on their age and quality. He knows many local families who now regret having thrown old stuff out, not appreciating its value at the time.

**Authentic souq**

**Antiques**

### Islamic Museum / Bayt Saeed bin Mohammed Al-Shamsi
(*45 minutes*)
Open 9am–1pm, 5–8pm. Closed Mondays.
Wednesdays ladies only 5–8pm. Tel: 353334
Extremely smart with glass automatic doors, this large merchant's house has been spaciously laid out as an Islamic Museum in its four corridors, and the courtyard is blocked off to visitors. The fully air-conditioned corridors display an impressive collection of illuminated Korans, early writing implements for calligraphy, glazed pottery from Iran, Afghanistan, Turkey and Syria, Iranian tiles and Islamic metalwork vases. One unusual item is the astrolabe, an early device for navigation from the stars invented in the Arab world before the sextant existed. The striking thing is that these items all come from elsewhere in the Islamic world.

**Immaculate displays**

### Majlis Ibrahim Mohammed Al-Midfa *(15 minutes)*

In the area around the Souq Al-Arsah are some other sites scheduled for renovation, one of which is the old Midfa merchant family house with its unique circular columned wind tower, very elegant and Persian in character. Located at the far end of Souq Al-Arsah, towards the sea, you will find the restored single room off a delightful small, courtyard which has the famous wind tower. A prominent intellectual family, the room displays some of their personal belongings including books, manuscripts and newspapers. Ibrahim Al-Midfa was an intellectual and started the first UAE newspaper called *Oman* in 1927. It was handwritten. His second newspaper *Sawt Al-Asafeer* (Song of Sparrows) founded in 1933, spoke out against the occupation of Arabia by foreigners. The rest of the house is in the process of being restored and will then be opened to the public.

**Prominent intellectual**

### Al- Husn/Old Ruler's Fort *(1 hour)*

Open 9am–1pm, 5–8pm. Fridays 4.30–8.30pm.
Closed Mondays. Wednesdays women only.

Originally built in 1822 and demolished in 1969, all that remained of this, the Emirates' most impressive fort, was a solitary tower left on the roundabout in the centre of Al-Burj Avenue, now known as Bank Street and lined with high-rise offices. Looking strangely out of place in such a setting, the original 4-towered fort has been restored and opened in April 1997, after the massive rebuilding project was completed and the huge green fence of scaffolding that had isolated it from the busy street was finally taken down.

**Restoration obsession**

Its restoration had become an obsession of Dr Sheikh Sultan. In his own words, "I was studying in Cairo when a friend told me that the fort was to be demolished, 28 years ago. I came home the same day and ordered the process stopped." All that remained however was a 12 metre tower. The ruler personally rescued doors and gates and whatever he could, and kept them with him till restoration work began. He also retrieved documents, old photos and pictures and took measurements to make certain the Sharjah Department of Culture and Information could recreate it faithfully. The main entrance faces inland and this is the most fortified aspect of the fort, especially the distinctive huge tower with vertical ridges called Al-Mahalwasa. The red stone for this tower was specially brought from Abu Musa island and mangrove poles from Zanzibar were used for the ceilings. The wooden stake in the outside forecourt of the fort was where criminals were tied up before execution by rifle. Inside, an old cinema reel shows footage of Sharjah in the days of the first Imperial Airways flights from London on their way to India in the 1930s and 1940s. This film really brings home how there was nothing here but sand and a few mud huts apart from this fort itself – no roads, no vehicles. The downstairs shows the jail of Al-Mahalwasa tower, a fine collection of old photos showing the British Trucial Oman Scouts and the early local dignitaries. There are also some displays of weapons and gifts to the ruler, while upstairs is an interesting room showing a model of the reconstructed fort, with photos and plans illustrating how the renovation was done. The courtyard has been glassed-in to make air-conditioning effective for the downstairs corridors that used to be open to the air. All labelling throughout is in Arabic and the whole fort is geared for Arab visitors rather than foreigners.

**Early photos and film**

### Sharjah Art Museum and Artists' Quarter (Half Day)

Open 9am–1pm, 5–8pm. Fridays 5–8pm. Closed Saturdays.
Tel: 511222

This huge three-storey Art Museum opened in April 1997 and is the biggest by far of its kind in the Gulf. Costing Dh20 million the architecture was designed to harmonise with the traditional Arab and Islamic buildings in the surrounding Art Zone. It exhibits contemporary art by local artists and has 32 exhibition halls spread over two floors, two libraries and a coffee shop. The basement is a huge underground car park. The main display which is worth visiting is the private collection of the ruler Shaikh Sultan, consisting of oriental paintings and prints including many David Roberts' scenes from all over the Near and Middle East, from Turkey right through the Holy Land, Lebanon, Syria and Egypt. This interesting collection occupies the first few halls to the left as you enter. The upstairs exhibition halls are unfilled at the time of writing, but the ambitious nature of the whole project is nevertheless impressive.

**Huge halls**

The other buildings of the Art Zone are not purpose-built like the museum, but are in newly renovated buildings.They are the Emirates Fine Arts Society, open for functions only, the Very Special Art Group (private to artists), the Artists' Souq and the Arts Library.

### Artists' Souq

**Sarah's Hospital**

Running parallel to the Creek all along this section is the main old souq alley, selling spices and knick-knacks, shoes and everything you can imagine. Linked now with the whole renovated Artists' Quarter, you enter the open courtyard area where the Arts Café is situated. Opposite is the Sharjah Art Centre *(Bayt Al-Serkal)* which gives art classes for groups of 10 or 15. In the past this building was the Sarah Hosmon Hospital, one of Sharjah's earliest hospitals, set inside the house of the former British political agent. It worked as a simple maternity hospital for some 40 years and was known simply as Sarah's Hospital.

### Arts Café

Opened in 1995 this traditional style café offers authentic Arab drinks such as hot milk with ginger, as well as simple Arab snacks.

A few cast-iron tables are set outside in the courtyard.

### Sharjah Art Galleries

**Magnificent plasterwork**

Set a little apart, by far the most impressive building architecturally is Bayt Obeid Al-Shamsi. The rooms here are now used as artists studios, both local and expatriate, and the guardian will show you round to look at the canvasses of Germans, Sharjans and Indians all sharing a group of rooms that would once have housed one section of the extended family of Obeid Al-Shamsi, a wealthy Sharjah merchant. The magnificent blue and white plasterwork decoration on the upstairs storey of this building fronting onto the corniche and souq, is the finest such building to be seen in the Emirates. At the time of writing the restoration process had not been completed and it is to be hoped that this decoration work is retained, especially in the upstairs colonnaded room.

**Old Airport Control Tower and Fort Resthouse** *(1 hour)*
This slice of modern history makes a fascinating trip and work
has now begun on its restoration, to convert the fire-blackened
old airport control tower to an Aviation Museum. The road
which runs south-east from King Faisal Mosque (the large
brownish building looking like a cross between a mosque and

*Old Airport
Control Tower,
scheduled to
become an
Aviation
Museum*

a multi-storey car park) beside the New Souq, was the former
runway, and if you follow it, now King Abdul Aziz Street, for
about one kilometre you will see the control tower on your left
set in waste ground some hundred metres back from the street
and partially obscured by the Immigration Building. Beside it
stands the enormous fort, already fenced in as restoration
work has begun on its outer walls.

This, the UAE's first Airport, was established here in 1932 because Sharjah's ruler offered the facilities. Imperial Airways, the forerunner of British Airways, had been seeking landing rights for their route to India after their agreement with the Persian government expired. Several other rulers were approached, but Sultan bin Saqr (father of the current ruler) made the offer partly hoping for a large annual income from it. He in fact under the agreement received 800 rupees a month rent for the landing strip built by the British. He also received landing fees and a personal subsidy of 500 rupees. In return he was to build the Resthouse for the crew and passengers.

**Incongruous relic**

During the Second World War Britain stepped up its use of the facilities and fortified the Resthouse with the tower gun emplacements which can still be seen in two of the corners. A new agreement was reached giving permission for use of the airport as an RAF base and it also later became the headquarters of the newly formed Trucial Oman Scouts.

**First political agent**

The consequent increased number of military personnel living in Sharjah led in 1948 directly to the appointment of a permanent British political agent for the first time. Up till then Britain had had a policy of non-involvement in the internal affairs of the shaikhdoms but now the increased British interests on the coast, together with the first negotiations for concessions for oil exploration, made it necessary to establish precisely where each ruling shaikh's territory began and ended.

Sharjah remained the centre of British presence until 1954 when the Creek began silting up, so the political agent moved to Dubai, whose newly dredged Creek meant that it became the trading centre for the coast and that the oil companies were therefore using it as their coastal headquarters. Dubai had been the first emirate to sign a concessionary agreement for oil exploration.

The Airport continued to be used till, in the mid-1970s, it was abandoned in favour of the new Sharjah International Airport. The huge Resthouse/Fort gives a vivid impression of the size of the British presence here, and part of the structure served at one stage as a British School. The whole place has a slightly British Foreign Legion feel to it.

Behind the control tower are a series of hangars, some inhabited by Indian families, and a disused aircraft still hides among the shrubs beside one of them. To judge from the debris inside, Indians almost certainly squatted in the rest of the control tower, and it would be a fair guess that their primus stove exploding led to the fire and shattering of glass in the control room windows.

**Explosion?**

## NEW SOUQS

Shopping in Sharjah is remarkably easy because of its wealth of souqs, all of them easily accessible by car and with an abundance of parking, unlike its neighbour Dubai, where parking in the souq area is a serious challenge. Even so, Sharjah merchants frequently complain that Dubai takes much of their business especially during the month-long Shopping Festival, and it is true that Dubai's souqs tend to be busier, even though they are generally more expensive.

**Al-Souq Al-Markazi,** New Souq/Central Souq *(2 hours)*
Open 9am–1pm, 4–10pm daily, Fridays 9–11am, 4–10pm.
Sharjah has taken the initiative in using traditional designs and as early as 1978 built the remarkable blue-tiled *Al-Souq Al-Markazi* (Central Souq in Arabic) in a barrel-vaulted spacious style and cooled by 10 wind towers. There are two separate sections separated by a road and linked by two bridges which themselves also have shops inside. The whole place has over 600 shops, the main barrel vaults having in their wide downstairs area electrical goods, videos, cameras, cassettes, perfumes, gold, jewellry, clothes and shoes. Upstairs in the more atmospheric alley-like corridors are the antique shops, carpet shops, traditional jewellery and a café. The clever design with high ceilings and open spaces ensures that it stays well-ventilated even in high summer, and its location on the edge of the lagoon catches the breeze and makes it a pleasure to shop in.

**Railway station souq**

**Souq Al-Majarra** *(1 hour)*
This extremely smart souq, designed by Halcrow's, opened in 1987. Its golden dome, arched windows and elaborate patterned stonework, look so smart that shop owners inside have complained that no one comes because people mistake it for a museum or some palatial mosque. Adding to its exclusive feel is the fact that all the entrances are kept shut

**Too smart**

**Bargaining techniques**

---
### PERSIAN CARPETS

Sharjah is reputed to be the cheapest place in the Gulf to buy carpets, since huge quantities come over in dhows from Iran. The upstairs shops of the Central Souq are probably the best places to buy from and offer a good variety. The cardinal rule when buying something like a carpet is never to show interest in the one you really like. Make sure your voice expresses dissatisfaction and always convey that it is not really quite what you were looking for. That way, your bargaining technique will be at its most effective. Never buy in a hurry, and ask the carpet dealer as many questions as you can think of, to help increase your knowledge for future purchases. It makes a big difference if you understand something about what you are buying. Some points to watch out for are:

- look at the closeness of the weave: the closer the weave and the smaller the knots on the backside, the better the quality and durability of the carpet. 900 knots is top of the range.

- check for artificial colouring by rubbing a damp handkerchief over a corner of the carpet.

- part the weave and see if the colour at the base is the same as on top.

- pinks and oranges in a carpet mean that it must have chemical dyes as these colours cannot be produced by natural dyes.

Most of the carpets on sale in the Emirates are new or newish. The dealer will always tell you this is his special price just for you, but no matter what he says, you will only be getting a good deal if you knock at least a third off his original asking price.

---

**Uncrowded**

because the inside is air-conditioned. Certainly very few shoppers seem to frequent the shops which sell clothing, shoes, handbags and perfumes. The only upstairs part is in the dome, decorated with the sky at night, where there is a café. Its souq atmosphere may be lacking, with no bustle and the sound of your own shoes clip clopping along the hallway, but it is certainly easy to shop here if you just want to pop in for something specific, rather than linger over the experience. Shop owners want to put up more signs advertising themselves and have even suggested changing the stone walls to glass so that shoppers can see in.

### Fish Souq and Fruit and Vegetable Souq *(1 hour)*

Just to the north of the roundabout opposite As-Souq Al-Markazi, where the bridge from Jazeerah Island crosses to the mainland, the Sharjah fish souq lies on the Creek edge, slightly hidden by its plain concrete buildings. On the other side however, the scene is alive with bustle, dhows unloading their catch and the stall owners laying it out on their slabs from 6am onwards, so the earlier you come the fresher the fish. In pre-oil days fish was the daily staple meal, with rice and the occasional vegetable as a treat. Today fast food outlets are altering the eating patterns of centuries, so the fish souq is no longer such a regular port of call for Sharjah inhabitants.

**Earlier the better**

The Fruit and Vegetable Souq is located, conveniently for shoppers, just opposite the fish souq, in a long low whitewashed building with a single corridor down the middle. There are over 120 stalls in all, and those that cannot fit inside, spill over onto the pavement area behind it. Ample parking is provided all round the souq.

### Plant Nursery Souq *(30 minutes)*

From the roadside corner of the Fruit and Vegetable Market, the Plant Nursery Souq begins, running in a series of stalls all alongside the dual carriageway that skirts the east side of the Creek, till it reaches the end to the right. Flower pots, trees, shrubs, flowers and seeds are all on display here, with prices considerably lower than in the Dubai equivalent nurseries by the Garhoud bridge. Such a souq is not part of the traditional heritage of course, because before oil the only flowering shrubs to be seen along this coast had seeded themselves from the wild. The nurseries have grown up recently to service the needs of villa owners intent on turning their sandy patches into colourful tropical gardens.

**Roadside lushness**

### The Animal Souq *(30 minutes)*

On the corner where the road along the Creekside bends right (north-east) into the Dhow Corniche, is a sign to the right to the Animal and Bird Market. The souq is at its busiest on Friday mornings, and by 11am it is fairly quiet. As well as sheep, goats, camels and horses, it sells chickens, ducks, pigeons and rabbits.

## MORE PROVERBS OF ARABIA

Clothes that protect you from the heat will protect you from the cold.

What is learned in youth is carved in stone.

When a man is satisfied he becomes an unbeliever.

If you wish to win renown, commit an atrocity.

When the son grows a beard, the father must shave his off.

If you cannot get the meat, drink the gravy.

Bring your hearts together, but keep your tents separate. (UAE Federation!)

How many friends had I when my vines produced honey, how few now that they are withered.

If God did not forgive, Paradise would be empty.

Having too much is the same as having too little.

Habit always triumphs.

When your house falls in ruins do not weep for the broken pots.

A woman's house is her tomb.

The rented donkey always dies.

The pleasure of food and drink lasts an hour, of sleep a day, of women a month, but of a building a lifetime.

Every generation curses its predecessor.

When one blind man leads another, both fall into the hole.

Every man is master of his own beard.

Many are the roads that do not lead to the heart.

Everyone is perfectly satisfied with his own intelligence.

Seek knowledge even though it be in China.

When the leader dies the nation's fire is put out.

Good luck comes to him who has it, not to him who seeks it.

### Old Souqs and Dhow Corniche

The main alley of the old Sharjah souq runs parallel to the Dhow Corniche, crossing Al-Burj Avenue in front of where the White Fort stands alone, backing onto the renovated Artists' Quarter described earlier.

**Ruler's Palace and Sharjah Women's Club** *(10 minutes, from outside only)*

Continuing along the corniche past the golden dome of Souq Al-Majarra you pass the Sharjah Continental Hotel that guards the entrance to the Creek and then you come to the Ruler's Palace also set on the coast  on your left with a beautifully landscaped area and gardens to your right. This is the palace to which the ruler moved after the old Al-Husn white fort was demolished in the late 1960s.

The Women's Club in pride of place on the coast beside the Ruler's Palace was built at the instigation of the ruler's wife Shaikha Jawaher.  She said that the women of Sharjah used to complain to her that they had nowhere to go in their leisure time, nowhere to exercise their bodies or their minds. The Shaikha had this large complex built which now offers full sporting facilities to women and male children under 10, with beach, pool and gym. The club also runs courses for women on computers and summer activity programmes for children. "The club should", she has said, "act as a haven for women to expand their capabilities."

*Excercise for mind and body*

The corniche after the Women's Club continues to the Coral Beach Hotel roundabout, beyond which you are in the emirate of Ajman.

**New Museums and Culture Roundabout**

Sharjah has more museums than any other emirate, a fact it is very pround of.  The new ones tend to be concentrated around Culture roundabout (also known as Book roundabout with its model of an open Koran as its centrepiece). The elegant green Cultural Centre on the roundabout is the largest of the buildings. The others are a pinkish mosque with minarets donated recently by the Ruler's mother and completed in 1997, and the Diwan, which used to be the old Archaeology Museum, an elaborately carved building behind the fence. The Cultural Centre's impressive flight of steps leads up into an Arabic library and an auditorium for a range of performances, many of them by Sharjah's own four amateur dramatic groups.

*Abundance of museums*

**Sharjah Science Museum** *(2 hours)*
Open 8.30am–1.30pm, 4.30–9pm on Sunday–Thursday.
Monday 4.30–9.00pm ladies only. Friday 4–9pm.
Closed Saturday. Tel: 06-541777.

**Modern design**

Opened in April 1996 this museum is unique in the Emirates. Located next to the TV station beside Culture roundabout, the new museum is set in landscaped grounds with ample parking and even stone slab benches and tables for picnics. Inside is a café and snack bar for sustenance to give you strength before, during and after your visit. There is a good shop and clean WCs. Children under 12 are free and there is a small entry fee for adults. Many schoolchildren come on school outings in the mornings. In addition to the fixed exhibition halls there are special showings at fixed times of films in the auditorium. At the time of writing the shows were the Planetarium each evening in English at 7.30pm and in Arabic at 7pm, and on the Internet at 6pm. There is usually a changing programme which, at the time of writing happened to be The Digestive System, 6.30pm English, 6pm Arabic. Telephone the museum in advance to check timings if these shows interest you. Thursday evenings are the busiest according to museum staff, and Wednesday evenings the quietest.

**Blinded with science**

The interior is extremely plush and beautifully laid out with no expense spared. After buying your ticket you turn left into the Exhibit Hall. Your first impression is to be literally blinded by science. The hall is a big open space with lots of random exhibits and no particular progression from one to the other, making it a bit of a free for all. The exhibits are almost all interactive and are designed to illustrate scientific properties like sound and light, colour, gravity. There are also some computers displaying children's software.

**Sharjah Archaeology Museum** *(2 hours)*
Open 8am–12pm, 5–7.30pm, Friday 5–7.30pm.
Closed Saturday. Tel: 06-366466

Opened in June 1997 the new swish Archaeology Museum stands just before the Science Museum on the way to Culture roundabout. It cost Dh20 million to build and was designed by a local company in an attractive blend of traditional Islamic and Arab architecture, completed amazingly in less than eight months by using pre-cast concrete. There is parking for 300 cars and the museum will be linked by a corridor to the Science Museum. There is a spacious cafeteria, and the inside displays were designed by Australian experts.

There is one main exhibition hall and three mini exhibition halls together with a conference theatre, a library and a workshop centre. There is an area by the foyer illustrating to children how an archaeological dig is conducted. The museum is arranged chronologically and on entering the "Gateway to the Past" you enter the oldest phase, 5000BC–3000BC, in which huge film screens in Arabic and English explain how early man here was a hunter-gatherer. Each chronological section is built up round a continuous film show, a computer database with archaeology-related games to play, written displays, showcases of finds from that period and models of types of horses and graves that came from each period. The accompanying sound and lighting effects are all ultra high-tech and can be a bit frightening for a younger child. After the hunting-nomadic phase came the settled phase of farmers, traders and craftsmen, 3000BC–1300BC, who learnt to cultivate and irrigate crops. Next came the oasis dwellers from 1300–300BC, who were able for the first time to build falaj systems, underground tunnels bringing water from the mountains. These Iron Age sites have been found at Al-Thuqeibah on the Madam Plain, and at Khor Kalba on the east coast.

**Audio visual displays**

The last section from 300BC–600AD, is dominated by exhibits from Maleihah, Sharjah's most extensive site. The settlement was lived in for 100 years and one notable feature were their tall tower tombs, a model of which is here. The towers rose up to four metres above ground, while the body itself was underground, buried with the finest possessions like jewellery and glass. The single most impressive exhibit is probably from the horse tomb, where the gold decorations of the horse bridal are displayed. The man was buried with his horses and gold, a signal of enormous wealth, the horse being more valuable than the gold. Much of their wealth was built on trading frankincense and myrrh. Alexander the Great sent a fleet to investigate these, and after his conquest, coins were introduced to the Gulf for the first time.

**Horse tomb**

In the final section of the museum the ruler's own collection

233

of objects is displayed, assembled from items found on the antiquities market.

Next to the Archaeology Museum on the same avenue, a gigantic shopping mall has been built, opened late 1997, designed with four castles at the corners, linked by glass walls. Outside are two cafeterias designed as castles, one for fast food, one for Arab food. It has been built and planned by the Sharjah Co-operative Society at a cost of Dh8 million.

**Glass castle**

**Sharjah Natural History Museum and Desert Park** *(3 hours)*
Open 9am–7pm on Sunday to Thursday. Closed Saturday. Friday 10am–8pm. Tel: 06-311411.
If you feel this Museum, opened in November 1995, set by itself a long way out of Sharjah, will not be worth the journey, you could not be more wrong. Far from housing a few stuffed animals and dried plants, this incredibly ambitious Museum tackles no less a subject than creation itself, using modern visual technology to the full, bombarding all the senses. Experts from the National Museum of Wales in Cardiff, where Sharjah's ruler got his PhD, are to be thanked for this. To get even a superficial understanding of what is being explained, the history of the earth from Sharjah's point of view, would take a whole day, so do not stint your timings here. There is an extremely pleasant café area serving snacks and excellent cakes, looking out through a plate glass window at the desert and with a pair of Arabian wolves in a glass enclosure beside you for company. It is located at junction 8 of the Sharjah-Dhaid Road, beyond Sharjah International Airport, and takes 45 minutes to one hour to reach it from Dubai, or 30 minutes from Sharjah. The reason for its location here is that a colony of spiny-tailed lizards lived on this spot but were threatened with extinction after the road made them accessible to humans. Sharjah's ruler came to hear of it and designated 2 square kilometres of land to be fenced in for the lizards. From this, Sharjah's first nature reserve if you like, the idea of the Museum and Desert Park evolved. There is a shop selling books and environmentally friendly souvenirs. Dr Marycke Jongbloed, who came to the UAE some years ago to work as a GP, has now become the director of the museum, a job to which she is perfectly suited through her deep interest in wildlife conservation, and as founder of the Arabian Leopard

**Excellent day's outing**

Trust. Under her supervision the museum is being extended to incorporate a Desert Park, with a breeding centre for leopards, small foxes, cheetahs, ibex, oryx and gazelles. A children's petting zoo for domestic animals has now opened near the museum entrance, with a demonstration bee hive, quail chick incubator, and milk and cheese fresh from the cow for tasting. There are outside stalls with camels, horses, donkeys, geese, ducks, pigeons and guinea fowl. All animals can be stroked and fed with food provided by the keeper. Pony rides are on offer. There will also be a zoo for animals of the Arabian peninsula, a collection which is far more diverse than one might imagine, which will be open to the public by the end of 1998. Dr Jongbloed is actively fund-raising from companies and has enabled five other areas in the emirates to be identified as wildlife reserves.

**Breeding zoo**

The museum itself plots a staggering journey through 4,500,000 years of time and relates how the geological processes have shaped the landscapes and how climatic changes have altered the life forms on the planet, and how oil was created as part of this biological process. It then goes on to look at various habitats for wildlife, from desert, mountains, valleys, flood plains, dunes, salt marsh and mangrove forests and the sea, the latter with a spectacular display. The final section looks at Man and the Environment, how man has altered the environment through his ability to irrigate, hunt and fish. His efforts however had little effect till recently, when oil wealth brought material prosperity, expanding populations, and consequent exploitation of natural resources.

**Journey through time**

The Koranic quotation that announces the start of the museum is apt:

Assuredly the creation
Of the heavens
And the earth
Is a greater matter
Than the creation of man:
Yet most men
Understand not.

*Sura 40, Verse 58*

### Sharjah Botanical Garden

On the way out to the Sharjah Natural History Museum you will pass this new garden on the Dhaid road about 15 kilometres out of Sharjah. It will serve as a research centre for plants in arid zones, and a traditional falaj irrigation system has been installed. The garden has plants from tropical zones, savannah, North and South America and the Far East. The garden was opened on the same day as the Sharjah Art Museum.

### Sharjah Children's City

**Kids' rule**

This brainchild of the ruler Dr Sheikh Sultan bin Mohamed Al-Qasimi is to have a special city built for children, run by children of all ages from across the country, with no interference from adults whatsoever. The plan is they will run their own TV stations, making their own TV programmes, have their own kitchens, laboratories and play areas, all of which they will be wholly responsible for maintaining. The Ruler says he has had this idea for a long time and will consult children all across the country to find out what they need and want. The thinking is that such an experience will enable the young to be more discriminating in their tastes, to counter the negative influences of commercial TV channels and adverts. Running their own kitchens and drawing up balanced menus will, it is hoped, help them understand a healthier diet and lifestyle, steering them away from fast food. Malnourishment is a recognised problem among the affluent in the UAE. Playgrounds are also to be designed by the children to provide the physical activity missing in many young lifestyles. So that local children also get exposure to global cultures there is planned to be a mini cultural centre, where plays, films, puppet shows and concerts from around the world can be shown.

### Sharjah National Park

Located on the Dhaid road beyond the Sharjah International Airport on the way to the Natural History Museum, this park is used by families at weekends for its spacious lawns and shady trees. A miniature Sharjah City is being built there for curiosity value, and the car parking facilities have been much improved.

**Drive Circuit of Sharjah City for Orientation** *(1¹/₂ hours)*
From a starting point of Dubai this drive will help you orient
yourself in this, one of the most difficult emirate cities to find
your way round in. Entering on the main Dubai-Sharjah
highway you simply stay on the flyovers that take you straight
ahead. The traffic in Sharjah is perilous and this road narrower
than most, so be especially vigilant. This street is Sharjah's
main modern shopping street, Al-Wahda Road, lined with
boutiques, restaurants and supermarkets. Try not to be too
distracted by it all, as you continue over another flyover and
through more roundabouts and traffic lights, always straight
on for 6 kilometres in total from the first flyover till you finally
arrived at Culture roundabout, one of the few signposted
roundabouts, recognisable by the open Koran in its centre if
you miss the sign. Here you will see the green Cultural Centre,
with the Science Museum and Archaeology Museum off on the
street that starts with the TV mast.

From this Culture roundabout take the exit between the
pinkish mosque and the brown and white Diwan, heading
straight for the coast. Keep straight through a series of
roundabouts for some 4 kilometres till you reach the coast at
Al-Muntazah Square, passing the Sharjah National Theatre on
your right.

Now turn left along the grand landscaped avenues of
palaces, past the Sharjah Women's Club till you reach the
Sharjah Continental Holiday Inn, an unsightly block on the
beach to the right. Continue along the corniche, past the
harbour areas and the dhows. The sea here is now the Creek
itself. On your left are occasional remnants of older buildings,
old housing with wind towers in a state of slum-like disrepair,
but probably eventually scheduled for restoration.

You now reach the gold dome of the fancy Al-Majarra Souq
selling clothes, shoes, perfume, handbags and other luxury
items. Keep your eyes open at each main turning to the left
from here on, to spot the white Ruler's fort, now restored and
open to the public, set between skyscrapers in the middle of
the road. You can go and park close to it in a side street to
explore it and the other restored areas of old Sharjah nearby.

Continue along the corniche as it now bends left and passes
the row of plant nurseries to your left, the Fruit and Vegetable
Souq to your left and the Fish Souq immediately opposite to

**Perilous traffic**

**Colourful
dhows**

237

the right on the Creekside. The series of shacks here are most active up till 11am.

Continue straight under the flyover to the new Central Souq where you can park easily and have a good look at the shops selling jewellery, electronic goods, watches, perfumes, Persian carpets, gifts and handicrafts.

Continue afterwards straight along the corniche to the Sharjah Dhow Restaurant where you can break for lunch if it is after 12 noon.

Then you pass the attractive Marbella Resort run by an Indian manager, owned by the Sharjah government, looking like something straight from the Spanish coast.

**Barasti coffee shop**

Further along the corniche is a barasti coffee shop on the lagoon edge, then a group of dhows for rent holding 15–20 people. Now complete your big loop of the lagoon, past the zoological gardens, back to the island on the other side. Go under the bridge here, to head back round towards Dubai, otherwise you are fed back over the bridge to the island Jazeerah Park. Alternatively by going under the bridge and straight on towards the coast, you can turn left to look at the beach corniche on this side of the Creek, where the beach hotels are concentrated, known for their prostitution rackets. After passing the hotels, take a quick look at the old fishing village of Al-Khan at the end roundabout on its sandy promontory, before heading back to Dubai, which is signposted back onto the main highway.

## BEYOND SHARJAH CITY

### Dhaid – Town and Oasis

Set in a fertile belt at the foot of the mountains before the sandy desert stretches to the coast, Dhaid has become Sharjah's agricultural capital. The location is strategically important because it commands the entrance to Wadi Siji which forms an easy natural route between Sharjah and its eastern dependencies of Khor Fakkan and Kalba. Water is drawn from deep wells tapping the ground water and even still from an ancient falaj system running underground from the mountains to emerge in the oasis itself, just beyond the walls of the old fort, now the police station. A range of crops are produced here, including remarkably the strawberry, which is exported to Holland, England, Hong Kong and Singapore in the winter months. Effective management of water resources is the major problem of the future.

Sharjah's camel race track is also located at Dhaid on the road south to Maleihah.

---

### SOCIAL HIERARCHY IN OASES

Land ownership in the oases reveals a complex stratification of the village population which the average westerner, with his romantic notions of idyllic pastoral life, would not readily imagine. Wealth was the most important factor, and the wealthy owned large herds of camels or had been successful in pearling and could therefore afford to buy up date gardens. Different tribes had different levels of dominance which dictated what functions they performed within the date plantations, from guiding the flow of the falaj to cutting off the lower branches of the palm trees. Beluch, immigrants from the Persian coast, usually drew water from wells and helped with building houses for which they earned a small wage. Beluch were not however permitted to marry Arab tribal girls. The date gardens could change ownership through inheritance or being sold. But the pattern increasingly was that those who worked in date gardens did not own them.

---

### Jebel Maleihah (Fossil Rock) and Archaeological Sites
*(2 hours)*

The stretch of land running in front of the Hajar mountains has a series of dramatic limestone outcrops, formed from the sea bed 70 million years ago. These outcrops are, not surprisingly, having been underwater till a mere 6,000 years ago, rich in fossils which illustrate the marine life of eons ago. They were also favoured by Man and three ancient settlements have now been found each one in the lee of such a mountain outcrop, all of which are thought to have been caravan trading cities, on the east- west route from one coast to the other.

**Dramatic outcrops**

The ancient town of Maleihah is the most extensive of these, in a major caravan city contemporary with Ad-Dour, a Hellenistic port in today's Umm Al-Quwain *(See later Umm Al-Quwain section)*. Goods were traded from Ad-Dour inland to Maleihah on the main caravan route along the western foot of

**Wealthy
ancient town**

the Hajar mountains. Its location and the high local water table created the right conditions for a large and wealthy town to establish itself, traces of which can still be seen scattered among the current farms of the area. Earliest excavations here were in 1972–73 by the Iraqis, who found a palace and cistern, and then from 1986 onwards by the French, who found the striking tombs and irrigation system. A small number of finds from the early digs are exhibited in the Al-Ain Museum, but the vast majority are in the new Sharjah Archaeology Museum. Their main significance for historians and archaeologists alike has been the number of inscriptions found here, more than on any other site in the UAE. One of the first discoveries was in fact a tombstone inscribed in the South Arabian script of the Yemen, showing that Arabs arrived in this area more than 2,000 years ago. Greek amphorae handles also showed Maleihah's trading links through to the Mediterranean. The sites today are interesting to the layman for their setting as much as anything else, as they have to be sought out among traditional old farms. The hulk of Jebel Maleihah itself, with its distinctive shape recognisable by its vertical drop on the south side, dominates the landscape and gives shape to the horizon. Walking in this area is very pleasant too, as there are many trees and the small red dunes lend colour and contour to the land. It is good picnicking territory.

**Distinctive
shape**

Approaching from Dhaid, turn south towards Madam and you will reach the modern town of Maleihah after about 20 kilometres. At 20.7 kilometres a track forks off left in an east/north-easterly direction towards the Shawka Pools. The sprawl of Maleihah is rather unappealing and lasts for about 1.5 kilometres till you look out for a wide track to your right that heads very obviously straight for Jebel Maleihah itself.

Go slowly and look out on your left after about half a kilometre for a small track which heads towards a cluster of trees on a raised mound near the corner of a fenced farm. Head for these trees (100 metres from the track) and just below the mound you will find the excavated palace found by the Iraqis, together with a little mud brick structure nearby, possibly a cistern. Both are about 2,000 years old. The area all around is scattered with pottery fragments. Continue on the track to Jebel Maleihah itself to arrive at a simple Arab village where

**Excavated
palace**

the people keep camel and goats, though now own 4WDs too. The track stops at their village and to reach the mountain itself you must undertake serious sand driving with deflated tyres or walk for 30–45 minutes. The great sand slide from the top of Jebel Maleihah is one of the ultimate tests for dune drivers.

**Sand slide**

To find the other main area of excavations you return to the main road and continue south for about 0.5 kilometres. To your right along the roadside you will also notice more excavated areas, which are probably about to disappear in the road widening project currently in progress here. Look out for the track on your left which brings you almost immediately to a fenced area. This fence has in fact been erected by the owner of the farm whose hut lies further on, and he has enclosed within his fence the area dug by the French from 1986 onwards. He does not mind however if you climb the fence to explore the excavated area, with its grouping of tombs and the nearby very big well. Camel skeletons and a horse skeleton are to be seen in some of the tombs, brought in alive and then ritually sacrificed with their dead master. In one of these, gold horse bridles were found, indicating the great wealth of the dead man, not just for the gold, but for the horse itself which was more highly prized. Large quantities of iron weapons – arrowheads, swords, daggers – were also found in these tombs, the earliest iron found in the UAE. These are the tombs illustrated in the Sharjah Archaeology Museum as the monumental tower tombs, built 3–4 metres above the ground, used to give offerings to the dead. Being closer to the main road and with fewer trees, this site is not so suited to strolling and picnicking.

**Animal sacrifice**

### Jebel Faya – Excavations and Fossils *(45 minutes)*
Just over half a kilometre further south along the main road, you come to the track off to your right towards Jebel Faya. At the foot of this mountain, also noted for its fossils, a large settlement dating to the first millennium BC has recently been found spread over one square kilometre at the foot of the mountain. Excavations are still in progress each winter, but so far a gigantic stone fence has been unearthed surrounding different architectural structures and the site of destroyed buildings. Many artefacts have already been discovered, including 3,000 year-old clay toys, and a large collection of beautiful copper rings.

**Large settlement**

### Jebel Buheis – Necropolis and Fossils *(45 minutes)*

From the Jebel Faya turn-off the main road continues south for another 11.5 kilometres to reach Jebel Buheis, where the track leads off to the right towards the outcrop, again noted for its fossils, near the tall radio mast. The site lies some 10km north of the Madam roundabout. Take the track that leads in between two farms to the mountain, heading for the guardian's conical tent. This track is exactly 1.5km after the ADNOC petrol station (on the right) if you are coming from the Madam roundabout. In early 1997 a German anthropological team made a number of interesting discoveries here finding skeletons of 180 humans dating back to the third millennium BC. The women were buried with large quantities of necklaces, pearls and precious stones. There are some 19 tombs grouped in two areas, and one of these tombs in particular, No. 66, has four interconnecting oval chambers and this is considered the most important because of its unusual shape. It was entirely underground, with a huge entrance and contained 30 human skeletons. Each of the chambers seems to have been kept for one family of the same tribe. One of the chambers contained a woman's skeleton with two young children on her lap. The mother was 25–30, and the older child 5. The younger child died of malnutrition, as revealed by a study of the bones. A man from one of the other chambers was seen by his skull to have met a violent end in his thirties. Many of the artefacts found in the tomb suggest that the people were very rich. Nearby a well preserved Iron Age settlement was discovered a year ago by the Antiquities Department of Sharjah in the Thuqeibah sector of the Madam plain. The fertile plains around Jebel Buheis were suited to grazing herds, hunting, collecting wild plants and fruits. Finely crafted flint tools were found for preparing skins and meat. Since 1995, 68 ancient tombs have been found by the Sharjah Local Archaeological Team in and around this area.

**180 skeletons**

**Interconnecting graves**

## SHARJAH PRACTICAL INFORMATION

### Airport
Sharjah International Airport opened 1977. 18 kilometres from Port Khaled, 15 minutes east from town centre. Direct flights to India, the Gulf and Iran. Tel: 06-581111.

### Hotels
Ranked in price order. All dry, that is, no sale of alcohol. Since there are relatively few hotels, the following is a fairly comprehensive list.

*Continental Holiday Inn\*\*\*\*\**
At the head of the Creek, near town centre and 20 minutes from Airport. 300 rooms. Sharjah's most expensive hotel with all five star facilities. Private beach, windsurfing, sailing, waterskiing. Tennis courts, gym, two pools, bowling alley.

*Sharjah Grand Hotel\*\*\*\*\**
Full five star facilities on the beach corniche. 20 minutes from Airport, next door to Carlton Hotel. 220 rooms. Well designed, semi-circle facing beach with pool nestling in centre. Attractive layout and sitting-out areas on beach.

*Sharjah Carlton Hotel\*\*\*\**
Near Al-Khan, 20 minutes from Airport, on the beach corniche. 150 rooms, 80 bungalows. Huge pool. Tennis court. Private beach. Tel: 06-283711.

*Coral Beach Hotel*
Cheaper than the Continental or Grand and all the others, but still on the beach corniche with full sports facilities. No gym.

*Marbella Club Resort*
2–3 bedroom villas. Private members club with good sports facilities and range of sports classes and lessons. Beautifully landscaped golf, Andalusian – Arab style, Caesar's Palace Italian restaurant. Gardens run down to the lagoon. Conferences, banquet scenes etc. Watersports on the lagoon and private pier. Pedaloes, lasers, catamarans.

**Restaurants**
No alcohol served.

*Sharjah Dhow Restaurant*
Open daily from 12 noon–12 midnight. This magnificent old dhow with arched windows and an open shaded top deck is the best ambiance of anywhere in Sharjah to eat. There is of

*Sharjah Dhow Restaurant with the Central Market in the background*

course no alcohol, but the Friday buffet is excellent value with endless cold hors d'oeuvres followed by meat or fish of your choice freshly cooked to order. Situated on Khaled lagoon just south of the Central Market. Tel: 06-730222.

*Snobar*
The best Lebanese food in Sharjah with an excellent range of mezze. It has a small terrace with a few trees onto the road where some tables are set out. Situated on the Al-Khan road, on the right hand side just before you reach the roundabout at the beach corniche.

**Beaches**
Public beach equipped with thatched sunshades and palm trees between Sharjah and Ajman. North of Hamriya, a long unspoilt beach beneath a steep dune.

## Car Rental
The big hotels all have agencies.

## Camel Races
Held on Thursday afternoons and Friday mornings in winter on the track among the red dunes at Dhaid, on the Maleihah road. Racing tends to rotate from here to Umm Al-Quwain (Falaj Al-Mualla) and Ras Al-Khaimah.

## Shopping
Sharjah is the cheapest place in the Gulf to buy Persian carpets. Of the souqs described, Souq Al-Arsah is the best for souvenir shopping. There is also Pinky's, a warehouse stuffed full of 'old' wooden items including furniture from India. Tel: warehouse 06-341714. Location: at first flyover coming from Dubai, turn right, after three roundabouts, turn left. The warehouse is opposite Sky Line College. Open 10am–1pm, 5–8.30 pm. Pinky's and its rival Khan's also have shops in the old unrestored section of souq between the Souq Al-Arsah and the *burj* area where the old fort stands. Both sell Indian 'antiques', from wooden pencil cases to dowry chests, at the best prices you will get in the Emirates.

## Driving
Acknowledged to be the worst in the UAE exacerbated by the narrow roads and lack of comprehensible road signs. Special care needs to be taken. Nobody obeys lane rules.

## Taxis
Plentiful but no meters, so bargaining is essential.

## Excursions
Orient Tours Tel: 06-549333. Trips into the desert and wadis, barbecues.
SNTTA Emirates Tours Tel: 06-548296.

## Golf
Sharjah Sand Golf Course.

### Cricket

Sharjah Cricket Stadium has two international tournaments a year. It was built by an Indian businessman in 1981.

### Amusement Park

On Jazeerah Island, with big wheel, water rides and miniature train. Opens Sunday–Thursday 3.30–10.30pm, Friday 9.30am–10.30 pm, closed Saturday. Monday women and children only.

### Nightlife

All nightclubs were closed in Sharjah when alcohol was banned in 1985.

### Cinemas

Al-Hamra on Al-Arouba Road has English films, one road inland from Al-Mujarra Souq parallel to the corniche.

### Walking

The best walking areas from among the places described in the Sharjah section are in Sharjah's hinterland:

Jebel Maleihah, the pleasantly green rolling landscape around the archaeological sites and the rock itself;

Wadi Shawka, approached by the new tarmac road that leads east just north of Maleihah village, and then bends south towards Hatta. This new road crosses the lush Wadi Shawkah, the unmistakeably wide wadi floor rich in vegetation. Leopard have been spotted here.

Jebel Buheis, the mountain itself is interesting to climb over in search of fossils;

Jebel Faya, the mountain itself is good for clambering, keeping an eye out for fossils and archaeological remains.

# Ras Al-Khaimah

*(Arabic, Cape of Tents)*

Area: 1,700 square kilometres
Population: 156,000

## Overview

**Seafaring tradition**

Geographically and scenically the most favoured of the emirates with a convergence of sand, sea, mountains and plains, Ras Al-Khaimah also boasted in the eighteenth and nineteenth centuries the most powerful tribe in the Emirates – the Al-Qawasim, a seafaring trading force with 60 ships and some 19,000 seamen, that controlled the entrance to the Gulf as well as many towns on the Persian coast. Their trading activities, together with the fact that they embraced Wahhabism, a strict sect of Islam from Saudi Arabia that advocated total adherence to the Koran and regarded all non-Muslims as heathens, inevitably brought them into conflict with the British, who were keen to maintain dominance of their trading routes with India. In 1819 these clashes of interest came to a head when the British naval fleet, without warning, raided Ras Al-Khaimah harbour and destroyed every single ship – over 300 in all. That accomplished, the British went on to do the same at the smaller ports of Ajman and Umm Al-Quwain. The ports of Dubai and Abu Dhabi were untouched as they had not been involved in the earlier attacks on British ships.

**Blessed by nature**

Ras Al-Khaimah's history is clearly strongly dominated by its maritime trading links, but complementary to that, it is the only emirate to be blessed with plains in front of the mountains, and these plains boast the most fertile agricultural soil in the UAE. Well watered by mountain run-off and fresh groundwater within 10 metres, this plain has been exploited by man for 4,000–5,000 years. If oil ran out, Ras Al-Khaimah is probably the only one of the Emirates in which life would continue to survive in much the same way as before.

**Southern enclave**

That said, commercially viable quantities of oil were found in 1997 and a drilling contract signed, so Ras Al-Khaimah may therefore be on the way to becoming an oil producer itself, freeing it from its current dependence on Saudi and federal aid. Because of tribal links, Ras Al-Khaimah also has a large southern inland enclave in the mountains, north of Hatta, separated from the main coastal part of the emirates by Fujairah's inland bulge along the Dhaid-Masafi road. The copper mines at Wadi Safarfir, Wadi Qawr and Wadi Hulw which lie in this southern enclave are all described later.

Today the atmosphere of Ras Al-Khaimah town and

emirates is pleasantly unhurried. It has the highest number of indigenous Arabs of any of the Emirates and there is a much smaller Indian and Persian community, and shops bow to Saudi pressure to close at prayer times. There is very little high-rise building and none of the frenetic commercialism of Dubai and Abu Dhabi. Little signs of affluence and changing lifestyle are creeping in through the styles of shops that are newly opening, like the superbly mistranslated 'Gym Fitness Centre' and the invidious fast food outlets. Traffic jams are not yet a feature of Ras Al-Khaimah rush-hour, though the long haul of traffic lights that runs through the main drag can be rather tedious.

*The beauties of mistranslation*

Always perceiving itself as somewhat apart from the others, Ras Al-Khaimah initially stayed out of the UAE Federation, but changed its mind very quickly when it realised the extent of federal aid it would get on joining. Today its main contribution to the federation is agricultural, supplying large quantities of vegetables, fruits, as well as chicken and dairy produce. Its northern mountains also supply important rock from their quarries used for cement breakwaters throughout the emirate.

To do the places described in this section justice would take a minimum of four days, ideally more like six, so the best way to visit from Dubai or Abu Dhabi is to plan a series of weekends over the winter months, basing yourself at one of the hotels described in the Practical Information section, selected according to your taste for alcohol. Government-owned hotels in Ras Al-Khaimah have bowed to Saudi pressure to go dry, therefore affecting their western tourist trade.

### Al-Jazira Al-Hamra *(2 hours)*

The drive northwards from Umm Al-Quwain roundabout into the emirate of Ras Al-Khaimah becomes increasingly scenic the further north you go, but before you really see the mountains or have the fine red dunes, there is one stop you should make to visit the abandoned town of Al-Jazira Al-Hamra. The turn-off is clearly signposted towards the coast and two watch towers to the inland side of the road mark the spread of the original settlement here. The name means the Red Island in Arabic, though it is a peninsula not a real island, **Modern ghost town** and it is unique in the emirate as a modern ruin, a town recently abandoned in favour of a newly built town provided by the Ras Al-Khaimah government. What it therefore offers is an unusual opportunity to poke at leisure around the houses of the pre-oil community to get a feel for their lifestyle and building techniques.

The area is extensive, several square kilometres, and you can simply drive round the edge to gauge the full extent, before then deciding which overgrown alleyway takes your fancy as a likely starting point.

Near the sea you can seek out a handful of fine traditional houses built of plastered coral blocks with highly ornate plasterwork window screens on the upper *majlis* (men's sitting area) to allow cooling breezes through. The smaller flat-roofed cottages are generally built round a courtyard. In the centre of town near the harbour is the strongly built Shaikh's fort and in the immediate vicinity is a whole area of the town which has **TV-set** been recreated as a film set for use in filming TV serials set in pre-oil days. The film set is authentic down to the last decaying aubergine in the market stall. Automatic lighting has been installed to come on at dusk, which can give you quite a start if you happen to be strolling round at that time.

The original inhabitants have left voluntarily to move into new housing on the other side of the main road which the government provided free of charge, equipped with electricity and plumbing, unlike the pre-oil houses. Some, one cannot help feeling, may miss the atmospheric soul of the old town, others are probably only too pleased to swap that for the mod cons.

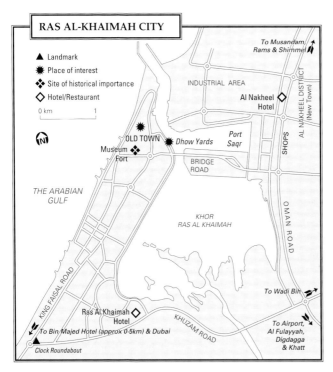

**RAS AL-KHAIMAH CITY**

▲ Landmark
✳ Place of interest
❖ Site of historical importance
◇ Hotel/Restaurant

0 km _____ 1

INDUSTRIAL AREA

To Musandam,
Rams & Shimmel

AL NAKHEEL DISTRICT
(New Town)

Al Nakheel
Hotel

OLD TOWN
Museum ❖
Fort

Dhow Yards

Port
Saqr

SHOPS

THE ARABIAN
GULF

BRIDGE
ROAD

KHOR
RAS AL KHAIMAH

OMAN ROAD

To Wadi Bih

KING FAISAL ROAD

Ras Al Khaimah ◇
Hotel

KHUZAM ROAD

To Airport,
Al Fulayyah,
Digdagga
& Khatt

To Bin Majed Hotel (approx 0·5km) & Dubai

Clock Roundabout

## Ras Al-Khaimah City

*Approach and Orientation*

Your arrival in Ras Al-Khaimah is imminent once the mountains loom and the high ridge of red dunes begins along the coast, blocking your view of the sea. A track leads off from the main highway down in front of these dunes, suitable even for a saloon car, so you can enjoy the sea and the dunes from the other side. Some wealthier members of society have built fine private villas along the crest of the dune and fenced themselves in, but considerable areas remain virgin.

The first real landmark is the Clock Roundabout at which the road bifurcates. The left side leads to the old town on the sandy spit, which is linked to the new town by a bridge across the Creek and harbour. In the old town lie the Museum/Fort, the souq area and old dhow fishing area. There is also a fine old mosque standing by itself in the northern extremity of the old town.

The fork to the right takes you to the inland route, past the

**Clock
landmark**

Ras Al-Khaimah Hotel, raised up on its mound to the left, then past the Ruler's Palace raised up on the right. At the end of the dual carriageway you hit a large roundabout, at which the right fork leads towards Khatt and the airport, and the left fork continues on through the new town, known as Al-Nakheel. This new part of town is rather unsightly and flashy, Indian dominated in comparison to the sleepy old Arab town.

**Museum/Fort** *(2 hours minimum)*
Open 8am–12noon, 4–7pm daily except Tuesday. Thursday ladies only day. No refreshment facilities. Tel: 07-333411.

The Ras Al-Khaimah Fort/Museum, opened in 1987, is the

**Authentic atmosphere**

most authentic-feeling of any such fort in the Emirates. Much of its charm derives from the lovely garden in the courtyard with its shady trees and benches. To protect the exhibits from dust, the previously sandy courtyard was paved with attractive rock from a nearby wadi, and when these rocks were cut into slabs, they revealed many fossils inside, which are still visible as you walk about the courtyard.

Like all such forts, it was the residence of the ruling Shaikh, in this case the Qasimis, and Shaikh Saqr the current ruler, lived here till the early 1960s. In the 1970s it served as the Police Headquarters and then as the prison, before preparations began in 1984 to convert it to use as a museum. Two expatriate characters were instrumental in these preparations: Major Tim Ash, a former officer in the Trucial Oman Scouts, whom Sheikh Saqr entrusted with the initial organisation and administration; and Miss Beatrice Di Cardi whom he instructed to conduct a full archaeological survey and to begin assembling material for that section of the museum. With the increasing number of archaeological finds, that section has turned out to be the largest of any of the display areas, now occupying three large halls.

The original fort dated to the mid-18th century, but only the square tower with the flag to the left of the entrance dates from that time, the remainder having been built within the last hundred years. The restoration that took place in the 1980s

**Original techniques**

used largely original methods, and even the gypsum plaster used to face the stonework was locally quarried, then burnt over a palm frond fire before being pulverised and brought to the museum, where it was mixed with water, then applied by hand.

The wind tower's effectiveness can be well tested in the room below, its constant cooling breeze far more congenial than any air conditioning. Open on all four sides, the tower could catch the breeze from any direction and channel it downwards. In winter the tower base was simply blocked off with matting or wooden planks to stop unwelcome draughts.

**Effective wind tower**

There is a nominal admission fee at the entrance to the fort which brings you in past the small shop selling mainly books, in the usual zig zag fashion to enter the courtyard. Steps lead up to the roof and upper floor, where you can visit the upper Qawasim majlis room with an interesting display of ship models and early documents on Ras Al-Khaimah's history, including the famous manuscript written by Vasco da Gama in 1498, describing his passage through the Straits of Hormuz, along with extracts from the current ruler of Sharjah's book 'The Myth of Arab Piracy in the Gulf', in which he sets out to prove the Qawasim were responsible traders, not pirates, as the British have always maintained.

**Myth of piracy**

The remaining displays are all downstairs on the ground floor in the museum proper, while the rest of the upper level is either rooftops or museum offices.

The Natural History section houses a large shell collection donated by a German expatriate after seven years of collecting from Ras Al-Khaimah beaches, all beautifully grouped and labelled. The fossil display was also a donation from the Emirates Ecology Group in 1987. Most are a staggering 135 million years old – the *Cretaceous* period as it was known – and were collected from fossil-bearing strata throughout the Emirates.

The archaeological exhibits are arranged in chronological order, starting from 5000–4000 BC (fifth millennium) when the earliest signs of human activity were flint tools, stone weapons and arrowheads for hunting.

The oldest and most important real settlement yet discovered in Ras Al-Khaimah is at Shimmel, 5 kilometres north of Ras el Khaimah, and dates from the second millennium, that is, from four thousand years ago. It extends over 3 kilometres and consists of a vast cemetery of 150–200 tombs for mass burials of 100–150 people at a time. Studies of the bones have shown average life expectancy at that time to have been 35 years. Buried with the men, women and children

**Mass burials**

was a considerable amount of jewellery such as bronze earrings, shell beads and necklaces of carnelian and agate. The tombs were built originally above ground, and the biggest, known as Tomb 99 is over 16 metres long by 10 metres wide.

**Stone-built tombs**

Most had a long chamber built of a double row of large stone blocks in-filled with rubble. Stone slabs were then put on top for the corbelling and roofing, while the entrance was two long vertical stones set on a doorstep slab supporting a large lintel stone.

Two other tombs of this age in Ras Al-Khaimah are at Dhayah, 6 kilometres north-east of Shimmel near the Dhayah fort, and at Ghalilah, known as Tomb 1 and Tomb 2.

In the far south of Ras Al-Khaimah, Wadi Qawr is a route to the east coast along which several tombs and settlements have been found. Those at the villages of Naslah and Fashga have been excavated and shown to have been last used in the Iron Age around 1500BC, though they may well have been built earlier and then re-used. Both villages are in Wadi Qawr in the stretch between Huwaylat (north of Hatta) and the east coast as the wadi runs west to east.

The archaeology section then displays an impressive collection of glazed pottery and glass mainly from Julfar, the most important town in Ras Al-Khaimah during the early Islamic period from the seventh century onwards. The pottery

**Chinese links**

is mainly of sixteenth and seventeenth century Chinese, Persian and Iraqi origin and shows the extent of Julfar's trading links throughout those centuries. Next comes an extraordinary coin collection from the tenth to the eighteenth centuries of silver, bronze and copper, generally found in hordes by farmers digging in remote wadis.

The ethnography section has some fascinating old photos of the various styles of houses lived in by the local people in the 1970s, the construction entirely suited to the climate, season, lifestyle and building materials available. The museum then has an excellent display of everything to do with

**Pearling explained**

pearling, mainstay of the coastal dwellers. It shows the white cotton suit the diver wore to protect from jellyfish stings and the leather finger guards to protect his fingers when he cut away the sharp oysters from the rocks with his small knife. Also on display is the complex pearl merchant's chest with his sieves, weights and scales to grade the pearls. Next come displays of fishing and agricultural tools, pottery and weaving. The courtyard outside has a life-size reconstruction of one of the pottery kilns as found at Wadi Haqil.

Camel saddles and associated camel gear are displayed in the Bedouin section. Stock breeding was the Bedouin means of gaining cash, and they would sell a racing camel for large sums of money. Falconry gear is the final display in the ethnography section.

In the last room before the entrance/exit comes a stunning collection of silver jewellery, used by women both for adornment and as an investment. The silver was traded as long ago as 2000BC in exchange for copper from Magan (the UAE/Oman peninsula). Many of the designs have their origins in the early civilisations of Iraq, Egypt and Ethiopia. The Maria Theresa dollar, first minted in Vienna in 1751 was often used in necklaces for its high and constant silver content, whereas today most of the silver comes from China in bars. Jewellery was worn constantly and therefore became old and battered. It was then melted down to make new, though the styles remained traditional, thus making it very difficult to judge the age of the piece. Few are thought to be more than 50 years old. The male decorative piece, though originally defensive, is the silver *khanjar* or curved dagger.

**Stunning silver**

**Melt the old to make the new**

In the same room are traditional costumes and weapons. Swords, shields of rhino hide, Shihuh axes, muskets and rifles dating from 18th to early twentieth centuries used by the British, weapons which originated in Persia, America, Turkey, Germany and Britain.

### Julfar/Kush *(1 hour)*

These two archaeological sites are manifestations of the same city, during different phases of its history, referred to as Julfar in Islamic records as early as 695AD. The city had to move to retain its harbour as the coastline changed, which is why the two sites are 2 km apart.

**Moving coastline**

The Julfar situated closer to the sea at present is, as you would expect, the younger site, dating from 14th to 17th century, and was discovered first by the British archaeologist John Hansman. His dating was made possible by the large finds of Chinese green Celadon ware and fine blue and white porcelain from the 16th and 17th centuries. He collected up to 90 surface sherds.

Digs were conducted there from 1973–4 by the British and have never resumed since then. The site is unprepossessing to the layman now, but determined ruin-spotters can reach it by taking the faded green sign pointing to the coast saying Julfar off the main highway some 5 kilometres north of Ras Al-Khaimah town. It lies near some houses close to a new mosque. The area is known as Darbahaniya, and a fair number of finds from the city are on display in the Al-Ain Museum, since the 1970s digs were conducted under the Al-Ain Department of Antiquities.

**More ancient tell**
The earlier part of Julfar is a large mud tell known by the local people as Kush. It lies further inland to the right hand side of the main highway rather than to the left like the later Julfar, some 4 kilometres north of Ras Al-Khaimah town on the way towards Rams. Once you have left the sprawling suburbs of Ras Al-Khaimah behind you, start looking out for the tarmac road with a proper exit lane, 2 kilometres after the Emirates petrol station. There is also a white sign with a UAE crest and big red arrow. Take this road and after less than 500 meters you will pass the local Islamic social club built of reddish stonework on your right, which announces itself as 'Shamal Flok (sic) Arts Society'. The rutted dirt track immediately past it leads you round to the fenced-in site of Kush in a wide semi-circle and back onto the tarmac again a little further on. A black sign in Arabic beside the locked gate prohibits playing about or destroying the site. The key is kept by the chairman of the social club who will happily let you in if he is there.

The Shell-sponsored excavations have revealed the remains of a thick mud brick wall 2.3 metres wide along the top of the tell (archaeological term for mound composed of the collapse of successive layers of buildings). The wall has been dated to the 11th century and can only have been defensive. The site is known to have been occupied from 4th century AD to 13th **9th–10th century peak** century AD, its peak of wealth being attained in the 9th and 10th centuries when its trade with Iraq was at its height. By the 11th century Iraq entered a period of decline and trade shifted away from the Gulf to the Red Sea and African coast. Dr Derek Kennet, leader of the recent excavation team and research fellow at Oxford University, says that this decline has been mirrored in the site, and there is a "general impoverishment"

## MORE ARAB PROVERBS

The whole world is nothing but the scraping of a donkey.

The date palm has its feet in water and its head in fire.

Three things prolong life: a big house, a swift horse and an obedient wife.

The beauty of a man is in his intelligence; the intelligence of a woman is in her beauty.

If I have regretted my silence once, I have regretted my chatter many a time.

Marriage is like a castle under siege: those within want to get out, those outside want to get in.

The beauty of man lies in the eloquence of his tongue.

Wisdom has lighted on three things; the brain of the Franks, the hands of the Chinese and the tongue of the Arabs. (Arabic is a rhythmic, musical and emotive language)

There is no messenger like money.

Honour the date palm, for it is your aunt.

If the captain of the ship loves you, you may wipe your hands on the ship's sails.

When one door closes, a hundred others open.

---

in their way of life evident in the decline from the mud brick to palm frond houses, till the site was abandoned in the 13th century. Excavations have been sponsored for three more winter seasons by Shell Markets, the British Museum and the British Academy and the National Bank of Ras Al-Khaimah. Major excitement was generated recently by the finding of a carbonised coffee bean dating to the 13th century, making this the earliest discovery of coffee beans in the Arabian peninsula. Before this, the earliest had been the 14th century found in Yemen. It is discoveries of this sort which archaeologists get most satisfaction from, rather than conventional "treasure", since this type of discovery sheds light on early lifestyles and trade development. Coffee is thought to have been introduced from Abyssinia. It did not reach Europe till the 16th century.

**Earliest coffee**

### Shimmel Area

**Concentration of sites**

Now that you have turned off onto this tarmac road towards Shimmel you have entered the richest concentration of archaeological sites to be found anywhere in the Emirates. A proper exploration of this area would take two days at least, if you are based in Ras Al-Khaimah, longer if you are coming on day trips from Dubai or Sharjah. The first day might consist of Sheba's Palace and the Shimmel Necropolis, while the second day might be Kush/Julfar, the People's Heritage Fort and Wadi Haqil with its pottery kilns. Picnicking with shade is straightforward in most of the places described.

### People Heritage Revival Association Fort (*30 minutes.*)

At the first major junction in the tarmac road after Kush/Julfar stands this imposing fort constructed 10 years ago of local stone. It has been built for local people rather than for foreign visitors and exists to re-create the old lifestyle of their grandfathers, to show today's children how everyone used to live just 20 or 30 years ago. The Bedouin of the northern Emirates were never truly nomadic, as the higher rainfall meant that there was nearly always enough grazing for the camels and goats. They therefore lived in barasti houses and irrigated the fertile plains from wells and falaj systems. On the coast houses tended to be built of mud brick or coral, while in the mountains they used stone and wood. The fort is most interesting for the reconstructions in its courtyard of the local

**Semi-troglodyte winter houses**

style of houses for winter and summer which were shown in the photos in the Ras Al-Khaimah museum. You can clamber down inside the winter house and sprawl onto its cushions. All the houses have basic furniture of the simplest kind, exactly as they would have done when they were inhabited.

### Sheba's Palace/Husn Shimmel (*1¹/₂ hours*)

By forking to the left of the Heritage Fort you take the tarmac road that leads you through the village of Shimmel to the foot of the mountains. The tarmac deteriorates to a dusty track, and then passes a small mosque. The exact method of approach does not really matter as long as you end up at the foot of the mountains north of the village. Look out for the fenced area at the mountain foot and follow it till you reach a green water tank raised up on stilts, near which you park. An alternative

approach is from the west thereby avoiding the centre of the
village. There have been accounts of villagers being unfriendly
to visitors, and children throwing stones, but such incidents
seem to have been controlled now by the village headman. It
is however important, since the site lies on the edge of a
village, to dress appropriately and to greet the villagers
courteously. The other approach involves staying on the main
Rams highway for 4 kilometres after the Emirates petrol
station on Ras Al-Khaimah's northern outskirts and taking the
track for just over 3 kilometres past the Necropolis tombs and
pyramid shaped rock (described later), to reach the same green
water tank/tower where you park. From here you will find a
gap in the fence and walk up the hillside for an energetic five
minutes or ambling 10 minutes, heading for the slight cleft in
the rock where a sort of path then becomes apparent. The
ascent is not difficult but requires better footwear than
flipflops as the terrain can be a little loose underfoot.

**Conservative
dress**

*Vista towards
the sea from the
summit of
pyramid rock at
Shimmel*

Referred to by the locals as Husn Shimmel (Shimmel Fort)
this is in truth a far more accurate name than our Sheba's
Palace. It is a medieval Islamic hill fort and defensive
settlement set on a natural plateau overlooking the plain
towards the sea and Ras Al-Khaimah, old Julfar. It has never
been properly excavated but the pottery found at the site dates
it to the 16th and 17th century. The name Sheba probably
comes from a misinterpretation of the Arabic Qasr Al-Zaba'
which means Palace of the High Plateau.

Once on top, the most impressive ruins are the oblong

**Dramatic
setting**

cisterns built to preserve vital rainwater, one of which still retains its domed roof. There are also complex water systems and a large well. Otherwise the site has clear defensive walls and a gateway visible as you make the ascent.

The charm of the site however lies less in its ruins than in its dramatic setting on its naturally defensive plateau with the spectacular mountain backdrop and the surprisingly green vegetation. The best time to visit is in spring after the first heavy rains, when the hilltop will be covered in grass and tiny flowers.

### Shimmel Necropolis *(2 hours)*

Here you have the most extensive and important concentration of ancient tombs in the Emirates, extending for some 3 kilometres along the base of the mountains, and centred round the weird pyramid-shaped rock of lighter colour. From the green water tank you head along the foot of

*Ruins in the Shimmel necropolis area*

the mountains towards the coast for about one kilometre till you see a track off through a gate heading towards the pyramid-shaped rock. The site was first excavated in 1976–77 by the British, and by the Germans from 1985 onwards. Over 60 tombs have been located here, all from the second millennium. The remains of the settlement itself lie behind the pyramid-shaped rock and for picnicking it is best to drive on to the shade of the trees from where you can get an overview of the site. Many hours can be spent here exploring the area

**Mysterious pyramid rock**

and especially the pyramid rock itself which conceals various extraordinary tunnels and caves. The ground everywhere is simply littered with pottery sherds, together with huge numbers of shells revealing that the sea once covered this area and also that shellfish comprised a major part of the local diet. 90% of the shells found here are the mangrove mud snail, *terebralia palustris*, a favourite food in ancient times. This proves that the Shimmel area must once have been rich in mangrove swamps, a similar landscape to that at Khor Kalba nowadays.

**Shellfish diet**

Studies of the bones found in the tombs showed that the locals also suffered severe teeth and jaw problems as a result of the high consumption of sugary dates. Life expectancy was 30–35 and the bones show that 45% of children died very young. The other contents of the tombs, like jewellery, weapons and pottery are displayed in Ras Al-Khaimah museum described earlier.

As the track continues towards the coast you will notice an old watchtower built of sandy rock and in its immediate vicinity are more large tombs, the more significant of them fenced-in. They are little more than foundations and to the layman rather difficult to decipher, though some sense of the scale of the stones used can be appreciated. The largest, a circular one, measuring 14.3 metres in diameter (Hili Grand Garden Tomb is 12 metres) would originally have stood three metres tall, and this makes it the largest tomb yet discovered in the whole Arabian peninsula. It has been dated as 4,300 years old, making it part of the Umm Al-Nar civilisation already found in Abu Dhabi, Ajman and Al-Ain, contemporary with the pyramids of Egypt. There were 12 separate burial chambers with over a hundred bodies. The quality of masonry is baffling archaeologists, who say that such high quality stone cutting is difficult even for twentieth century masons to achieve. These skills may well have been acquired from trading partners in Mesopotamia and the Indus Valley, the two sophisticated cultures of that time to whom they exported copper, the basis of the UAE and Oman's wealth at that time. *(See also pages 143–145).*

**Largest Arabian tomb**

*Pottery kiln at*
*Wadi Haqil*

### Wadi Haqil *(2 hours)*

Leaving the Heritage Fort on your left you continue along the tarmac road till you see a military camp and large Etisalat satellite dish. Just before the military camp and some 200–300 metres before the satellite dish you take the track to the left which leads in towards the hills. Bearing left whenever there is a choice, you reach the new settlement of Wadi Haqil within 2 kilometres or so, now approached by a tarmac road from Shimmel.

**Ruined**
**potters' village**

Wadi Haqil is a dead end valley ringed with hills and beyond the new settlement, at the foot of the hills to the seaward side of the wadi, are the stone-built huts of the potters, with the pottery kilns sunk into the ground scattered among them. The houses cover an extensive area but are very rewarding to explore, especially as they were only abandoned in the 1970s when the new town was built. Look out for one well preserved house that still retains its internal tiny wooden door to the inner windowless big chamber, but watch out for spiders webs (those of the harmless but ugly Orb spider are plentiful here) and scorpions. In spring the whole area is delightfully green with lush grass carpeting the wadi bed. The kilns themselves date from the fourteenth century and remained in use till the 1970s. The tribe of potters were the **Tribe of** Bani Shumaili, and they made cooking and storage pots for all **potters** purposes like storing dates, grain and water. The pottery was simple and unglazed, made from the mountain clay found in the wadi floor. The clay was pounded and sieved, tempered with pulverised shells for strength, then water added. The base of the pot was shaped by hand before being set on the potter's wheel. The only other pottery sites in the area are at Buraimi and at Bahla, where the local clay was also suitable.

Right at the end of the wadi, diligent observation will reward you with the discovery of a track which leads up and onto a plateau hidden from below by a steep cliff. Here stands the attractive village of Al-Halla, now abandoned, in which sixteenth century Chinese blue and white porcelain fragments have been found.

**Rams** (*2 hours for shelling beach*)
After emerging from the Shimmel track back onto the main north-south highway by the Eppco Ready Mix Beton factory, you can if you have time continue your exploration of the coastline northwards to the Omani border at Ash-Sham. From the map this stretch looks as if it should be very scenic, with the mountains close up behind the shore, but in practice it is heavily industrialised with the busy port of Mina Saqr at Khor Khowair shipping out huge quantities of quarried rock and cement from the mountains which are gradually being cut away to provide the vast amounts of building material required by the richer emirates of Abu Dhabi and Dubai.

Rams itself, 12 kilometres north of Ras Al-Khaimah, is unremarkable as a town, just boasting a few simple watchtowers. Driving through the town towards the sea however, you will notice a rickety old bridge over an inlet, and **Rickety bridge** this is what you must cross to reach the 7 kilometre-long Rams shelling beach, frequented by locals and foreigners alike. The locals, especially on Fridays, like to exercise their 4WDs up and down the beach, while the foreigners peer at the tide mark for shells. Old hands go to the furthest point between the last breakwaters, knowing there will have been least disturbance there. The beach driving requires confidence rather than experience, but things are usually fine if you keep your speed up. There is a track that runs through the scrubland on the edge of the beach, so you can drive to the furthest point along the bay, then park and walk to the beach if you are feeling

**Fishermen and turtles**

energetic and the season is not too hot. Local fishermen use the beach, and turtles have been known to get caught in their nets and dumped here. The best times to see shells are after storms, when a lot will be washed up, at low tides, and in the hot summer months when no one else is crazy enough to come, so you have a month's pickings to yourself. *For more details on shells see the Shells and Marine Life section.*

### Dhayah Fort *(1¹/₂ hours)*

Continuing north from Rams on the main highway you reach the village of Dhayah after 3.5 kilometres set amid a lush date plantation. The famous fort, to which the inhabitants of Rams retreated when the British fleet landed in 1819, rises above the palms before the plantation and is deceptively difficult to reach. The British laid siege to the fort for four days, before the local people surrendered.

Do not attempt to broach the oasis by the direct route to the fort, as you will soon encounter lanes which are too narrow for a vehicle. Instead you pass the fort, turning right immediately after the white mosque and grocery shop beside it. This dirt

**Tricky approach**

track swings round to the right behind the village. Follow it for some 500 metres till you reach another grocery shop called Al-Adal. Pass to the left of the shop and keep following the track for another 300 metres. Where you reach a fork, keep straight, leaving the main track to fork left, and keep going to pass an old watchtower on your left after about 250 metres. The track winds on to the right and left for a further 400 metres. You then turn right for the final 300 metres heading straight towards the hill, to park on its northern side.

The ascent takes 15–20 minutes and the terrain is loose rock and this makes the descent rather slippery. The whole conical hillside is covered with shells, indicating that it was under the sea a few millennia ago. The best approach is along the western side of the hill (the side facing the sea) crossing towards the far southern side as you ascend, so that you can enter from the southern gate, the only means of entry. Inside, the fort is extremely simple and makes you realise how small the population of Rams must have been to fit in here. The crumbling walls have recently been restored.

**Scrambling ascent**

### Ghalilah and Ash-Sham *(1 hour)*

The main highway continues for a further 15 kilometres to reach Ash-Sham on the Omani Musandam border, passing through a succession of cement factories which are undeniable blots on the landscape. By Mina Saqr, the industrial port, you pass Ghalilah, site of an oval second millennium tomb excavated by the British in 1977, whose foundations only are still visible.

The village of Ash-Sham itself is ringed with mountains and is unremarkable except for the number of little shops it seems to have, lining the roadside.

From here the border crossing into Oman enables you to drive the spectacular route along the coast to the tip of the Musandam at Al-Khasab, from where dolphin viewing and diving trips are organised. Accommodation is available at the somewhat basic Khasab Motel or at the larger villas which can be booked in advance (Khasab Travel and Tours Tel: 5-830464.)

**Into Oman**

### Al-Falayyah Fort and Ruins *(1 hour)*

Returning from the Rams highway to the centre of Ras Al-Khaimah town you should definitely visit the interesting group of ruins known as Al-Falayyah, which make a good lunch spot for a picnic. They were the former garden and summer residence of the ruling Qawasim family. From the main roundabout you reach from Rams after the succession of traffic lights, you cross straight over following signs to Khatt and the airport, leaving the road back to the Ras Al-Khaimah Hotel and Dubai on your right. Just 2.9 kilometres from the roundabout the road crosses a bridge and the cluster of ruined buildings lies to your left immediately after the bridge.

**Former summer palace**

First is the tiny mosque with its outside courtyard and

265

pillars. Further in is a fort tower which still has steps to the second floor, and at the far end is a kind of long fortified farm house, getting quite heavily overgrown. Historically the site is significant as the place where the 1820 peace treaty was signed with the shaikhs of all the Emirates and the British, after which the Pirate Coast became known as the Trucial Coast, thereby laying the cornerstone which preserved the national integrity of the shaikhdoms and enabling them to form the independent UAE 151 years later. Because of its historic significance, the site was originally chosen as the location of the Ras Al-Khaimah museum. The large concrete unfinished building by the roadside is the original Ras Al-Khaimah Museum, the project abandoned in favour of the old fort as a setting. It is interesting to explore the inside of this structure, graffiti and all.

**Significant setting**

### Khatt Hot Springs *(1 hour)*

From Falayyah the road continues for 3.5 kilometres where it reaches a turn-off to the left towards the hot springs. The road takes you through the typical farming land of Ras Al-Khaimah with many small villages till at 7.7 kilometres you join a road from your right and continue swinging round to the left for the final few kilometres, till you reach the dead end at Khatt itself. A couple of old watchtowers stand on the nearby mounds. Until the 1980s these hot sulphur and mineral springs were delightfully informal out in the open under the palm trees. Now proper segregated bathing houses have been built, along with a restaurant, and the ambiance has been lost in the name of progress.

### Digdaga and Camel Race Track

Returning from Khatt you can drive through the fertile agricultural land towards Digdaga, where the first cattle farm in the UAE was started in 1969 with a herd of 30 black and white Fresians. There are now well over a thousand. In summer they are kept cool by fine spraying of water in their sheds. A poultry farm also began here in 1978. The chicks are hatched and allowed to roam for 40 days before they are slaughtered. They would never get any bigger anyway because of the climate and you will have noticed that UAE chickens are indeed uniformly small. Chicken is the only local meat. Beef, lamb and pork are all imported from Australia,

**Small chickens**

Ireland, Holland and the UK. Between Digdaga and Kharran as you head back towards the coast look out for the yellow sign off to the left to Ras Al-Khaimah's Poultry and Feeding Company. This road leads you to the Ras Al-Khaimah camel race track, an 8 kilometre circuit and one of the UAE's best. Set in an area of red sand and grey-green trees, the spot is very attractive and is known locally as Wafi. Actual races are held on Thursday afternoons and Friday mornings from 6–9.30am, when much money changes hands – camel racing is big business. Entry is free but find yourself a safe place to watch, away from the careering 4WDs which speed after the camels.

**Scenic spot**

**Wadi Bih** *(Full day, 4WD only)*
The day trip drive through Wadi Bih from Ras Al-Khaimah across the southern Musandam mountains to emerge on the east coast at Dibba is one of the most spectacular on offer in the UAE. It passes through quite a large chunk of Omani territory and you must make sure to have your car licence, driving licence and everyone's passport with you before setting off. There is a police post checkpoint at which all these documents must be shown, otherwise you will not be allowed to proceed. Try to avoid Fridays as it really gets quite busy now, this is such a well driven route. The drive is fairly tough on the vehicle, with steep gradients as you go over the mountain pass built by the Omani military, and over the rocky terrain in the narrow gorge of Wadi Bih itself as it nears the east coast. It is therefore essential to make sure your vehicle has been checked and well prepared before setting off. There are no facilities or refreshments en route so you must have a full tank of petrol and all your own food and drink. By making a 7.30 or 8am start from Dubai, the trip can be completed in a tiring day, returning to Dubai by 8pm.

**Spectacular trip**

**Be well prepared**

From the Clock roundabout on Ras Al-Khaimah's outskirts, fork right to bypass the old town and continue the 5 kilometre stretch past the Ras Al-Khaimah Hotel to the roundabout on the edge of the new town. Cross straight over here to the Coffee Pot roundabout which you again cross straight over till, after another five kilometres, you reach a fork in the road at which you turn right, skirting round a green and white domed house set behind trees. Follow this road for 2.6 kilometres to reach the signposted turn-off to Wadi Bih Dam. From here it

*The Wadi Bih reservoir with its clay bottom*

is worth making the short detour to the left to see the dam before returning to the track and continuing into the wadi itself. From this point on, there is only one track all the way to Dibba, so there is no scope for getting lost.

Steps climb up to the dam wall from which you can survey the size of the lake behind, fluctuating according to the season. It has been a project of mixed success. Its intention was to

**Dubious dam**

replenish the groundwater levels by allowing collected rainwater run-off from the mountains to sink down into the ground. However it appears the soil is heavy in clay and not therefore very keen to allow water to penetrate. As a result huge quantities of water are being lost in evaporation before they have a chance to seep underground.

Continuing now into the wadi proper, the track skirts the lake along the eastern side and heads into the wide approach to Wadi Bih. You need to keep a very careful eye open here for the abandoned villages of the Shihuh tribesmen, built of rock

**Camouflaged villages**

and extremely well camouflaged since their colour is identical to that of the mountains. There are several here in this early stage before the police post, often built into the foot of the mountains. Even more invisible are the Shihuh trails, tiny footpaths which zigzag up apparently sheer cliffs. The wadi beds of gravel are full of acacia and the largest and most attractive Arabian tree the *ghaf (Prosopis)* which can reach up to 25 metres. The ghaf leaves and pods are used for animal feed and the nectar-rich flowers are favoured by bees in their honey production. Also plentiful in the wider stretch of rocky valley are the *sidr* (*zizyphus*, Arabic *shu'*) which bear edible berries, and the flowering almond Morenga trees, growing high up in rocky crevasses. The amount of vegetation and trees is surprising here.

If you make an early start from Dubai or Sharjah you will reach the Omani border post at around 10am. It generally takes some 10–15 minutes to pass through and you then continue to reach the start of the military pass, announced by signposts at the bottom. The ascent is quite magnificent, winding on endlessly in hairpin bends, with stunning vistas of the Ru'us Al-Jibaal (Arabic Heads of the Mountains) on all sides, becoming more and more bare as you climb. The rock strata here are a geologist's dream.

**Mountain pass**

You will reach the summit around 12.30pm, a suitable

---

### THE SHIHUH, MOUNTAIN TRIBESPEOPLE

In 1900 the Shihuh numbered about 20,000. In the cooler winter months they lived high on fertile terraces in the Ru'us Al-Jibaal mountains of Musandam, irrigated by rainfall and lived in rough stone houses. No springs or wells exist in these mountains, so rainwater was collected in underground cisterns which had to last the entire winter for men, crops and the goats which were herded. In the summer when the mountains became unbearably hot, they would move to barasti huts in the palm groves of the towns, mainly at Ash-Sham and Ghalilah, or live by fishing from the coastal villages that fringed the mountains. Some also took part in the summer pearl dives.

The Shihuh considered themselves basically independent but as allied to the Sultan of Oman who kept a *Wali* (governor) at Khasab. Those that were based at Ash-Sham and Ghalilah on the Ras Al-Khaimah coast owed their allegiance instead to the Qawasim tribes.

Today the mountain Shihuh bemoan their lot and wish they had joined up with the UAE rather than with Oman, as they felt they would have been better provided for financially. The Arabic root of their name means to be avaricious, a name thought to originate from the fact that they had to eke out such a meagre existence in an inhospitable environment, which made them appear avaricious in the eyes of other Arab tribes.

Because of the importance of land in the mountains and down in the date gardens, Shihuh were especially rigorous about marriage within the family, usually to the daughter of the paternal uncle. That way land did not pass into the hands of other tribes.

picnicking time, though shade of course is sorely lacking. Binoculars are useful here for examining the Shihuh villages on distant terraces. A mere fraction of these are inhabited now, the once semi-nomadic population having gone to settle in new breeze block houses built by the government down on the plains, thereby bringing to an end the lifestyle of centuries. The pattern of life beforehand was for the Shihuh to move to the coast at the beginning of the summer season (end May), returning to their mountain villages during the transition to winter (early November). Just a few elderly men remain in the mountain villages now, those who have no family and who are not prepared to change the habits of a lifetime. They are reduced to begging from tourists, something they seem prepared to do with no great shame attached, and will sometimes sell some piece of handicraft like the small Shihuh axe, its slim handle made from the wood of a small tree (*mizi*) known for its strength and straightness. Much bad feeling has been aroused by foreigners coming to the Shihuh villages and helping themselves to such items as carved doors and old pots. Though they may no longer live here, and though the old Shihuh beggar seems to live in a house with a TV aerial where he no doubt watches *The Bold and the Beautiful*, they still regard these villages as their property and get rightly incensed by strangers coming in and stealing things. The houses themselves have stone walls and roofs of wooden beams covered with earth. Beware of walking on these roofs for they are frequently close to collapse.

**Remaining few**

The village most readily visited because it is closest to the road lies in the lee of Jebel Aqaba and is around 2 kilometres below the summit on the approach to Dibba to the left of the track.

**Narrowing gorge**

The descent continues past the helicopter landing pad used by the military for dropping supplies, and proceeds into the increasingly narrow wadi. The boulder-strewn floor shows how flash floods regularly wreak havoc, but the track is continuously maintained, so even after floods bulldozers generally come and sort it out within days. From your 8am departure time you will reach the narrowest part of the gorge around 4pm. By 5pm you will emerge across the plain and onto the beach north of Dibba, in time to have a refreshing swim before sunset. The drive back to Dubai from Dibba on the tarmac takes two hours via Masafi.

## SOUTHERN ENCLAVE

**Wadi Al-Safarfir copper mines** *(4WD only, 1 hour)*
This small but attractive site is an easy one hour detour from a trip to Wadi Qawr or Wadi Hulw, in the southern enclave of Ras Al-Khaimah. It is reached from Hatta, and after the Hatta Fort roundabout you take the first tarmac road to your left signposted Huwaylat. The road winds through barren hillsides for 8.3 kilometres till you reach a small wadi-crossing, with the wadi valley to your left. The approach from here is very rocky, so continue up and over the hill to the next dirt track fork to the left which brings you back down into this wadi after the rocky patch has passed. Continue to the point where the wadi divides into two, and park over by the left bank of the left fork under a large *ghaf* tree. The remnants of the copper mining villages are difficult to spot at first but persistence will eventually be rewarded by the discovery of steps leading to the mine shaft, a few small houses and a mosque, and a small Islamic graveyard on the terrace above. On the opposite side of the wadi are piles of shiny black melted slag lying below a row of ruined furnaces. The stone outer walls of these furnaces have been dated back to the third millennium BC, contemporary with the Umm Al-Nar culture which owed its wealth to trading copper from mines such as these. The rock from the mine shafts would have been transported across the wadi, and put in the furnaces to melt away the surrounding rock, while the copper ran off into a crucible. Bits of ore with bright green copper traces are still littered about.

**Difficult to find**

Copper is known to have been mined in these mountains for over five thousand years, and in the 10th century ingots from here were transported to the Omani coastline and distributed along trade routes to production areas throughout the Abbasid (Arab dynasty with Baghdad as its capital) empire. Of the metals known in antiquity – copper, silver, gold, iron, tin, mercury and lead – it was not iron (the most abundant), that was discovered first. The Bronze Age came before the Iron Age because it was easier to extract the copper and tin used for bronze (8:1 or 10:1) than it was to extract iron from its ore. Copper is thought to have been discovered by accident, through pieces of the ore used in fireplaces coming into contact with hot charcoal and the molten metal spilling out.

**5,000 year old mines**

**Wadi Qawr, tombs** *(1 hour detour off-tarmac)*

From the Hatta Fort roundabout, the tarmac road to Huwaylat is some 10 kilometres. Recently the tarmac road here has been extended and now continues all the way to Muna'i and beyond. By turning down into Huwaylat and following the road across the wadi bed you will enter the Wadi Qawr heading due east towards the coast. The wadi passes by several villages en route to the coast and at two of them, Naslah and Fashga, tombs have been discovered. At Naslah **Graves reused** two tombs were first used 4,000 years ago and then reused in the Iron Age. The Iron Age objects recovered from the tombs are on display in Ras Al-Khaimah Museum. At Fashga the stone-built tomb was found to contain over 30 people along with 100 pots and 60 soft-stone vessels, as well as beads, shells and bronze arrowheads. Again these items were Iron Age, 3,000–2,500 years old, but the tomb itself is thought to be older, as at Fashga. There are several settlements along the wadi, including a hill fort, which are all thought to be Iron Age.

*Hilltop settlement at Wadi Hulw, with a ruined village in the valley beyond*

**Wadi Hulw, ruins** *(4WD only, Full day)*

From the Hatta Fort roundabout, this wadi is reached by heading north 10 kilometres past Huwaylat, then straight on to Muna'i some 4 kilometres further on. On the outskirts of Muna'i look out for a generating station on the right of the road with a large pylon. Take this road, past a repair garage raised up on your left, and head on towards the mountains

*Prolific tombs on the plain behind Kalba*

Above: *Shihuh watchtowers in the Musandam Mountains*

Right: *The mosque at Khatwa Oasis, focal point of the village*

Above: *Fujairah Fort, scheduled to become the new museum*

Left: *Graves at Wadi Hulw, Ras Al-Khaimah*

*Deep tombs at Maleihah, Sharjah*

eastwards. Then look out for the electricity pylons heading eastwards in the distance, and cross the wadi bed to reach them at what is clearly the entrance to Wadi Hulw. (*Hulw* means beautiful in Arabic.) This first section runs for 5.6 kilometres past extensive quarryworks which are far from appealing, to reach the settlement of Hulw itself. From here on, the scenery improves dramatically, with unspoilt views, lots of water in the wadi bed, and lush vegetation with flowering pink oleander to introduce colour. Look out on your left for an extensive ruined settlement which runs right over to the foot of the mountain, with walls still standing over two metres high in places. Immensely thick defence walls still stand to an impressive height, and one tomb can still be climbed down into, while on the western edge of the settlement is an enormously wide well, its diameter at least five metres. Traces of green glazed pottery indicate trading links with Persia and Iraq.

**Beautiful wadi**

The scenery continues to be spectacular and the track continues eastwards towards the coast. A new road has recently been forged to the left over the mountains towards Fujairah, but stay on your track to the east and within a couple of kilometres you will see ruins of another extensive settlement to your right, set in a grassy dell between two hills. Climb the hill to the east (left) and you will be rewarded with the discovery of an ancient tower house on the summit, and several other buildings on the way up, all in surprisingly good condition. From this vantage point you can see across the track into the valley opposite, where the ruins of some 20 houses can be spotted. This is thought to be an ancient copper mining village, and occasional pieces of jet black copper slag, as well as the tell-tale green-tinged stones, can be found. From recent studies very little copper remains today in these mountains in commercial quantities.

When you reach the next T-junction be sure to turn left, as right will take you into Oman. The track now winds out towards the coast through increasingly open and less dramatic hills towards Ghayl with its fort, described later with Khor Kalba and Kalba under the Fujairah section, with which it fits geographically, but in fact belongs to the emirate of Sharjah.

## RAS AL-KHAIMAH PRACTICAL INFORMATION

### Airport
Ras Al-Khaimah has its own small airport 15 kilometres south of the town city on the road to Khatt, which takes flights from a handful of airlines, mainly to other parts of the Arab world and India. There are none to Europe.

### Hotels
*Bin Majid Beach Hotel* Tel: 07-352233 fax: 07-353225
P O Box 1946. 140 rooms.
The first hotel you come to, named after Ahmad bin Majid, the famous Arab navigator of the sixteenth century who lived here, the Bin Majid is at the approach to Ras Al-Khaimah town, before even reaching the Clock roundabout. It is signposted 'Hotel' towards the sea and from the car park and outside the hotel looks singularly unprepossessing. Once inside, and especially once outside again on the seaward side, its facilities are rather more impressive, with an attractively landscaped pool area with gardens and playground, and steps down onto a fine private beach with sunshades. The rooms themselves are disappointingly small, but well designed. Owned privately by a Scandinavian company, the hotel is not subject to the alcohol ban and therefore serves the full range of liquor in its bars and restaurants. Package tours from Scandinavia and the CIS countries comprise the bulk of the clientèle, but local Arabs also use its facilities for large scale functions like weddings. The hotel rates itself 4 star and has a fixed room rate with no weekend or special discounts. Waterskiing, windsurfing and diving are all on offer.

*Ras Al-Khaimah Hotel* Tel: 07-352999 fax: 07-352990
P O Box 56. 90 rooms.
This, Ras Al-Khaimah's first quality hotel, has lost much of its foreign clientèle to the Bin Majid since going dry (alcohol-free) some years ago. Originally under private ownership like the Bin Majid it is now government owned and thus Saudi pressure has forced the decision to stop serving alcohol. Its rooms however are more spacious than those of the Bin Majid and therefore more comfortable, if you need mattresses on the floor to accommodate children. The dining room also has an

interesting bird cage along one side providing endless fascination while you wait for your food. The food itself is adequate though probably not as varied as that of the Bin Majid. By way of compensation, room and food are some 20% cheaper than the rival. Outside it has no beach of course, being set on a mound on the edge of the mangrove lagoon, but has a good sized rectangular pool, sauna, gym, tennis and squash courts, and a pleasantly grassy playground area with superb swings, strong enough for grown ups. It offers a good two-night weekend rate for Thursday and Friday.

*Al-Nakhil Hotel* Tel: 07-222822. 60 rooms.
Cheaper than either the Bin Majid or the Ras Al-Khaimah Hotel, the Al-Nakhil has little else to recommend it, being really a business hotel set in the modern centre of Ras Al-Khaimah. Its bar does serve alcohol and is known to be the cheapest in town, so it draws the clientèle to match.

### Taxis
The Ras Al-Khaimah taxi rank is just south of the Bin Majid Hotel on the outskirts of town. Service (shared) taxis run from here to Dubai, Sharjah, Fujairah and Abu Dhabi. Town taxis have no metres but rates are cheap.

### Car rental
Cars can be rented from the hotels.

### Tours
A range of organised day or half day tours are offered from the Bin Majid and the Ras Al-Khaimah hotels. They are an expensive and generally unsatisfactory way of seeing the place if there is more than one of you.

### Restaurants
Apart from the hotel restaurants Ras Al-Khaimah has a Pizza Inn open 11am–midnight . Tel: 334040.

### Walking

The best walking areas from among the places described in the Ras Al-Khaimah section are:

Al-Jazira Al-Hamra, several hours can be spent exploring these ruins;

Shimmel necropolis, the mountains behind and all around Sheba's Palace;

Wadi Haqil, the large dead-end valley and the little village of Al-Halla above;

Dhayah Fort, the oasis all around and the mountains behind;

Camel race track near Digdaga, the green dunes and heavily wooded foothills;

Wadi Safarfir, the valleys beyond the copper mines;

Wadi Hulw, the wadi itself and the mountains round the ruined copper mining village.

# Fujairah

Area: 1,300 square kilometres
Population: 73,000

## Overview

Fujairah has as yet no proven oil resources, but it has two other exploitable advantages – its geography and its location. Its **Mountainous coast** geography with mountains coming right to the sea and little or no desert plain, have given it the most beautifully scenic coastline of any of the Emirates, an attraction which is gradually drawing more and more tourists. Its location on the east coast of the UAE, outside the Arabian Gulf, gives it a more temperate climate than the other emirates, with less extremes of temperature and fewer storms. Ships berthing here are also spared the journey round and up through the Straits of Hormuz, often a politically turbulent waterway.

Fujairah's economic hopes now and long-term are pinned on its port traffic and associated Free Zone. A new port, it only received its first ship in 1982, but its growth has been impressive, becoming the world's third largest tanker refuelling and bunkering (crew-changing) station. Ships can then off-load onto smaller ships which go directly to the various destinations, or can be transported by road or by air from Fujairah's International Airport. All this growth and development is still very much in its early stages, and the emirate, with its small population of a mere 73,000, does not yet at any rate convey the impression of a booming industrial centre.

Until 1976 there was not even a tarmac road from Fujairah connecting it with the rest of the Emirates. The current ruler Shaikh Hamad bin Mohamed Al-Sharqi, succeeded his father **Youngest ruler** Shaikh Mohamed in 1974, and is the youngest of the Emirates' rulers. The Al-Sharqi family have ruled Fujairah for over a century and trace their origins to Yemen. Since their arrival in this mountainous terrain some 2,000 years after the collapse of the great Marib Dam in Yemen, they have had many struggles to retain their independence against other neighbouring tribes. The emirate was finally recognised by the British as a separate entity in 1952, having previously been part of Sharjah, and it then joined the UAE federation in 1971.

## Orientation and Approach

The only tarmac road that links Fujairah with the other main centres like Sharjah and Dubai starts from Dhaid and then heads on a dramatic and scenic dual carriageway through the

Hajar mountains to reach Masafi near which a lively street market lines both sides of the road for about one kilometre, selling everything from plants and pots to fruit, vegetables and carpets. Like many markets it is at its most lively after dark. For clay pots you may do even better for variety and price by forking right shortly after the turn-off to Manama on your left (some 12km earlier), following the sign to Thorbann Pottery.

**Pottery**

At Masafi the road divides, north towards Dibba and south, following the course of Wadi Ham, towards Bithna and then Fujairah town itself. The total drive from Sharjah is one and a half hours to Fujairah town, from Dubai two hours, and from Abu Dhabi three and a half hours. Fujairah is the only emirate to have all its land on the east coast. Along this 60 kilometre stretch of coastline, Fujairah's territory is interrupted by the Sharjah enclaves, first at Dibba, then at Khor Fakkan and its hinterland, and again at Kalba and Khor Kalba. Inland from Qidfa there is also a curious mountain enclave belonging to Oman.

### Environment

Fujairah has recently recognised the problem of plastic rubbish disposal along its beaches and is seeking to educate its nationals to minimise use of blue plastic bags and to clear up in its litter. Campaigns are run by the Municipality in schools and elsewhere, with organised beach clean-ups. The Municipality has also erected many signposts in the city in an attempt to increase public awareness of the environment and trees in particular. So far it still has quite a long way to go to catch up with Sharjah Municipality, easily the most advanced in civic pride after Abu Dhabi. On the beaches, much of the tar and debris has been washed up from ships dumping their waste offshore. 90% of the passing oil tankers dispose of the waste illegally in territorial water, while only 10% gives it in to the floating slop and waste disposal facilities at the port. With over 40 giant oil tankers a day passing through, the problem is a serious one, with oil slicks that, though they may be dispersed on the surface by winds and tides after a few days, have heavy sediments which sink to the sea bed and pollute sea life. The sea off Kalba has been especially badly hit and local fishermen have to stay ashore for days waiting for it to

**Beach problems**

**Threatened fish**

disperse rather than have their nets and tackle ruined. The fishermen say that the pollution over the last five years is causing the fish to go further out to sea and there are already some types that no longer exist. The authorities are well aware of the problem and are actively seeking solutions.

Being such a mountainous emirate, Fujairah is better able than the other emirates to trap the rainfall at dams like at Wadi Siji, and then control its use for agriculture in the valleys or especially on the fertile coastal plain.

### Bithna, Fort and Tomb *(1½ hours)*

This is described in full later in this section, but you can visit it on the way through to Fujairah if you have left yourself enough time.

### Fujairah, New Town

The new town is very spread out for such a small place and can be quite disorienting and difficult to judge distances. If you head for the sea and then turn north you will reach the Fujairah Hilton, the most useful landmark of the town.

### Fujairah Museum *(1 hour)*

Open 8am–12noon, 4–6pm daily. Friday 4–6pm.
Closed Saturday. Tel: 09-229631.

From the outside this small but recently expanded modern building looks rather insignificant and unprepossessing, but inside it is more interesting than you might expect. From the roundabout by the Fujairah Hilton where the new Ottoman-style Abu Bakr mosque is being built, the biggest mosque yet on the east coast, take the exit inland and the museum is on your right at the next roundabout. Inside its courtyard is a life-size barasti hut decked out in traditional furnishing. To complement this, the ethnographic room inside shows costumes, weapons, tools and household articles, together with a collection of old photos showing life in the pre- oil era. It is worth noting here that the differing geography of Fujairah and its lack of deserts, has meant that the camel and the falcon play no part in the local traditional lifestyle. Fujairah is the only emirate which still has no camel race track. Instead Fujairah has developed its unique sport of bull-fighting, with humped bulls, fighting against each other. Fattened up to

**No deserts or falcons**

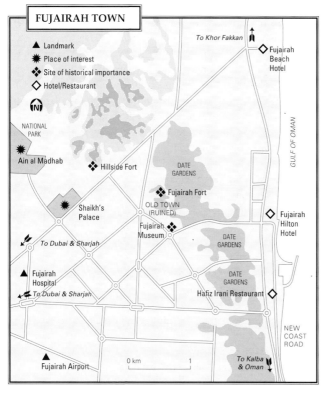

**FUJAIRAH TOWN**

- ▲ Landmark
- ✳ Place of interest
- ❖ Site of historical importance
- ◇ Hotel/Restaurant

NATIONAL PARK

✳ Ain al Madhab

❖ Hillside Fort

DATE GARDENS

❖ Fujairah Fort

OLD TOWN (RUINED)

✳ Shaikh's Palace

Fujairah Museum ❖

To Dubai & Sharjah

▲ Fujairah Hospital

To Dubai & Sharjah

Hafiz Irani Restaurant ◇

DATE GARDENS

DATE GARDENS

To Khor Fakkan

◇ Fujairah Beach Hotel

GULF OF OMAN

◇ Fujairah Hilton Hotel

NEW COAST ROAD

▲ Fujairah Airport

0 km          1

To Kalba & Oman

weigh about a ton, fed on milk, honey and meal, the hump-backed bulls have a contest of strength with no blood-spilling, to see which can force the other to the ground. This sport is practised at weekends throughout the winter.

**Bulls, not camels**

The archaeological rooms display the results of the excavations at the tombs of Qidfa, Badiyah and Bithna up to the time of 1991 when the museum opened, along with more recent finds. The old palace of the ruler borders the museum, a palace the present ruler's father only moved out of in the late 1960s. The museum will move into the fort once restoration is completed in 1999.

### Fujairah Old Town and Fort *(1 hour)*

Lying behind (north of) the Museum, the fort catches your eye first, raised up as it is on a natural rock outcrop. All around it the ruined mud brick houses of the old town lie part abandoned, part inhabited by sub-continental labourers who

**Oldest fort**

so often seem to move into the old houses vacated by nationals in the 1960s when new housing was built. The fort, built 360 years ago, has been partially restored in a rather concrete slab kind of way, that is already showing signs of cracking. Some of this repair work dates to earlier this century, when the British, following a dispute between the British political resident and Shaikh Hamad, the current ruler's grandfather, ordered the gunboats to bombard the castle, severely damaging the three towers that face the sea. If the original structure, as the authorities claim, really is over 300 years old, it is quite an age for a mud brick fort, as most are less than 100 years old. For the next two years the fort and surrounding area will be cordoned off while restoration takes place, culminating in the transfer of the museum here in 1999.

### Fujairah Heritage Village National Park and Hinterland
*(2 hours)*

Also known as Ain Al-Madhab Garden and open from 10am–10pm, this park was once the property of the ruling Al-Sharqi family. It has now been given over to become a public park and mineral spa, with chalet accommodation. Located on the outskirts of Fujairah town, it is laid out like a grassy park with playgrounds, and the Heritage Village display is set in one area showing the old pre-oil lifestyle through traditional costumes, food, pottery and utensils. Fujairah authorities are very keen to preserve awareness of traditional lifestyles, not for the benefit of tourists so much as for their own youth, whose knowledge of their own heritage is minimal. With drugs, alcohol and irresponsible driving on the increase in the national youth, the authorities are increasingly aware of the need to educate the young of the dangers and to bring them back to Islam and their Arab traditions.

In the valley beyond, traces of ancient copper smelting furnaces can still be seen, together with an Iron Age fort, raised up on a bluff on the east side of the valley. The whole valley is ringed with mountains and the series of little tracks which criss-cross all over it make peaceful picnic areas with plenty of shady trees.

**Peaceful
valley**

## Bithna , Fort and Tomb *(1¹/₂ 1hours)*

On the main approach road from Masafi, some 12 kilometres before you get to Fujairah, this village guards the main pass through the mountains, and is especially attractive at sunset when the reddish hue of the mountain rock takes on a special glow. The town itself is rather scruffy but should be visited for its fort and for its unique T-shaped tomb, the finds from which are in a detailed display in the Fujairah Museum. You will spot the fort from the main dual carriageway, its flag waving from the tower, but when you take the Bithna exit, do not head straight for it but continue on the dirt track at right angles to the main road till you go down the lip of the hill. Only then do you turn right to follow the track for some 600 metres, keeping left when there is a choice, and then crossing the wadi to reach the fort on its bluff to the right. Pleasanter, if you are not in a rush, is to leave your car in the wadi and walk the last 300 metres to give you a chance to enjoy the surrounding mountain landscape and the oasis farming beside the fort.

*Bithnah, viewed from the top of the fort*

The guardian, a mountain villager who thinks he is probably 90-ish, is usually about, since this is his home. He ushers visitors in through the tiny door and lets them explore, staying mainly below himself with his stick and stiff limbs. At the base of the tower, the circular room is his bedroom, his clothes and blankets hung from the line strung across the diameter. From this room, an iron ladder leads up to the roof of the tower which he encourages you to climb. Having a

**Ancient guardian**

resident caretaker who used to be a local shepherd certainly adds to the interest and enjoyment of the visit, making it one of the very few opportunities foreigners get to come into contact with nationals.

The T-shaped tomb is much less exciting to the layman, set in a scrappy open space within 200 metres of the main dual carriageway. For those who want to see it, since it is the only one in the UAE, it is recognisable by its wire fence and makeshift corrugated iron roof on poles over the tomb itself. On your way back up towards the main road, look out for the last track to your left and follow it as it runs parallel to the main tarmac road, till you get to the large red and white pylon. The site lies beside the pylon. There are holes in the fence that enable you to scramble through to the tomb, now full of

**Startled goats**  rubbish. Your arrival is likely to startle goats seeking peace and shade in the tomb. Some 10 skeletons were found here buried in the deep stone-lined walls between 1350BC and 300BC, though the tomb itself is thought to be older than this. It was excavated in 1988. Bithna is also famous for its

**Famous bees**  mountain honey, very expensive at Dh150 per kilo, but said to cure insomnia if taken in water at bedtime, as well as curing colds and respiratory disorders. The farmers who collect the honeycombs insist that the stings are good for rheumatism.

### Qidfa, tomb *(15 minutes)*

Heading along the Fujairah corniche road to the north, you reach the village of Qidfa after 18 kilometres. It was here that a 500BC Iron Age horseshoe communal tomb was found

**Bulldozed**  during some bulldozing work, identical to another horseshoe
**tomb**  tomb found at Wadi Qawr. Rescue excavations were carried out by Al-Ain Department of Antiquities in 1986–87. It turned out to be the richest tomb ever found in the UAE, its grave goods from the large number of bodies undisturbed, with large quantities of bronze bowls, arrowheads, daggers, anklets, bracelets, much pottery and an excellent collection of chlorite (soapstone) boxes and bowls. These are on display in the Fujairah Museum. Despite the importance of the site, there is virtually nothing for the layman to see here today.

Just inland from Qidfa a sign points up a turning into the little Omani enclave, governed by the Omani governate of Musandam because of its inhabitants' tribal links to that country rather than to Sharjah or Fujairah.

### Khor Fakkan, town and port *(1 hour)*

This town, the largest after Fujairah on the east coast belongs in fact to Sharjah. Its name, meaning Creek of Two Jaws, is easily the most attractive of any along the east coast, more enclosed, with mountains right down to the sea. It has a successful container port to rival or complement that of Fujairah, and its corniche and civic surroundings are generally very well maintained in a way that is typical of Sharjah's civic pride. Roundabouts abound with flowers and there is greenery and trees all along the corniche. Its tourism potential has been restricted by Sharjah's ban on alcohol, which is why most westerners head for Fujairah's Sandy Beach Motel and Holiday Beach Motel to the north, rather than Sharjah's Oceanic Hotel. The town also has a lovely traditionally designed souq near the corniche close to the landscaped Persian restaurant, Hafiz Irani, typical of Sharjah's style and love for the traditional. An old tower in the Al-Khorba area and some heritage houses in the old town are scheduled for restoration. In the port area and therefore, alas, not accessible to the public, are some recently discovered graves set up on a hillside. The new Sharjah Archaeology Museum has film footage of them in one of its displays, which is the closest you will get.

**Pretty landscaping**

Offshore, floating shipwrecks have recently been converted to diving platforms behind Khor Fakkan seaport where they would be out of the way, and used partly as artificial reefs to help increase the fish in the area.

**Converted shipwrecks**

### Badiyah, mosque and watchtowers *(45 minutes)*

Your attention will be drawn here as you drive through this town 8 kilometres north of Khor Fakkan, by the much photographed little white mosque, the oldest still in use in the UAE. In front it has a well and everyone, foreigners included, is welcome to stop and use the water, then enter the walled courtyard of the mosque, before going into the cool single room, whose amazingly quaint four domed roofs are supported by astonishingly thick walls and a gigantic pillar in the centre. No wood at all has been used in its construction, a fact generally held to be responsible for its survival, though its exact date is not known. The Fujairah authorities say it is 400 years old. It is sometimes referred to as the Ottoman mosque, but this is simply a corruption of Othman, the man reputed to

**Quaint domes**

have built it, and nothing to do with its age. The only other known building of similar style is in Oman, a mosque in the town of Bilad Beni Bin Ali. A small Heritage Village has recently been set up beside the mosque.

In the 16th century the Portuguese built a fort here but all trace of it has vanished now, and all that remains from that time are the two watchtowers perched on rocky outcrops behind the white mosque. Near the mosque is a graveyard in the middle of which is the long passage tomb dating to 1,000BC whose contents are on display in the Fujairah Museum. Just south of Badiyah in front of a small hill behind the Emirates Mineral Water plant, are some 20 Iron Age tombs, all robbed long ago.

**Snoopy Island**

Continuing north you reach after 6 kilometres the Sandy Beach Motel opposite the island known as Snoopy Island, famous for its coral reefs, excellent for snorkelling. It also runs diving courses.

### Ziqt, dam and old village (30 minutes)

A signpost points inland to this several kilometres after the Sandy Beach Motel. The tarmac road leads straight through the new village and out the other side to reach the massive dam and enormous reservoir. The ruins of the old village lie just before the dam and are interesting to explore.

### Dibba, town and Islamic cemetery (1 hour)

The coastline continues along lovely if polluted beaches passing the recently built Holiday Beach Hotel till it rounds the headland of Ras Dibba to arrive at Dibba itself.

Dibba was not accessible by land at all till 1968, when the steep Wadi Tayyiba was opened for Land Rovers from Masafi, and passes were at much the same time blasted through rocky headlands on the coast, to enable road communication with the other Sharjah dependencies of Khor Fakkan and Kalba down the coast. Dibba, weirdly, is divided between three municipalities – Fujairah, Sharjah and Oman, in that order as you approach from the south, though it is virtually impossible to notice the difference as you drive through. It is an attractive spot, ending in the forbidding mountains of the Musandam, which come right down to the sea, making any further coastal exploration impossible except by boat. The town is pleasant, but there is little of historical interest beyond the fort in Dibba

**Three municipalities**

Hisn (Sharjah) which has been used as the police station till its recent restoration.

Inland there is the track that leads into Wadi Bih, the route described in the Ras Al-Khaimah chapter. Also inland, though you may have trouble finding any local who can tell you where it is, is the site of a famous early Islamic battle in 633 AD. The vast necropolis of 10,000 rock headstones is an eerie sight today, between Dibba and the Omani border. The battle occurred the year after the Prophet Mohamed's sudden death, when Arabians who had been Muslims, broke away and became apostates in what became known as the Ridda Wars (Arabic for apostasy). Victory was won by the first Caliph Abu Bakr against the pagan Omanis, a significant victory for early Islam in its conquest of Arabia before it moved on to conquer Syria, the Levant and Egypt all in the space of 30 years.

**Eerie necropolis**

### Kalba, Fort, Ruler's Palace, Garden Site and Tombs
*(1¹/₂ hours)*
Although Kalba belongs to the Municipality of Sharjah, a fact which is evident to visitors immediately from its carefully landscaped corniche and the recent restoration projects of the Fort and the Ruler's Palace, it will be treated here since it fits with the geography. The administration of Kalba was much in dispute in the 19th century, with it changing hands frequently between the Sultans of Muscat and the Qawasim rulers.

The White Fort stands just back from the corniche and is entered by a curious white spiral staircase to the side, bringing you to the door set high in the outer defence wall. The guardian lives just beside the fort and is on hand to open it at most times. Inside one room has been turned into a display of traditional arms and tools, while another room has interesting old photos on its walls. Wooden rungs set into the corners enable you to climb up to the tower.

**White Fort**

Across the main corniche dual carriageway, much closer to the sea, stands the attractive Shaikh Saeed bin Saqr Al Qasimi Ruler's Palace, undergoing restoration to become a museum of traditional household items. The palace has fine decorative plasterwork above some of its doors, and its own private mosque. The Sharjah Heritage Department has insisted that the same materials be used in the reconstruction as in the original, so stones and gypsum were brought from nearby wadis for the renovation.

**Spectacular
"Garden" site**

By driving inland at right angles to the coast, leaving the White Fort on your right, you can visit the new archaeological digs known as the Kalba Garden Site, a spectacular fortress still under excavation by a British team under Carl Philips. Digs first began here in 1994. At the first little roundabout, continue straight inland following the dirt track for about 2 kilometres till you come to the green-fenced area a little to your right. To your left is a huge stone building set up on a mound, referred to by the locals as a cistern. The gate to the site is not locked, but you should obviously take great care not to disturb anything, and certainly do not attempt to climb down into the often deep excavation pits where the fortress walls have been uncovered. The guardian at the White Fort will gladly escort you to the site if you want a guided tour.

In the flat plain before the mountains a little further inland from here, are a whole series of tombs. Some of the Umm Al-Nar type can be visited. The larger and more important have been fenced and two even have roofs for protection, but there are literally tens of them simply lying out on the plain as they are. The best way to see them is not from the Kalba Garden Site, as the maze of tracks leading inland from here is very confusing. Instead you should head back to the little roundabout just inland of the White Fort and head parallel to the coast towards Khor Kalba. Follow this main tarmac road for some 3–4 kilometres, till, in a built up suburb of Kalba, you notice on your right (the inland side of the road) a decaying building called the National Cinema. Turn inland here and follow the tarmac road till it runs out, bending slightly to the right. Looking out onto the plain in a northerly direction (i.e. back the way you have just come), you should from here be able to make out the tell-tale heaps of stones and find a track over to them. The terrain is firm and not very rocky, so a saloon car can manage this, if driven carefully. Spread out in a line running northwards parallel to the coast for the next 3 kilometres or so, there must be at least 50 tombs of various sorts, some cairns, some circular Umm Al-Nar and some long and thin. The whole area is like a gigantic necropolis.

**Giant
necropolis**

### Khor Kalba, mangrove swamp and beach

Just to the south of Kalba, Khor Kalba too belongs to Sharjah and there are restoration plans for the old mosque and the old fortress.

What most people come this far to see are the mangrove swamps of the Kalba lagoon *(Khor)*, a dramatic landscape which you reach by continuing south on the tarmac road, past the Marine Hotel and over the bridge onto the spit of land separated by the water inlet. Across the bridge a children's playground area stands, in what must be one of the loveliest natural settings in the UAE, with the dark green of the mangroves, the blue water in the foreground and the fine jagged mountains behind. From here a series of sandy tracks leads off in various directions round the mangrove creek edge or over the dunes onto the beach itself. 4WD is required for some but not all of these tracks. There are many delightful spots to find where total quiet reigns and the birdlife can be observed at leisure. The whole area is huge, at least 8 kilometres long, before you reach the Omani border, and going inland for some 2–3 kilometres. It has now been designated a nature reserve by the Ruler of Sharjah, conscious of the potential for eco-tourism. There is a big tidal zone, and at low tide you can wade out into the semi-freshwater lagoon and even see old boat wrecks in places. Crabs abound, as well as green turtles and the many birds breeding here include Reef Herons and Booted Warblers. The unique bird which is a breeding resident here, and nowhere else, is the White-Collared Kingfisher, with its bright turquoise body and wings and white head with black collar running across from its eyes. These mangrove swamps have been here thousands of years and are easily the most extensive in the UAE. Globally they are known to be dwindling.

**Mangroves and mountains**

**Dwindling**

The beach here is much used by local fishermen in 4WD trucks and the sand is often covered with their nets drying. Overfishing has in fact been a problem too, for the nets are too fine to allow younger fish to escape. Since they are too small to be commercially viable, the fishermen simply throw them out to die on the sand, which is beginning to have an adverse effect on the numbers. The fishermen say they have been doing this for years and no one has ever explained that it is not good practice.

From south of Kalba, just before the big white building marks the Omani border post, a new highway heads across the mountains, announced as the Ghail to Mudiqq new road. A few kilometres further north just before Khor Kalba, a single tarmac road leads to Al-Ghail, the village on the edge of which

*Al-Ghail Fort*

stands Al-Ghail fortress, on a hill dominating the plain, another Sharjah project scheduled for renovation. This is the point where you emerge from the mountains having come overland from Hatta *(see the Ras Al-Khaimah section,* southern enclave). In Al-Ghail itself Sharjah Municipality is building new housing for villagers, simple blocks of six identical houses in rows.

## EXCURSIONS

### New Discoveries

**Giant fortress** An Australian team of archaeologists led by Professor Dan Potts has recently excavated remains of a giant fortress measuring 100 metres by 50 metres with walls two and a half metres thick dated to 800BC. The site is at Al-Awhala, about one hour's drive south of Fujairah. Its design and elaborate entrance are similar to contemporary Assyrian cities like Nineveh and Nimrud (northern Iraq) and large quantities of pottery have been unearthed. The new Ghail-Mudiqq road leads to the villages of Wadi Mai and Al-Awhala and the hot bubbling sulphur spring of Ain Al-Ghammour. When finished it will eventually link up to the new tarmac road that runs from Hatta northwards through Huwaylat and Muna'i, emerging near Dhaid via Wadi Shawka.

### Overland to Hatta *(4WD only, Full Day)*

See Ras Al-Khaimah section for description and simply reverse the direction.

The old summer
palace of the
ruling Fujairah
shaikhs at Wadi
Hayl

**Wadi Hayl, old summer palace** *(4WD or saloon car on quarry road, Half to full day)*
This enjoyable trip to the ruined summer palace of the Fujairah rulers can be an easy half day from Fujairah or turned into a longer day's excursion if you want to walk and explore the valleys beyond. It is just possible from Dubai or Sharjah in one day, but works better as the subject of a camping trip.

**Day trip or camping**

Leaving Fujairah and heading inland towards Bithna on the main road, the turn-off is 2 kilometres from the first roundabout of Fujairah town (or 25 kilometres from the Masafi-Fujairah junction if you are coming from Dubai or Sharjah). Look out for the turn-off left (south-west) opposite the police station. This road is tarmac to begin with for 2.5 kilometres and continues to pass a large military camp on your right. The tarmac road then forks left to head towards some quarries, but you take the first track to your right to continue in a southwesterly direction. After about 5 kilometres you arrive at the new village of Hayl. Passing through the village the rough track (4WD only) leads out and leftwards along the bank of the wadi. A bumpy few kilometres then brings you to within sight of the fort and you almost immediately join a newly graded wide track that finishes the final approach to the fort. This track, as you will soon realise, has been built for lorries using the newly dug quarry further inland beyond the Hayl palace, and the peace of the location is somewhat marred by regular truck traffic throwing up clouds of dust. One benefit however is that this makes the ruins and Hayl accessible now to saloon cars, who can use this track instead of the first described one. Having passed the military camp and the first track to the right, continue on the tarmac till you reach another much wider track heading in the same southwesterly direction.

**Unique ruined palace**

Unique in the UAE, these ruins are quite delightful, the palace itself down below, with traces of grandeur left in the decorated plasterwork and pillars, and the fort set above on the hill, guarding the wadi approach. Both can still be climbed to their upstairs levels by ladders. An expatriate was prevented not long ago from removing the carved window frame of the palace, by a field worker for the Arabian Leopard Trust who happened to be working nearby. The mountain setting is spectacular, the jagged peaks reaching 1100 metres, with the greenery of the oasis set a short walk below the track, and many rock pools teeming with wildlife. Water flows here all summer and you can walk upstream to explore the dense almost jungle-like greenery of the oasis, with an abundance of toads and little fish. A few of the pools where the wadi curves are deep enough to swim.

In this wadi, but more especially in Wadi Furfar to the north, you may spot ancient rock drawings, known as petroglyphs. These drawings often show such things as snakes or men on horseback.

### Wadi Wurrayah, waterfall *(2 hours)*

This trip used to involve a very bumpy 18 kilometres off tarmac each way, much of it is along the rocky wadi bed itself, so 4WD was essential. Now the tarmac road is signposted about 5km north of Khor Fakkan. It passes close by the impressive waterfall, the only one in the UAE to run right through the summer months. It is some eight metres tall but with higher rapids above. You turn to the right along the wadi bed to reach the falls and can then climb up to a plateau above to see how they begin. The mountain scenery all about is stunning and is designated a potential nature reserve, making

**Graffiti**

the thoughtless graffiti on some of the rocks near the waterfall all the more distressing.

# FUJAIRAH PRACTICAL INFORMATION

## Airport
Fujairah International Airport is served by Gulf Air to Oman and Bahrain and ·by Air India to Bombay. Expansion is planned.

## Hotels
The Fujairah hotels only provide some 400 beds, and the Fujairah Tourism Bureau wants to encourage investors to build more luxury hotels and restaurants, as well as shopping malls and other entertainment facilities. They are all around one and a half hour's drive from Dubai or Sharjah.

*Fujairah Hilton* Tel: 09-222411/5. 92 rooms and chalets, some with fun circular sunken baths, recently renovated, with two new restaurants – Neptunia with varied menu for businessmen and tourists, and Octavia, a bistro with lighter cuisine and mellow music. 12 chalets for 4. Children's playground.

*Sandy Beach* Tel: 09-445354. First opened 1980. Set opposite Snoopy Rock just 100 metres offshore, so you can wade across at low tide and the best snorkelling is round the sides of the island. There are older style chalets equipped with their own barbecues, popular with western expatriates, and a newer hotel wing has opened in 1997 which nationals and tour groups prefer. A fitness centre, new restaurant and tennis court are planned.

*Oceanic at Khor Fakkan (Sharjah)* Tel: 09-385111. No alcohol. 162 rooms. Sailing and waterskiing, fenced private beach, gym, diving centre, rooftop restaurants with music. pool.

*Al-Siji Hotel (previously Fujairah Plaza)* in town centre. No beach. Bowling alley. Self-catering apartments. Opened 1993.

*Fujairah Beach Motel* Cheaper than the others, can attract Russians. 100 rooms.

*Holiday Beach Motel* Tel: 09-445540. 45 single and double chalets, near Dibba. Diving instruction centre, marine sports, beach rather rocky.

*Marine Motel, Kalba (Sharjah)* Tel: 06-778877/8. Simple low- rise motel before the mangrove swamps. Beach restaurant, no alcohol. 13 kilometres south of Fujairah.

## Restaurants

The hotels have the most reliable restaurants.

*Khor Fakkan (Sharjah)* – Hafiz Irani Restaurant on the corniche near the central market. Tables outside surrounded by flowers. No alcohol.

Fujairah has a Pizza Inn open from 10am–midnight Tel: 222557.

Dibba has seafront restaurants offering fresh fish. No alcohol.

## Car Rental

There is a car rental office opposite the Fujairah Hilton.

## Driving

The Emirate has a reputation for atrocious driving which it is trying to rectify. Statistics show that 80% of traffic accidents involved locals speeding and frequently no other car was involved. Roaring up and down the beach in 4WDs is another favourite pastime, especially at night, which can make beach camping less peaceful than one might hope.

*Fujairah skyline from inland*

## Walking

The best walking areas from among the places described in the Fujairah section are:

The valley ringed with hills behind the Fujairah Heritage Village National Park;

Bithna beyond the oasis agriculture into the mountains;

The Kalba Mangrove swamps, all round the shoreline;

Wadi Hayl, the wadi bed itself makes an excellent nature walk, below the ruins;

Wadi Wurrayah, the mountains all around the waterfall, which are designated a nature reserve.

# Umm Al-Quwain

Area: 777 square kilometres
Population:  35,000

## Overview

**Escape from commercialism**

Probably the simplest and most unassuming of the seven emirates, Umm Al-Quwain, lying half way between Dubai and Ras Al-Khaimah, can be a welcome breath of fresh air if you are looking for a change from commercialism, traffic and high-rise development. It and Abu Dhabi have but one thing in common – unlike all the other emirates, neither has a separate enclave in the hinterland.

Sometimes unkindly referred to as a windswept backwater, this is in practice Umm Al-Quwain's very attraction. In summer its thin peninsula jutting out into the Gulf always catches the breeze, and the main road between Sharjah and Ras Al-Khaimah bypasses it, thereby ensuring peaceful and traffic-free roads. With its many offshore islands and the lagoon of Khor Al-Baidha, it offers some of the best sailing in the UAE.

From Dubai the drive to Umm Al-Quwain takes an hour, and from Sharjah's Culture roundabout, half an hour in normal traffic conditions. It is the second smallest emirate after Ajman, and has never had any significant industry but fishing and shipbuilding. The Dhow yards at Umm Al-Quwain are still some of the most active in the UAE, and its very name means 'Mother of the Powers', a reference to its long seafaring background. Earlier this century Umm Al-Quwain was building about 20 dhows a year compared to Dubai's 10.

Inland at the fertile oasis of Falaj Al-Mu'alla there is some date cultivation and a large poultry farm supplying eggs and chickens to the markets of Abu Dhabi, Dubai and Sharjah. Umm Al-Quwain's camel race track is also at Falaj Al-Mu'alla.

**Excellent water**

The drinking water of the Emirate is excellent, supplied from the wells of this inland town.

Oil and gas have so far not been found here in commercially viable quantities, so the emirate is dependent on aid from the federal budget. In attempts to generate income for itself, Umm Al-Quwain's ruler Shaikh Rashid bin Ahmad Al-Mu'alla (viz. the Al-Mu'alla tribe from Falaj Al-Mu'alla ) has recently embarked on a tourism drive, with new hotels opening, the Umm Al-Quwain Tourist Centre and the extraordinary Aquapark on the main Ras Al-Khaimah road, hoping to lure families from neighbouring emirates to come for a day's fun outing. Otherwise, its additional revenue is from its port and small Free Trade zone.

One of Umm al-Quwain's least known assets is its archaeological heritage, boasting the two major sites of Ad-Dour and Tell Abraq. Umm Al-Quwain's Museum, when it opens in years to come, will surprise all with the wealth of its antique treasures, currently in the basement of the Diwan building. To explore the places described fully, a two night stay at one of the listed Umm Al-Quwain hotels (*see end of this section*) is warranted.

**Archaeological assets**

### Orientation and Approach

Orientation in Umm Al-Quwain town could hardly be more straightforward. The signposted turn-off from the main Sharjah – Ras Al-Khaimah road leads directly on to the headland of Umm Al-Quwain, passing several wealthier houses and basic shops, through a series of roundabouts, till you reach the municipal park with its trees and playground areas. By forking to the right you enter the old part of town with the conspicuous fort, flying its flag ahead of you, and by winding down onto the creek front you will pass the Fish Souq and come to the Umm Al-Quwain Tourist Centre. The tip of the headland is a bare windswept area, but out on the extremities beside the new port is the Ministry of Agriculture and Fisheries which houses the Aquarium. By looping round onto the western more exposed and windswept side of the headland you can eye up the row of wealthy smart private houses and palaces that line the sea shore, past the Umm Al-Quwain Beach Hotel, culminating in a splendid shaikh's palace. Many such palaces stand empty for much of the year, fully tended by servants and gardeners, awaiting the brief occasions when their master comes to stay. Nothing in Umm Al-Quwain is more than two storeys high.

**Empty palaces**

### Umm Al-Quwain town
### Ruler's Palace Compound (*15 minutes*)
Having turned off the main Sharjah-Ras Al-Khaimah highway towards Umm Al-Quwain town, you will shortly notice to your right on the shore a large two-storey white building set within extensive grounds. Take the first road to your right to reach it, past the red and white water tower, and you will be able to see from the perimeter fence, the ruler's emus and

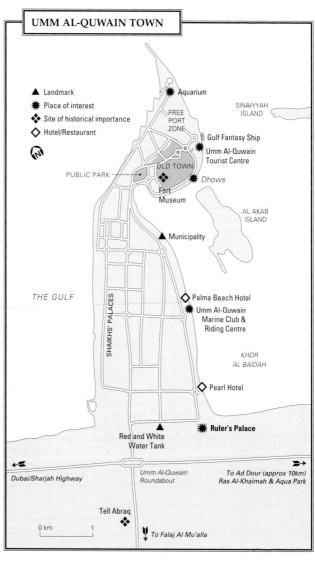

UMM AL-QUWAIN TOWN

▲ Landmark
✴ Place of interest
❖ Site of historical importance
◇ Hotel/Restaurant

Aquarium

SINAIYYAH ISLAND

FREE PORT ZONE

Gulf Fantasy Ship

Umm Al-Quwain Tourist Centre

PUBLIC PARK

OLD TOWN

*Dhows*

Fort Museum

AL AKAB ISLAND

▲ Municipality

THE GULF

SHAIKHS' PALACES

◇ Palma Beach Hotel

✴ Umm Al-Quwain Marine Club & Riding Centre

*KHOR AL BAIDAH*

◇ Pearl Hotel

▲

✴ **Ruler's Palace**

Red and White Water Tank

Dubai/Sharjah Highway

Umm Al-Quwain Roundabout

To Ad Dour (approx 10km)
Ras Al-Khaimah & Aqua Park

Tell Abraq
❖

0 km          1

To Falaj Al Mu'alla

**Unassuming palace**

gazelles which wander freely, along with the topiary elephants and camels that have been shaped from the huge bushes. The palace itself is the most unassuming of any of the rulers' palaces, certainly quite modest compared to those of the Abu Dhabi and Dubai ruling families.

### Old Fort/Museum *(1 hour)*

Umm Al-Quwain's picturesque old fort served as the town's police station until very recently, and one wing of it is still decked out in the tacky carpet typical of police offices. It is currently undergoing an extensive restoration programme and while work is ongoing the door is generally open and you are free to look around. The supervisor will gladly escort you, making sure you don't walk on areas where the floor is unsafe. The most attractive room by far is the upstairs majlis with its carved wooden verandahs and high ceilings. The air conditioning, through an ingenious system of strategically placed holes in the wall, can be checked and found to be very effective. This was of course the reason that the main majlis was housed upstairs, better to catch the breeze, which in Umm Al-Quwain was predominantly from the west, and buildings were oriented accordingly.

*Picturesque fort*

*The Ruler's old fort, undergoing restoration*

Downstairs are mainly storeroom and kitchen areas, and piles of old cannon balls can be seen gently rusting in one corner. Upstairs, the bathroom complexes are quite luxurious and relatively well-planned, with the slopes of the floor away to the drainage holes, more carefully designed than in the average modern house! All the old carved doors have been saved and will eventually be re-hung in the restoration which will probably not be completed before 1999. At that point the fort will open as the emirate's Museum, displaying all the treasures from the local sites.

**Old Palace** *(15 minutes)*

Immediately behind the fort are the crumbling remains of an old palace also due for restoration once funds become available. The stairs have totally collapsed, leaving the highly decorated plasterwork of the upstairs majlis tantalisingly out of reach. This would not have been the Ruler's Palace, since he lived in the fort itself, but that of another local Shaikh.

*Collapsed stairs*

**Sinaiyyah Island** *(3 hours)*

Directly opposite the main town lies this very flat barrier island. The community of Umm Al-Quwain used to live on the island till its sweet water dried up, and it now serves as a private retreat for the Umm Al-Quwain ruling family and as a nature reserve. Two ancient towers mark the location of the old island settlement. Today the island is occasionally accessible by prior arrangement to specialist naturalists and to field trips of such groups as the Dubai Natural History Group. Between September and January it is home to the world's largest breeding colony of Socotra cormorants. The cormorants are unpopular unfortunately, as fishermen see them as competitors and their breeding colonies have an unpleasant smell. In 1995 none bred here because of excessive 4WD activity. A small group of gazelles have also been introduced. The lagoon area created by the barrier of Sinaiyyah Island is called Khor Al-Baidha (White Creek), an area of diverse marine and birdlife, with one of the UAE's largest concentrations of mangrove swamps. There are strong tidal currents here.

*Unpopular birds*

**The Aquarium** *(1 hour)*

Unique in the UAE is this aquarium which is part of the Marine Research Centre of Umm Al-Quwain's Ministry of Agriculture and Fisheries. Situated right out on the headland beside the New Port, the aquarium is open to visitors during normal Ministry hours of 8am–1pm daily except Friday. Thursday it is 8–11am, and you can simply drive in through the gates to park by the building straight in front of you.

*Research Centre*

It takes about an hour to have a proper look at the 20 or so large tanks of live fish together with the dried and pickled varieties in jars. First set up in 1984 for marine research purposes, the aquarium is now a little tired-looking and is suffering from the usual lack of maintenance. For fish-eating fans, the labels on the tanks tell you whether the fish is good to eat, and it is worth jotting down the odd name to help you on your next visit to the fish souq. The larger tanks have green turtles, whip-tailed rays and even the odd black-tipped reef shark. Of the dried displays the huge saw fish and ray are the most impressive.

**Reef sharks**

## Beach and Riding facilities

Umm Al-Quwain is most visited by expatriates for its riding centre and water sports facilities which it is striving to develop. These and the new Aquapark are fully described in the Practical Information at the end of this section.

## Tell Abraq, ruins and excavations *(1 hour)*

Located less than half a kilometre from the Umm Al-Quwain roundabout on the road to Falaj Al-Mu'alla, Tell Abraq is a little-visited archaeological mound which was first excavated in 1973. The Arabic word *tell* means mound and this has come to be the archaeological term for a settlement in which successive ages piled on top of each other, one town built on another, till the final effect is a man-made hill. The mound lies on raised ground to the right of the road and a track forks off to circle its base. The spot makes a pleasant picnic site, raised up to catch the breeze, though there is no shade. The Iraqis were the first to excavate here, and it was they who dug the trench across the bottom of the mound, thereby revealing the foundations of two third millennium BC defensive towers. The area is currently covered in protective blue plastic sheeting but in between gaps you can still make out the distinctive white so-called 'sugar lump' blocks which were characteristic of the stones used in the exterior facing of the early Umm Al-Nar style tombs.

**Excavated foundations**

There was then a gap in excavations until a Danish team came and worked here for three successive seasons of 1989, 1990 and 1991, and were on the verge of important discoveries when they were told to stop because of a border dispute. Sharjah and Umm Al-Quwain had been arguing about which emirate the site of Tell Abraq belonged to, and the compromise was finally reached that the border went straight through the centre of the site. Whilst this solution satisfied the local

**Border dispute**

authorities, the consequence was that all digs stopped and have never resumed. The white trigometer erected in recent years on the summit of the mound is thought to mark the border. Before stopping excavations the Danish team was able to conduct digs near the summit of the mound which revealed the Iron Age wall, the best preserved, and a well inside the tower, a large oven and fireplace. They also found a tomb with 20 skeletons.

In its heyday Tell Abraq was 300–400 metres from the coast, and if you look carefully at the stones you will see they have been cut from reef rock, with the shells inside, made up from calcified sand and rock. The iron pegs that are visible in the excavated areas are left over from the archaeologists measuring out their grid system which enables them to mark the exact co-ordinates of items that were unearthed during the dig.

**Ad-Dour, Hellenistic Site** *(4WD or careful saloon car, 2–3 hours)*

**Extensive ruins**

This remarkably extensive archaeological site belongs unquestionably within the territory of Umm Al-Quwain and is unique in being the only site of what is known as the Hellenistic period in the whole of the Emirate, and the site of the UAE's first known temple. Hellenistic is the name given to the period after Alexander the Great's death, in which Greek influences spread outward from Greece into the lands conquered by Alexander and his generals in the first century BC. It comes from the Greek *hellenistes* meaning 'imitator of the Greeks' and was an era of great cultural activity, stimulated by the cross-fertilisation of Oriental and Western cultures. The city of Ad-Dour would originally have been a coastal site and is known to have been inhabited from 200BC till the 3rd century AD, but most of the extant ruins date from the first century AD. Its heyday was therefore contemporary to the Parthian empire in the East and the expanding Roman empire in the West.

The inland areas of the site are very good for picnicking as there are many tall ghaf trees for shade. Try to avoid Fridays as you may have to share it with Arab families who see the tracks as designed for their children's sand buggies and the ruins as an adventure playground for the children to romp all over.

The landmark to help pinpoint it is the Emirates Petrol Station on the right-hand side of the main highway as you head towards Ras Al-Khaimah, roughly 10 kilometres from the Umm Al-Quwain roundabout turn-off. Just 200 metres before the Emirates Petrol Station and a long-necked giraffe billboard, look out for a small track that leads up onto a mound overlooking the road, with some insignificant-looking stone foundations on top.

**Giraffe landmark**

Excavations at the site, which extends over an area of one kilometre inland from the road and four kilometres in width, were first begun in 1973 by the Iraqis, continued in the 1980s by an international team from France, Great Britain, Belgium and Denmark, and then the last digs took place in 1994 by the Belgians. These digs yielded a rich range of antique artefacts all of which are currently in the basement store of the Diwan in Umm Al-Quwain, awaiting completion of the restoration of the fort which will then be converted to a museum.

The roadside bluff with foundations is thought to be a Governor's House because of its exceptional size and design, and the layout reveals three circular fortification towers. One male skeleton was found together with a camel, which by its posture was revealed to have been sacrificially slaughtered at the burial of the male, a fairly common Arabian practice, especially if it was a riding camel. Two eagle statues, both headless, were found flanking the entrance door, which archaeologists have seen as reminiscent of a similar style of building to Hatra (a town 90 kilometres south-west of Mosul) in Mesopotamia. The eagle was worshipped in pre-Islamic Arabia as a god called *Nasr* (Arabic eagle) and their presence here, together with other burnt offering traces found, suggests that the house also served some funerary temple purpose. The stone used is locally available limestone or beach rock, in which a high percentage of undecomposed shells are visible.

**Governor's House**

**Eagle god**

From the roadside hill, the track continues inland across the site and out through a makeshift gate in the fence. You should close this gate after you, to keep animals from straying into the site or onto the road. Heading inland across the red dunes, you can stop after about one kilometre where two tall ghaf trees stand beside the track. The track presents no problems for a carefully driven saloon car. Scattered about in this area are literally hundreds of tombs. From the trees a footpath leads

**Square Fort**

further inland towards the fort dated to the 4th century AD by the Iraqis who first dug here in 1973. The fort itself is roughly 20 metres square with 70 centimetre thick walls and circular towers 4 metres in diameter at each corner. In the centre was a two-roomed building roughly 6 metres square.

A total of over 350 coins have been found at Ad-Dour, evidence of the wealth and active trading of the city. All but a handful were minted in Arabia. No other UAE site has such a profusion of coins. These trading activities are also shown by the wealth of coloured green and turquoise glazed pottery littering the desert, which would have originated in Persia, Iraq and Syria, at that time part of the Parthian empire.

All around the fort are small houses of the same period which digs have found to be built on top of earlier 1st century BC houses. Some 20 metres to the left (east) of the fort is an elaborate tomb with a corbelled roof and flagstone floor. Inside were found a female aged 25–30 and a male aged around 40 with sword, beads, glass, a bronze wine set with a cauldron and sieve and bull's head spout. All but two of the tombs found so far had already been robbed for their precious metal

**Mountains of pottery**

in earlier centuries. Mountains of pottery are to be found all around, sorted into piles by previous digs.

As you continue walking round in a big loop towards the shed with its green corrugated iron roof, erected as an animal pen by the local Bedouin farmer in recent years and nothing to do with the dig, you pass some stone wells which were sunk down to the fresh groundwater. Despite the proximity to the sea the groundwater here was always, and still is, unusually

**Fresh water**

fresh because of the rainwater run-off from the mountains. Near the green shed close to a group of large trees is the largest of the houses in this area, a four- roomed building, one room of which has a square mud brick platform. Some of the walls show traces of white gypsum plasterwork.

Returning to the car you now continue along the road track for other 400 metres till you reach the next large tree, conveniently located close to the temple area of the site, the most inland part. A footpath leads the 50 metres to reach the simple square of the temple itself, still standing over two metres high and dated to between 100BC–100AD. Nothing was originally visible here but a sandy mound, and when the Belgians dug it out in 1989, they had no instructions to preserve it or back-fill it. As a result the deterioration in the structure has been considerable and the original white gypsum plasterwork facing which had been superbly crafted into ashlar block styles to mimic stonework, with traces of yellows and ochres and friezes of meandering vine leaves, has suffered greatly and is now partially visible on the southern wall only. The piles of stones around were originally altars two metres high, now collapsed, bearing a 9-line inscription in Aramaic about Shams, the Sun God of Mesopotamia. (*Shams* is also Arabic for sun). This temple is therefore thought to be a sun temple. One 'sugar lump' large white block inside the temple with a small depression hollowed out is reckoned to have been borrowed from a nearby Umm Al-Nar style tomb and the basin carved out for some sacrificial ritual. More evidence of sacrificial practices is to be found in the water channel cut into the northern wall which leads downwards from the well, for water to run into the temple. A Roman oil lamp was also found inside the temple, indicating that worship continued in this temple till the first century AD. Near the temple are more graves scattered about. The settlement is thought to have declined and disappeared when the *Khor* (Creek) on which it depended silted up with tidal movements, thereby cutting it off from its lifeline, the sea.

**Tiny temple**

## UMM AL-QUWAIN PRACTICAL INFORMATION

### Airport
None of its own – Sharjah is the nearest.

### Hotels
All the Umm Al-Quwain hotels serve alcohol, and the Pearl has a sort of off-licence/hole in the wall at the back, where liquor can be bought over the counter by anyone.

*Palma Beach Hotel*  Tel: 06-667090, fax: 06-667388.
Best of the beach hotels with pleasant if basic portakabins lining the beach and round the pool just in from the beach. There are three sizes of portakabin, all have a fridge and washing-up area, but no cooker. Bring your own barbecue for outside cooking on the large terraces. Each portakabin has its

own shower and toilet in which the plumbing can be temperamental. There is no restaurant, but there is a reasonably-priced and comprehensive room service menu. Thursday nights are best avoided as the local clientèle can become extremely rowdy. The gardens are well-tended and there is grass round the pool. Alcohol is served. Motorboats, jetbikes and horses can be rented by the hour from the next-door Marine Club and Riding Centre.

*Pearl Hotel* Tel: 06-666678.
Set on the beach a little south of the Marine Club and Riding Centre, the Pearl has 20 chalets round a pool. Pleasantly landscaped but with rather too much paving and too little greenery. It has a proper restaurant attached to the main reception area, open to passing travellers too.

*Umm Al-Quwain Beach Hotel* Tel: 06-666647
The oldest of Umm Al-Quwain's hotels, a series of 22 portakabins on the windy west side of the spit. The pool is raised up and hidden behind wind-sheltering walls. There is a grand entrance through landscaped gardens, though the portakabins themselves are rather bare, all set on tarmac with no verandahs. The Umm Al-Quwain Beach Restaurant is separate in the adjacent plot of land on the beach. Alcohol is served. Live entertainment on Thursday and Friday evenings with a circular stage and seating for 250.

*Barracuda Beach Hotel* Tel: 06 - 681555 fax: 06 - 681556.
Beside Aquapark Dreamland on the main Ras Al-Khaimah road. 11 chalets on the beach, bleak and windswept. Not a place for families, with plenty of smashed glass from beer bottles in the sand. Its odd restaurant functions in the evenings only, with a live band.

## AquaPark Dreamland
Open 9am–10pm.
Located on the sea in a large plot just beside the main Sharjah-Ras Al-Khaimah highway, this new fun park is conspicuous because of its huge white dinosaur-teeth fencing. It sells itself as being 30 minutes drive from Dubai. Specialising in water rides it offers a series of interconnecting tunnels to shoot through for those who love to terrify themselves. When totally

finished it will be the largest water park in the world, and will include villas and bungalows and a 320 room 5 star hotel. A free transport system will be launched covering all the UAE to encourage visitors. Children under five are free. The entry fee includes all rides. There are plans for a Dolphin Show and a parachute and sky-diving club. The first phase cost Dh95 million as opposed to the early estimate of Dh40 million. The park has two aqua- restaurants, a shopping arcade, a 'lazy river', a 'crazy river', black holes, Kamikazes, an amphitheatre and swimming pool for children. The management says it is geared for 8,000 visitors a day.

**Ambitious rides**

### Marine Club and Riding Centre Tel: 06-665446
The well-kept stables offer a good range of riding with jumps, dressage and hacking. It is a delightful family club with realistically priced membership. The clubhouse building offers simple food and snacks, ice-cream and drinks. The Marine Club has yachts, motorboats and jetskis for rent, and the beach has shaded picnic tables, beside which camping is permitted, making use of the shower facilities provided. It has recently acquired a tourist dhow, traditionally furnished, catering for up to 150 people, making twice daily trips to nearby islands and beaches.

**Family club**

### Umm Al-Quwain Tourist Centre Tel: 06-651185, fax: 06-651186.
Located by the old town opposite Sinaiyyah Island and the sheltered lagoon, and right beside the huge white liner Gulf Fantasy that was impounded here some years ago. This newly opened centre has a jetty from which it offers boat trips to the islands to view the birdlife and also offers marine life study trips. It has a full range of boats for hire including catamarans and glass bottom boats. The sheltered nature of this large seawater lagoon makes it ideal for watersports, though when swimming you will feel quite a pull when the tide is going out. They also offer sailing instruction. There is a licensed bar, kitchen facilities for barbecueing and simple snacks, beach showers and sun shades. There is an attractive grassy area by the bar.

**Boat trips**

### Heritage Camp
10 kilometres north-east of Umm Al-Quwain roundabout in the desert this camp shows the Bedouin lifestyle and offers camel and horse tours.

### Walking
The only area for uninterrupted walking among the places described in the Umm Al-Quwain section is the archaeological site of Ad-Dour, with its attractive rolling hills covered in grass and plenty of trees.

# Ajman

Area: 259 square kilometres
Population: 91,000

## Overview

Tiniest of the seven emirates Ajman is noticeably less affluent than its neighbour Sharjah to which it appears at first glance to be a mere extension. The trained eye however detects little signs in the housing, less well-finished, and the streets less well provided with street lighting. Its attraction for most is its cheaper housing, for those who work in Sharjah or even Dubai. Fishing and dhow building are its two mainstays, from its own small creek.

**Mountain enclaves**

Besides its coastline between Sharjah and Umm Al-Quwain, Ajman has two inland enclaves given to it because of its tribal links from the pre-oil era. One enclave is Masfut at the edge of the Hajar mountains just before Hatta, where the coastal Ajmanis used to retreat for the hot summer months to escape the humidity, and the other is at Manama on the road to Masafi and Fujairah. The ruler, Shaikh Humaid Bin Rashid Al-Nuaimi, succeeded his father Shaikh Rashid Al-Nuaimi in 1981.

## Ajman Corniche

As you pass through Sharjah along the corniche and out beyond the Sharjah Ruler's Palace and the Sharjah Women's Club with their beautifully landscaped roundabouts and avenues, you come to the roundabout at the Coral Beach Hotel. Beyond this is the border with Ajman, so immediately after the roundabout the next corniche is Ajman's, noticeably poorer and less well facilitated than Sharjah's, with a beach bare of amenities.

**Bare beach**

## Ajman Transit Highway

As you pass through Sharjah and out beyond Culture roundabout to meet the main highway towards Ras Al-Khaimah you cross a large stagnant-looking inlet of what could either be a shallow seawater creek or a lake of industrial effluent. Wading birds seem undeterred by which of the two, and stalk about intent on the next meal. Blue plastic bags flutter merrily and rubbish tips sparkle with broken glass. Billboards and adverts hideous by any standards, line the roadside, but in a setting such as this, can hardly be called a blot on the landscape.

**Well-adjusted birds**

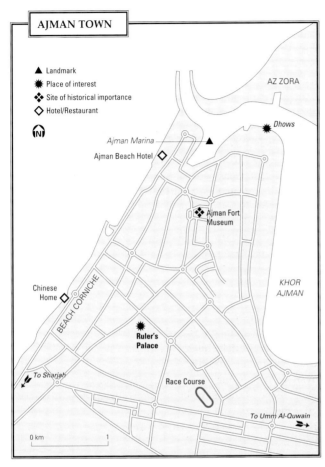

AJMAN TOWN

▲ Landmark
✹ Place of interest
❖ Site of historical importance
◇ Hotel/Restaurant

AZ ZORA

Ajman Marina ▲
Ajman Beach Hotel ◇
✹ Dhows

❖ Ajman Fort Museum

Chinese Home ◇
BEACH CORNICHE
KHOR AJMAN

✹ Ruler's Palace

To Sharjah
Race Course
To Umm Al-Quwain

0 km                1

## Ajman Souq
A small traditional-style series of domes in white with green patterning, this souq sits to the left of the road a little forlornly, looking as if few people bother to visit.

## Ajman Tombs
These two important tombs were excavated by the Al-Ain Department of Antiquities in 1986. One is a circular Umm Al-Nar tomb dating to the late third millennium, the first building of such date ever found north of Abu Dhabi. The second adjacent tomb was oblong, both originally located close to the old shoreline.

**Ajman Museum** Tel: 06-423824/428222
Open 9am–12noon, 5–8pm daily, Friday 5–8pm only.
Closed Saturday.
Set a little inland, this very attractive museum converted from the Ruler's old fort is nevertheless best reached via the corniche route from Sharjah. Leaving Sharjah at the Coral Beach roundabout, continue along the Ajman corniche till you reach the Ajman Beach Hotel. Take the main dual carriageway turn-off inland some 100 metres before the hotel and continue straight over at the next roundabout. After about 200 metres you will see the Fort Museum on your left and then fiddle across the carriageway to park in its carpark. There is a nominal entry fee and no photography is permitted inside. In the far left corner of the courtyard is a simple cafeteria offering sandwiches and grilled chicken, fizzy drinks, tea and coffee.

This and the Ras Al-Khaimah Fort Museum have the most authentic feel to them as forts, and both museums have been extremely well laid out, making them a pleasure to explore.

*Ajman Fort and Museum*

**The real thing**

The outer courtyard with its display of dhows and other boats and beautifully constructed replicas of authentic winter and summer houses of the pre-oil era, is quite charming and it is here at sunset with the dusk calls to prayer ringing round the town and the museum staff kneeling to prayer on the grass, that one can have that rare experience in the UAE of feeling, if only for a moment, surrounded by natural indigenous culture.

Also in this outer courtyard, just to the right of the entrance gate, is the reconstructed pair of tombs 5,000 years old, completing the sense of dominant local culture.

Passing through the main fort gateway into the inner courtyard you can begin in the left hand corner by visiting the archaeology room in which the surprisingly rich finds from the two tombs are displayed. The clay and carnelian necklaces and bracelets which adorned the bodies of the buried are in excellent condition, as are the pots, characteristic of the Umm Al-Nar period with their black wavy lines. That some of these are still in one piece after 5,000 years is truly remarkable. The soapstone boxes and containers are also surprisingly well-crafted, as are the bronze tools. One somewhat gory exhibit is a clay jar about the size of a baby, inside which a child's body was found, a common way of enterring the young at that time.

**Still intact**

The display rooms continue upstairs and the little staircases and tiny series of rooms furnished as authentically as possible with coarse string matting and carved old chests, are a delight to explore. The weapons' display is very impressive, and among the more unusual exhibits are the traditional games, showing just how inventive the children could be in the days before plastic toys. Also unusual is the Police exhibition, with its tear gas bombs and photos of a police execution by gunfire. The fort doubled till fairly recently as the police headquarters. Outside in the courtyard is an interesting equivalent to the stocks, where five prisoners could be tied by the wrists to the wooden beam and left on view to feel the shame.

**Police history**

Another rather gory section is the large exhibit hall of Traditional Medicine, showing what extraordinarily primitive techniques the people resorted to in the days before drugs and hospitals.

The Traditional Wedding room explains that costumes were for girls from 12 onwards and for boys from 17 onwards.

The pearling and fishing displays are extremely well done with charming models of the boat and the divers, each on the end of his rope, pulled up by his helper on board when he gives a tug. On average each diver collected 10 oysters per dive.

**Boat models**

No one can visit this museum without coming away with an enhanced awareness of the importance of the palm tree. Apart from the vital element in the local diet of the date itself, almost everything in people's everyday lives was made from the various parts of it. The branches were strung together to make the summer and winter houses, the fronds were woven

313

into baskets, food trays, conical fly covers and fans. 25 types of date palm trees grow in the Emirates and the palm is regarded as a blessed tree mentioned even in the Koran, without which people could not have survived in this harsh environment.

### Ajman Creek

From the Ajman Beach Hotel you can skirt right round the edge of Ajman's Creek to see the Dhow building yard and the port which Ajman is dredging and improving. The main player here is Arab Heavy Industries, one of the UAE's largest ship repair companies, equipped to repair and maintain oilfield supply boats, tugs and cargo ships. The company is part owned by UAE citizens and the Ajman government, and part by Japanese companies.

## AJMAN PRACTICAL INFORMATION

### Airport

Ajman has no airport of its own. The closest is that of Sharjah, half an hour away.

### Hotels

*Ajman Beach Hotel* Tel: 06-423333

50 rooms. Unlike neighbouring Sharjah, Ajman is not dry, so this simple Beach Hotel attracts lots of Russians and CIS clientèle for its cheapness and alcohol. Its large shaded open terrace on the beach makes a good lunchtime stop with a tasty selection of Arabic *mezze* (dips and starters) and kebabs. You can swim and use their beach showers if you come prepared with towels and swimwear.

A new hotel is under construction on the beach.

*Lilley's Club*

This ex-club of the Lilley construction company is a relic of the past, offering the most basic facilities. A scruffy fence on the beach gives privacy to the somewhat seedy club which has one shower, a pool table, and beer. Its bar is known as the 'Star Wars' bar, from its unusual clientèle. Set on the beach between the Coral Beach Hotel and the Chinese Home Restaurant.

*Chinese Home Restaurant* Tel: 06-422202
Open 12.30–3pm, 7pm–midnight.

Incongruously set beside the Venice Italian fast-food restaurant in the strange circular building on the Ajman corniche, this small Chinese restaurant is run by Danny Chen and serves a good range of reasonably priced Chinese food for take-away as well as in-house consumption. He serves alcohol – beer, wine or whisky – as 'special tea' in a teapot, so as not to offend local sensitivities.

*Venice Italian fast-food Pizzeria*
No alcohol. Run by a cheerful blonde Italian lady, this surprising place has a good range of home made pizzas and fresh pasta according to what was made that day – ravioli, cannelloni, lasagne etc. It also does hamburgers and chips. Situated on the corniche, the distinctive circular two-storey building cannot be missed. Inside, she keeps a few birds in cages and a tiny terrapin. Going through her circular hall and out onto the somewhat decaying white ballustraded terrace, the sea breezes are cooling even in the hot summer months. Water pipes (hubble-bubbles) are popular here.

*Ajman Marina* Tel: 06-423344.
Set on the creek near the Ajman Beach Hotel, this is Ajman's sports and health club with a pool, health club and jacuzzi, gym and squash courts. Membership fees are considerably lower than in other emirates, and you can also pay a one-off entry fee as a non-member. The Falcon Restaurant here is a popular place for barbecues on Thursday evenings and brunch on Friday mornings.

# FURTHER READING

**Mohammed al-Fahim**, *From Rags to Riches*,
London Centre of Arab Studies, 1995

**Mohammed al-Murr**, *Dubai Tales*, Forest Books, 1991
*The Wink of the Mona Lisa*, Motivate, 1994

**Simon Aspinall**, *Status and Conservation of the Breeding Birds of the UAE*, Hobby Publications 1996

**Geoffrey Bibby**, *Looking for Dilmun*,
Penguin Travel Library, 1972

**Donald and Eloise Bosch**, *Seashells of the Arabian Gulf*,
Motivate, 1994

**Peter Dance**, *Seashells of Eastern Arabia*, Motivate

**Dubai Municipality**, *Dubai Tourist and Business Guide*, 1994

**Encyclopaedia of Islam**, *edited HAR Gibb*,
Brill and Luzac, 1960

**Donald Hawley**, *The Trucial States*, Allen and Unwin, 1970

**Frauke Heard-Bey**, *From Trucial States to United Arab Emirates*,
Longman 1996

**Heinzel, Fitter, Parslow**, *The Birds of Britain and Europe with North Africa and the Middle East*, Collins, 1984

**Peter Hellyer**, *Fujairah An Arabian Jewel*, Motivate, 1991

**Marycke Jongbloed**, *The Green Guide to the Emirates*,
Motivate, 1991

**Shirley Kay**, *Emirates Archaeological Heritage*, Motivate, 1986
*Sharjah Heritage and Progress*, Motivate, 1992

**Liz Kirkwood**, *UAE: A MEED Practical Guide*, MEED, 1995

**Anne Love**, *Gardening in Oman and the Gulf*,
Apex Publishing, 1995

**Paul Lunde and Justin Wintle**, *A Dictionary of Arabic and Islamic Proverbs*, Routledge, 1984

**Alistair MacKenzie**, *Dubai Explorer*, 1996

**Patrick Osborne**, *Desert Ecology of Abu Dhabi*, Pisces Publications, 1996

**Jonathan Raban**, *Arabia through the Looking Glass*, Picador, 1981

**Colin Richardson**, *The Birds of the United Arab Emirates*, Hobby Publications, 1990

**Gordon Robison**, *Arab Gulf States*, Lonely Planet, 1993

**Wilfred Thesiger**, *Arabian Sands*, Longman, 1959

**Peter Vine**, *Natural Emirates*, Trident Press, 1996

**Tony Woodward**, *Beachcomber's Guide to the Gulf*, Motivate, 1994

**Dariush Zandi**, *Off-Road in the Emirates*, Motivate, 1991
*Off-Road in the Emirates 2*, Motivate, 1994

# INDEX